CONFLICT
AND
TENSION
IN THE
FAR EAST

Key Documents,
1894-1960

CONFLICT AND TENSION IN THE FAR EAST

KEY DOCUMENTS, 1894-1960

BY JOHN M. MAKI

UNIVERSITY OF WASHINGTON PRESS
SEATTLE   1961

PREFACE

The documents in this collection are related to international conflict and tension in the Far East from 1894 to 1960. They fall into three broad categories: treaties and agreements designed to relieve tensions or to safeguard national interests in the face of threatened conflict; official policy statements relating to situations of conflict or tension; and treaties or agreements which brought major wars or military conflicts in the Far East to an end.

This collection is designed to be a supplementary textbook for courses dealing with Far Eastern international relations or diplomatic history. Much of the material also relates to United States policy in the Far East; much of it will also be useful for an understanding of the general history of the Far East in the twentieth century. There are excellent accounts and analyses of the conflicts and tensions covered by this collection, but both the general and the specialized studies offer only limited selections of documents. It is my hope that this broader selection of documents will be an aid to the student and a convenience to the scholar.

I have not attempted to supply complete documentation on any problem. However, through a judicious use of the sources quoted the interested student should find it reasonably easy to assemble fairly complete documentation for any topic dealt with herein.

The concentration on international conflict and tension has resulted in the omission of some topics which would normally be dealt with in courses for which this collection is designed. For example, colonialism and its dissolution are covered only as they have involved international conflict; thus the Korean and Indochinese conflicts are dealt with, but not the struggle in Indonesia. Civil wars, most notably the one in China which reached its climax in the late 1940's, are not dealt with, though they may have had a significant bearing on international relations. Internal political developments,

v

even though they may have been intimately related to international conflict and tension (for example, military-civilian struggles for power in Japan in the 1930's and the political issues of the Chinese civil war) are also not covered.

The brief introductory statements in each chapter are designed only to provide a thread of continuity for the documents.

John M. Maki

Seattle, Washington

CONTENTS

1 *The Rise of Japan: 1895-1910*   3

2 *The First World War and Its Aftermath: 1914-25*   26

3 *The Manchurian Crisis: 1931-35*   62

4 *The Second World War in the Far East:*   77
  First Phase, 1937-41

5 *Japan's Wartime Diplomacy: 1941-45*   106

6 *Japan: The Lost War and the Peace*   117

7 *China: The United States and the Soviet Union,*   156
  1945-50

8 *The Problem of Korea: 1945-*   178

9 *Truce in Indochina: 1954*   202

10 *Free World Security in the Far East*   213

Notes   233

Bibliography   239

Index   241

INTRODUCTORY NOTES

To the greatest extent possible I have relied on official sources for the texts of documents. However, in a few cases I have had to depend on unofficial sources which, for the most part, are accepted as authoritative. I have included the complete texts of some items because of their outstanding importance or their brevity, but in a number of instances I have omitted meaningless formal verbiage, especially introductory or concluding paragraphs of treaties, without indicating the omission.

In some documents I have omitted material either because it was repetitious or because it consisted of details not essential to an understanding of the basic significance of the document in question. In these cases, I have indicated omissions by the following devices: (1) the use of the standard dots; (2) bracketed statements either summarizing or describing the omitted material; or (3) the retention of the original number of an article or paragraph so that gaps in the numbering will indicate omission, e.g., Article 5 followed by Article 9. The citation of the source of each document enables the interested reader to check the original for omitted material.

I have made no alterations in the text of any document. Consequently, there is no consistency in such matters as spelling, punctuation, capitalization, and so forth.

CONFLICT
AND
TENSION
IN THE
FAR EAST

Key Documents,
1894-1960

1

THE RISE OF JAPAN: 1895-1910

The critical period between 1895 and 1910 witnessed the emergence of Japan as the dominant power in the Far East. In 1895 it defeated Imperial China in war and ten years later it administered a similar defeat to Imperial Russia. In 1910 it completed its territorial expansion as an empire by annexing Korea. Only shattering military defeat thirty-five years later by a non-Far Eastern power ended the domination of the Far East that Japan had achieved by 1910.

In 1894-95 Japan for the first time in its modern history resorted to war as an instrument of national policy. The ease of its victory and the extent of its economic and territorial gains at the expense of China demonstrated that Japan had come of age militarily. In the quarter of a century between roughly 1870 and the outbreak of this war Japan had created a national army, based on universal conscription, equipped with modern weapons, trained in the tactics and strategy of the Western military powers of the time and backed by an emerging system of industrialization. The attack on the collapsing Imperial Chinese government revealed not only military readiness but its eagerness to resort to force to achieve its goals in foreign policy.

The transcendent significance of the Japanese victory was that it established the relationship between Japan and China that was to prevail until the end of the Second World War: Japanese domination and Chinese forced submission. Consistently and almost without interruption Japan pursued an aggressive diplomatic, economic, and military policy toward China that was ended only by military defeat, inflicted by a United States that over the years had taken a stronger and stronger stand against Japan's policy on the continent.

The Open Door policy of 1899 resulted from American reaction to the closely related events of the Japanese victory over China and the "carving of the Chinese melon" by the Western powers which had

3

taken place after the Japanese triumph had so convincingly demonstrated the great weakness of China. Since the essence of the policy consisted only in gaining the commitment on the part of the other powers that they would not harm the United States position in China, it hardly strengthened that position in any positive fashion. However, it revealed an attitude toward China, its problems and the United States relation thereto that was to characterize United States policy through the Second World War. It was this policy as it was pursued over the years that drew the United States ever more deeply into the problems of Chinese-Japanese relations.

The Three-Power Intervention was the immediate and effective reaction of Russia, Germany, and France to the Japanese victory. Though Japan was forced to yield at the time, the resentment created among the Japanese was certainly one factor that led Japan to go to war with both Russia and Germany within the next twenty years. The principal issue involved in the intervention, the Liaotung Peninsula, brought Manchuria into the main arena of Far Eastern international relations; and it remained one of the key areas of tension in Far Eastern international relations into the 1950's.

The Japanese victory over Russia in the war of 1904-5 was additional and even more convincing proof of Japan's newly developed capacity to wage war. Imperial Russia was one of the world's great powers at the beginning of the century and the Japanese victory could not be explained away as a lucky one at the expense of a backward neighbor as had been the victory over China a decade earlier. The economic drain on Japan was considerable and victory almost eluded the Japanese forces; nevertheless, the Treaty of Portsmouth gave Japan substantial gains, especially in Manchuria and Korea. Of equal, if not greater, significance was the fact that it blunted the Imperial Russian thrust into the Far East. Forty years later one of the most powerful motives for the Soviet Russian attack on Japan in the closing days of the Second World War was the desire to regain the position lost by Imperial Russia at Portsmouth.

The conclusion of the first Anglo-Japanese Alliance in 1902 was a major diplomatic victory for Japan. In the first place, it was a necessary preliminary for the war to come with Russia. In the second place, to become allied with what was generally accepted as the great world power of the time was a major achievement for Japan which had been regarded as a mere international upstart and which, additionally, had escaped from the onerous burden of the unequal treaty system only three years earlier. The alliance also provided the means for Japan to become involved in the First World War at the expense of Germany, one of its principal rivals in China.

It likewise created for the United States a disturbing diplomatic problem that was not solved until the Washington Conference twenty years later. Increasing United States concern over the alliance was another measure of the growing tension between that country and Japan.

The annexation of Korea in 1910 was the final act in the territorial expansion of the old Empire of Japan. Although Japan later brought vast areas under its control, it was never again to absorb foreign territory directly and formally into the empire. The acquisition of Korea was the result of both Japanese penetration into Korean affairs and the elimination of two rivals, China and Russia, from the peninsula. Thirty-five years of colonial existence under Japanese rule inhibited the development of Korean national life to such an extent that it became almost automatically entangled in a new web of international rivalry and conflict after the Japanese defeat.

Military victories at the expense of its two rivals for power in the Far East, the annexation of a continental neighbor, and an alliance with the greatest power of the period securely established Japan as the leading nation of the Far East by 1910. These achievements revealed the extent to which Japan had mastered the techniques of power politics which characterized international affairs at the time. The basic pattern that emerged was a simple one: an economically, diplomatically, and militarily strong Japan, increasingly aggressive and increasingly willing to resort to war to achieve its foreign policy goals; a progressively weaker China, enfeebled not only by internal problems of great magnitude but also by increasing pressure from Japan; and a group of Western powers, uneasy over the rise of Japan and the collapse of China, but unable effectively to deal with either problem. Out of this situation there developed an increasingly complex interplay of tensions within the Far East and on the world scene which progressively pulled the Far East into the full current of world affairs.

No. 1. Treaty of Peace between Japan and China, "Treaty of Shimonoseki," Signed, April 17, 1895[1]

Article I. Independence of Korea. China recognizes definitely the full and complete independence and autonomy of Korea, and in consequence the payment of tribute and the performance of ceremonies and formalities by Korea to China, in derogation of such independence and autonomy, shall wholly cease for the future.

Article II. Cession of part of Fengtien Province. China cedes to

Japan in perpetuity and full sovereignty the following territories, together with all fortifications, arsenals and public property thereon:

(a) The southern portion of the province of Fengtien, within the following boundaries:—

The line of demarcation begins at the mouth of the River Yalu and ascends that stream to the mouth of the River An-ping; from thence the line runs to Feng-huang; from thence to Haicheng; from thence to Ying-kow, forming a line which describes the southern portion of the territory. The places above named are included in the ceded territory. When the line reaches the River Liao at Ying-kow, it follows the course of that stream to its mouth where it terminates. The mid-channel of the River Liao shall be taken as the line of demarcation.

This cession also includes all islands appertaining or belonging to the province of Fengtien, situated in the eastern portion of the Bay of Liao-tung and in the northern part of the Yellow Sea.

(b) The island of Formosa, together with all islands appertaining or belonging to said island of Formosa.

(c) The Pescadores Group, that is to say, all islands lying between the 119th and 120th degrees of longitude east of Greenwich and the 23rd and 24th degrees of north latitude.

Article III. Delimitation of ceded territory. The alignments of the frontiers described in the preceding Article and shown on the annexed map, shall be subject to the verification and demarcation on the spot, by a Joint Commission of Delimitation consisting of two or more Chinese and two or more Japanese Delegates to be appointed immediately after the exchange of the ratifications of this Act. In case the boundaries laid down in this Act are found to be defective at any point, either on account of topography or in consideration of good administration, it shall also be the duty of the Delimitation Commission to rectify the same.

The Delimitation Commission will enter upon its duties as soon as possible and will bring its labors to a conclusion within the period of one year after appointment.

The alignments laid down in this Act shall, however, be maintained until the rectifications of the Delimitation Commission, if any are made, shall have received the approval of the Governments of China and Japan.

Article IV. War Indemnity to Japan. China agrees to pay to Japan as a war indemnity the sum of 200,000,000 Kuping Taels. The said sum is to be paid in eight installments. The first installment of

50,000,000 Taels to be paid within six months and the second installment of 50,000,000 Taels to be paid within twelve months after the exchange of the ratifications of this Act. The remaining sum to be paid in six equal installments, as follows: The first of such equal installments to be paid within two years; the second within three years; the third within four years; the fourth within five years; the fifth within six years; and the sixth within seven years, after the exchange of the ratifications of this Act. Interest at the rate of 5 *per centum per annum* shall begin to run on all unpaid portions of the said indemnity from the date the first installment falls due.

China shall, however, have the right to pay by anticipation at any time any or all of said installments. In case the whole amount of the said indemnity is paid within three years after the exchange of the ratifications of the present Act, all interest shall be waived and the interest for two years and a half or for any less period if then already paid, shall be included as a part of the principal amount of the indemnity.

Article V. Inhabitants of ceded territory. The inhabitants of the territory ceded to Japan, who wish to take up their residence outside the ceded districts shall be at liberty to sell their real property and retire.

For this purpose a period of two years from the date of the exchange of the ratifications of the present Act, shall be granted. At the expiration of that period those of the inhabitants who shall not have left such territories shall at the option of Japan be deemed to be Japanese subjects.

Each of the two Governments shall immediately upon the exchange of the ratifications of the present Act, send one or more Commissioners to Formosa to effect a final transfer of that Province and within the space of two months after the exchange of the ratifications of this act, such transfer shall be completed.

Article VI. Treaty of commerce and navigation to be negotiated. All treaties between Japan and China having come to an end in consequence of war, China engages, immediately upon the exchange of the ratifications of this Act, to appoint plenipotentiaries to conclude with the Japanese plenipotentiaries a treaty of commerce and navigation and a convention to regulate frontier intercourse and trade. The treaties, conventions, and regulations now subsisting between China and European Powers shall serve as a basis for the said treaty and convention between Japan and China. From the date of the exchange of the ratifications of the Act until the said treaty and convention are brought into actual operation the Japanese Government, its officials, commerce, navigation, frontier intercourse and trade, industries, ships and subjects shall in every respect be accorded by China most-favored-nation treatment.

China makes, in addition, the following concessions, to take effect six months after the date of the present Act:—

I. The following cities, towns, and ports, in addition to those already opened, shall be opened to the trade, residence, industries, and manufactures of Japanese subjects under the same conditions and with the same privileges and facilities as exist at the present open cities, towns, and ports of China:—

1. Shashih, in the province of Hupeh.
2. Chungking, in the province of Szechuan.
3. Suchow, in the province of Kiang Su.
4. Hangchow, in the province of Chekiang.

The Japanese Government shall have the right to station consuls at any or all of the above-named places.

II. Steam navigation for vessels under the Japanese flag for the conveyance of passengers and cargo shall be extended to the following places:—

1. On the upper Yang-tsze river, from Ichang to Chungking.
2. On the Woosung river and the canal, from Shanghai to Suchow and Hangchow.

The rules and regulations which now govern the navigation of the inland waters of China by foreign vessels shall, so far as applicable, be enforced in respect of the above-mentioned routes, until new rules and regulations are conjointly agreed to.

III. Japanese subjects purchasing goods or produce in the interior of China, or transporting imported merchandise into the interior of China, shall have the right temporarily to rent or hire warehouses for the storage of the articles so purchased or transported, without the payment of any taxes or exactions whatever.

IV. Japanese subjects shall be free to engage in all kinds of manufacturing industries in all the open cities, towns, and ports of China, and shall be at liberty to import into China all kinds of machinery, paying only the stipulated import duties thereon.

All articles manufactured by Japanese subjects in China shall, in respect of inland transit and internal taxes, duties, charges, and exactions of all kinds, and also in respect of warehousing and storage facilities in the interior of China, stand upon the same footing and enjoy the same privileges and exemptions as merchandise imported by Japanese subjects into China.

In the event additional rules and regulations are necessary in connection with these concessions, they shall be embodied in the treaty of commerce and navigation provided for by this article.

Article VII. Subject to the provisions of the next succeeding article, the evacuation of China by the armies of Japan shall be completely effected within three months after the exchange of the ratifications of the present Act.

Article VIII. As a guarantee of the faithful performance of the stipulations of this Act, China consents to the temporary occupation by the military forces of Japan of Wei-hai-wei, in the province of Shantung.

Upon the payment of the first two installments of the war indemnity herein stipulated for, and the exchange of the ratifications of the treaty of commerce and navigation, the said place shall be evacuated by the Japanese forces: provided the Chinese Government consents to pledge, under suitable and sufficient arrangements, the customs revenue of China as security for the payment of the principal and interest of the remaining installments of said indemnity. In the event no such arrangements are concluded, such evacuation shall only take place upon the payment of the final installment of said indemnity.

It is, however, expressly understood that no such evacuation shall take place until after the exchange of the ratifications of the treaty of commerce and navigation.

Article IX. Immediately upon the exchange of the ratifications of this Act, all prisoners of war then held shall be restored, and China undertakes not to ill-treat or punish prisoners of war so restored to her by Japan. China also engages to release at once all Japanese subjects accused of being military spies or charged with any other military offences. China further engages not to punish in any manner, nor to allow to be punished, those Chinese subjects who have in any manner been compromised in their relations with the Japanese army during the war.

Article X. All offensive military operations shall cease upon the exchange of the ratifications of this act.

Article XI. The present Act shall be ratified by their Majesties the Emperor of Japan and the Emperor of China, and the ratifications shall be exchanged at Chefoo on the 8th day of the 5th month of the 28th year of Meiji, corresponding to 14th day of the 4th month of the 21st year of Kuang Hsu.

In witness whereof the respective plenipotentiaries have signed the same, and have affixed thereto the seals of their arms.

Done at Shimonoseki, in duplicate, this 17th day of the 4th month of the 28th year of Meiji, corresponding to the 23rd day of 3rd month of the 21st year of Kuang Hsu.

No. 2. The Three-Power Intervention:
Russian Note to the Japanese Government[2]

The Government of His Majesty, the Emperor, my August Master, in examining the conditions of peace which Japan has imposed on China finds that the possession of the peninsula of Liao-tung claimed by Japan, would be a constant menace to the capital of China and at the same time it will render illusory the independence of Corea, that henceforth it would be a perpetual obstacle to the permanant peace of the Far East. Consequently, the Government of His Majesty, the Emperor, my August Master, would give a new proof of his sincere friendship for the Government of His Majesty, the Emperor of Japan, by advising it to renounce the definitive Possession of the peninsula of Liao-tung.

No. 3. Reply of the Japanese Government to Russia,
Germany, and France[3]

The Imperial Government have most carefully examined the memorandum which has been addressed to them by His Excellency the Envoy Extraordinary and Minister Plenipotentiary of His Majesty the Emperor of Russia in the name of his Government. The Government of His Majesty the Emperor, taking into consideration the friendly recommendation of the Imperial Russian Government, and being desirous to give new proof of the value which they attach to relations of good friendship which unite the two Empires, consent, after the honour and dignity of Japan shall have been satisfied by due exchange of ratifications of the Treaty of Shimonoseki, to introduce by a Supplementary Act the following modifications in the said Treaty:—

First. –The Imperial Government consent to renounce their definitive possession of the Feng Tien [Liaotung] Peninsula, excepting the province of Kinchow, reserving for subsequent adjustment with China the question of a reasonable pecuniary compensation for the abandoned territory.

Secondly. –It is, however, understood that the Imperial Government shall have the right to occupy as a guarantee the above-mentioned territory pending the complete performance by China of her Treaty engagements to Japan.

No. 4. Convention for the Retrocession by Japan to China of the Southern Portion of the Province of Feng-Tien (i.e., the Liaotung Peninsula), November 8, 1895[4]

Article I. Territory Retroceded. Japan retrocedes to China in perpetuity and full sovereignty the south portion of the Province of Feng-Tien, which was ceded to Japan under Article II of the Treaty of Shimonoseki . . . together with all fortifications, arsenals and public property thereon at the time the retroceded territory is completely evacuated by the Japanese forces. . . .

II. Compensation in Lieu of Territory. As compensation for the retrocession of the southern portion of the Province of Feng-Tien, the Chinese Government engage to pay the Japanese Government 30,000,000 Kuping taels on or before [November 16th, 1895]. . . .

III. Mode of Payment. Within three months from the day on which China shall have paid to Japan the compensatory indemnity of 30,000,000 Kuping taels provided for in Article II of this Convention, the retroceded territory shall be completely evacuated by Japanese forces.

No. 5. Convention for the Lease of the Liaotung Peninsula, March 27, 1898[5]

Article I. For the purpose of ensuring that the Russian naval forces shall possess an entirely secure base on the littoral of northern China, H. M. the Emperor of China agrees to place at the disposal of the Russian Government, on lease, the Ports Arthur (Liou-choun-kow) and Ta-lien-wan [Dairen], together with the water areas contiguous to these ports. This act of lease, however, in no way violates the sovereign rights of H. M. the Emperor of China to the above-mentioned territory.

Article IV. . . . the entire military command of the land and naval forces and equally the supreme civil administration will be entirely given over to the Russian authorities. . . . No Chinese military land forces whatsoever will be allowed on the territory specified. . . .

Article VIII. The Chinese Government agrees that the concessions granted by it in 1895 to the Chinese Eastern Railway Company, from the date of the signature of the present agreement shall be extended to the connecting branch which is to be built from one of the stations of the main line to Ta-lien-wan and also, if deemed necessary, from the same main line to another more convenient point on the littoral of the Liaotung Peninsula. . . .

No. 6. Secretary of State Hay's "Open Door"
Correspondence[6]

A. Mr. Hay to Mr. White [Ambassador to Germany]

Department of State
Washington, September 6, 1899

Sir: At the time when the Government of the United States was informed by that of Germany that it had leased from His Majesty the Emperor of China the port of Kiaochao and the adjacent territory in the province of Shantung, assurances were given to the Ambassador of the United States at Berlin by the Imperial German Minister for Foreign Affairs that the rights and privileges insured by treaties with China to citizens of the United States would not thereby suffer or be in anywise impaired within the area over which Germany had thus obtained control.

More recently, however, the British Government recognized by a formal agreement with Germany the exclusive right of the latter country to enjoy in said leased area and the contiguous "sphere of influence or interest" certain privileges, more especially those relating to railroads and mining enterprises; but, as the exact nature and extent of the rights thus recognized have not been clearly defined, it is possible that serious conflicts of interest may at any time arise, not only between British and German subjects within said area, but that the interests of our citizens may also be jeopardized thereby.

Earnestly desirous to remove any cause of irritation and to insure at the same time to the commerce of all nations in China the undoubted benefits which should accrue from a formal recognition by the various Powers claiming "spheres of interest" that they shall enjoy perfect equality of treatment for their commerce and navigation within such "spheres," the Government of the United States would be pleased to see His German Majesty's Government give formal assurances, and lend its cooperation in securing like assurances from the other interested Powers, that each within its respective sphere of whatever influence—

First. Will in no way interfere with any treaty port or any vested interest within any so-called "sphere of interest" or leased territory it may have in China.

Second. That the Chinese treaty tariff of the time being shall apply to all merchandise landed or shipped to all such ports as are within said "sphere of interest" (unless they be "free ports"), no matter to what nationality it may belong, and that duties so leviable shall be collected by the Chinese Government.

Third. That it will levy no higher harbor dues on vessels of another nationality frequenting any port in such "sphere" than shall be levied on vessels of its own nationality, and no higher railroad charges over lines built, controlled, or operated within its "sphere" on merchandise belonging to citizens or subjects of other nationalities transported through such "sphere" than shall be levied on similar merchandise belonging to its own nationals transported over equal distances.

The liberal policy pursued by His Imperial German Majesty in declaring Kiao-chao a free port and in aiding the Chinese Government in the establishment there of a custom-house are so clearly in line with the proposition which this Government is anxious to see recognized that it entertains the strongest hope that Germany will give its acceptance and hearty support.

The recent Ukase of His Majesty the Emperor of Russia declaring the port of Talien-wan [Dairen] open during the whole of the lease under which it is held from China to the merchant ships of all nations, coupled with the categorical assurances made to this Government by His Imperial Majesty's representative at this capital at the time, and since repeated to me by the present Russian Ambassador, seem to insure the support of the Emperor to the proposed measure. Our Ambassador at the Court of St. Petersburg has in consequence been instructed to submit it to the Russian Government and to request their early consideration of it. A copy of my instruction on the subject to Mr. Tower is herewith enclosed for your confidential information.

The commercial interests of Great Britain and Japan will be so clearly served by the desired declaration of intentions, and the views of the Governments of these countries as to the desirability of the adoption of measures insuring the benefits of equality of treatment of all foreign trade throughout China are so similar to those entertained by the United States, that their acceptance of the propositions herein outlined and their cooperation in advocating their adoption by the other Powers can be confidently expected. I enclose herewith copy of the instructions which I have sent to Mr. Choate on the subject.

In view of the present favorable conditions, you are instructed to submit the above considerations to His Imperial German Majesty's Minister for Foreign Affairs, and to request his early consideration of the subject. Copy of this instruction is sent to our Ambassadors at London and St. Petersburg for their information. I have, etc.

John Hay

B. Mr. Choate to Lord Salisbury

Embassy of United States
London, September 22, 1899

. . . While the Government of the United States will in no way commit itself to any recognition of the exclusive rights of any power within or control over any portion of the Chinese Empire, under such agreements as have been recently made, it can not conceal its apprehensions that there is danger of complications arising between the treaty powers which may imperil the rights insured to the United States by its treaties with China. It is the sincere desire of my Government that the interests of its citizens may not be prejudiced through exclusive treatment by any of the controlling powers within their respective "spheres of interests" in China, and it hopes to retain there any open market for all the world's commerce, remove dangerous sources of international irritation, and thereby hasten united action of the powers at Peking to promote administrative reforms so greatly needed for strengthening the Imperial Government and maintaining the integrity of China, in which it believes the whole western world is alike concerned. It believes that such a result may be greatly aided and advanced by declarations by the various Powers claiming "spheres of interest" in China as to their intentions in regard to the treatment of foreign trade and commerce therein. . . .

C. [Foreign Minister] Count Von Bulow to Mr. White

Foreign Office
Berlin, February 9, 1900

Mr. Ambassador: Your Excellency informed me, in a memorandum presented on the 24th of last month, that the Government of the United States of America had received satisfactory written replies from all the Powers to which an inquiry had been addressed similar to that contained in Your Excellency's note of September 26 last, in regard to the policy of the open door in China. While referring to this, Your Excellency thereupon expressed the wish that the Imperial Government would now also give its answer in writing.

Gladly complying with this wish, I have the honor to inform Your Excellency, repeating the statements already made verbally, as follows: As recognized by the Government of the United States of America, according to Your Excellency's note referred to above, the Imperial Government has, from the beginning, not only asserted, but also practically carried out to the fullest extent, in its Chinese possession absolute equality of treatment of all nations with regard to trade, navigation, and commerce. The Imperial Government entertains no thought of departing in the future from this principle, which at once excludes any prejudicial or disadvantageous commercial treatment of the citizens of the United States of America, so long as it is not forced to do so, on account of considerations of reciprocity, by a divergence from it by other governments. If therefore, the other Powers interested in the industrial development of the Chinese Empire are willing to recognize the same principles, this can only be desired by the Imperial Government, which in this case upon being requested will gladly be ready to participate with the United States of America and the other Powers in an agreement made upon these lines, by which the same rights are reciprocally secured.

I avail myself, etc.

Bulow

D. Instructions sent Mutatis Mutandis to the
United States Ambassadors at London, Paris, Berlin,
St. Petersburg, and Rome, and to the United States
Minister at Tokyo

Department of State
Washington, March 20, 1900

Sir: The ----- Government having accepted the declaration suggested by the United States concerning foreign trade in China . . . and like action having been taken by all the various Powers having leased territory or so-called "spheres of interest" in the Chinese Empire . . . you will please inform the Government to which you are accredited that the condition originally attached to its acceptance—that all other Powers concerned should likewise accept the proposals of the United States—having been complied with, this Government will therefore consider the assent given to it by -----as final and definitive.

You will also . . . convey to him [the Minister for Foreign Affairs] the expression of the sincere gratification which the President feels at the successful termination of these negotiations, in which he sees proof of the friendly spirit which animates the various Powers interested in the untrammeled development of commerce and industry in the Chinese Empire, and a source of vast benefit to the whole commercial world.

I am, etc.

John Hay.

No. 7. Agreement Relative to China and Corea (Anglo-Japanese Alliance), January 30, 1902[7]

The Governments of Great Britain and Japan, actuated solely by a desire to maintain the *status quo* and general peace in the Extreme East, being moreover specially interested in maintaining the independence and territorial integrity of the Empire of China and the Empire of Corea, and in securing equal opportunities in those countries for the commerce and industry of all nations, hereby agree as follows:

Article I. The High Contracting Parties having mutually recognized the independence of China and Corea, declare themselves to be entirely uninfluenced by any aggressive tendencies in either country. Having in view, however, their special interests, of which those of Great Britain relate principally to China, while Japan, in addition to the interests which she possesses in China, is interested in a peculiar degree, politically as well as commercially and industrially, in Corea, the High Contracting Parties recognize that it will be admissible for either of them to take such measures as may be indispensable in order to safeguard those interests if threatened by the aggressive action of any other Power, or by disturbances arising in China or Corea, and necessitating the intervention of either of the High Contracting Parties for the protection of the lives and property of its subjects.

Article II. If either Great Britain or Japan, in the defence of their respective interests as above described, should become involved in war with another Power, the other High Contracting Party will maintain a strict neutrality, and use its efforts to prevent other Powers from joining in hostilities against its ally.

Article III. If, in the above event, any other Power or Powers should join in hostilities against that ally, the other High Contracting Party will come to its assistance, and will conduct war in common, and will make peace in mutual agreement with it.

Article IV. The High Contracting Parties agree that neither of them will, without consulting the other, enter into separate agreements with another Power to the prejudice of the interests above described.

Article V. Whenever, in the opinion of either Great Britain or Japan, the above-mentioned interests are in jeopardy, the two Governments will communicate with one another fully and frankly.

Article VI. The present Agreement shall come into effect immediately after the date of signature, and remain in force for five years from that date.

In case neither of the High Contracting Parties should have notified twelve months before the expiration of the said five years the intention of terminating it, it shall remain binding until the expiration of one year from the day on which either of the High Contracting Parties shall have denounced it. But if, when the date fixed for its expiration arrives, either ally is actually engaged in war, the alliance shall, *ipso facto,* continue until peace is concluded.

No. 8. Agreement between Great Britain and Japan, August 12, 1905[8]

Preamble. The Governments of Great Britain and Japan, being desirous of replacing the agreement concluded between them on the 30th January, 1902, by fresh stipulations, have agreed upon the following Articles, which have for their object:

(a) The consolidation and maintenance of general peace in the regions of eastern Asia and India;

(b) The preservation of the common interests of all Powers in China by insuring the independence and integrity of the Chinese Empire and the principle of equal opportunities for the commerce and industry of all nations in China;

(c) The maintenance of the territorial rights of the High Contracting Parties in the regions of Eastern Asia and of India, and the defence of their special interests in the said regions:

Article I. It is agreed that whenever in the opinion of either Great Britain or Japan, any of the rights and interests referred to in the preamble of this Agreement are in jeopardy, the two Governments will communicate with one another fully and frankly, and consider in common the measures which should be taken to safeguard those menaced rights or interests.

Article II. If, by reason of an unprovoked attack or aggressive action, wherever arising, on the part of any other Power or Powers, either Contracting Party should be involved in war in defence of its territorial rights or special interests mentioned in the preamble of this Agreement, the other Contracting Party will at once come to the assistance of its ally, and will conduct war in common, and make peace in mutual agreement with it.

Article III. Japan possessing paramount political, military and economic interests in Corea, Great Britain recognizes the right of Japan to take such measures of guidance, control and protection in Corea as she may deem proper and necessary to safeguard and advance those interests, provided always that such measures are not contrary to the principle of equal opportunities for the commerce and industry of all nations.

Article IV. Great Britain having a special interest in all that concerns the security of the Indian frontier, Japan recognizes her right to take such measures in the proximity of that frontier as she may find necessary for safeguarding her Indian possessions.

Article VI. As regards the present war between Japan and Russia, Great Britain will continue to maintain strict neutrality unless some other Power or Powers should join in hostilities against Japan, in which case Great Britain will come to the assistance of Japan, and will conduct the war in common, and make peace in mutual agreement with Japan.

Article VIII. The present Agreement shall . . . remain in force for ten years. . . .

No. 9. *Agreement between Great Britain and Japan, July 13, 1911*[9]

Article IV. Should either High Contracting Party conclude a treaty of general arbitration with a third Power, it is agreed that nothing in this Agreement shall entail upon such Contracting Party an obligation to go to war with the Power with whom such a treaty of arbitration is in force.

No. 10. *Treaty of Portsmouth, September 5, 1905*[10]

Article I. There shall henceforth be peace and amity between Their Majesties, the Emperor of Japan and the Emperor of all the Russias, and between Their respective States and subjects.

Article II. The Imperial Russian Government, acknowledging that Japan possesses in Corea paramount political, military, and economical interests, engage neither to obstruct nor interfere with the measures of guidance, protection and control which the Imperial Government of Japan may find it necessary to take in Corea.

It is understood that Russian subjects in Corea shall be treated in exactly the same manner as the subjects and citizens of other foreign Powers, that is to say, they shall be placed on the same footing as the subjects or citizens of the most favored nation.

It is also agreed that, in order to avoid causes of misunderstanding, the two High Contracting Parties will abstain, on the Russo-Corean frontier, from taking any military measure which may menace the security of Russian or Corean territory.

Article III. Japan and Russia mutually engage:

(1) To evacuate completely and simultaneously Manchuria except the territory affected by the lease of the Liao-tung Peninsula, in conformity with the provisions of the additional Article I annexed to this treaty; and

(2) To restore entirely and completely to the exclusive administration of China all portions of Manchuria now in the occupation or under the control of the Japanese or Russian troops, with the exception of the territory above-mentioned.

The Imperial Government of Russia declare that they have not in Manchuria any territorial advantages or preferential or exclusive concessions in impairment of Chinese sovereignty or inconsistent with the principle of equal opportunity.

Article IV. Japan and Russia reciprocally engage not to obstruct any general measures common to all countries, which China may take for the development of the commerce and industry of Manchuria.

Article V. The Imperial Russian Government transfer and assign to the Imperial Government of Japan, with the consent of the Government of China, the lease of Port Arthur, Talien, and adjacent territory and territorial waters, and all rights, privileges, and concessions connected with or forming part of such lease and they also transfer and assign to the Imperial Government of Japan all public works and properties in the territory affected by the above-mentioned lease.

The two High Contracting Parties mutually engage to obtain the consent of the Chinese Government mentioned in the foregoing stipulation.

The Imperial Government of Japan on their part undertake that the proprietary rights of Russian subjects in the territory above referred to shall be perfectly respected.

Article VI. The Imperial Russian Government engage to transfer and assign to the Imperial Government of Japan, without compensation and with the consent of the Chinese Government, the railroad between Chang-chun (Kuan-chang-tsu) and Port Arthur, and all its branches, together with all rights, privileges, and properties appertaining thereto in that region, as well as all coal mines in the said region belonging to or worked for the benefit of the railway.

The two High Contracting Parties mutually engage to obtain the consent of the Government of China mentioned in the foregoing stipulation.

Article VII. Japan and Russia engage to exploit their respective railways in Manchuria exclusively for commercial and industrial purposes and in no wise for strategic purposes.

It is understood that this restriction does not apply to the railway in the territory affected by the lease of the Liao-tung Peninsula.

Article VIII. The Imperial Governments of Japan and Russia, with the view to promote and facilitate intercourse and traffic, will, as soon as possible, conclude a separate convention for the regulation of their connecting railway services in Manchuria.

Article IX. The Imperial Russian Government cede to the Imperial Government of Japan in perpetuity and full sovereignty, the southern portion of the Island of Saghalien and all islands adjacent thereto, and all public works and properties thereon. The fiftieth degree of north latitude is adopted as the northern boundary of the ceded territory. The exact alignment of such territory shall be determined in accordance with the provisions of additional Article II annexed to this treaty.

Japan and Russia mutually agree not to construct in their respective possessions on the island of Saghalien or the adjacent islands any fortifications or other similar military works. They also respectively engage not to take any military measures which may impede the free navigation of the Straits of La Perouse and Tartary.

Article X. It is reserved to Russian subjects, inhabitants of the territory ceded to Japan, to sell their real property and retire to their country; but if they prefer to remain in the ceded territory, they will be maintained and protected in the full exercise of their industries and rights of property, on condition of submitting to Japanese laws and jurisdiction. Japan shall have full liberty to withdraw the right of residence in, or to deport from, such territory any inhabitants who labor under political or administrative disability. She engages, however, that the proprietary rights of such inhabitants shall be fully respected.

Article XI. Russia engages to arrange with Japan for granting to Japanese subjects rights of fishery along the coasts of the Russian possessions in the Japan, Okhotsk, and Behring Seas. It is agreed that the foregoing engagement shall not affect rights already belonging to Russian or foreign subjects in those regions.

Article XII. The Treaty of Commerce and Navigation between Japan and Russia having been annulled by the war, the Imperial Governments of Japan and Russia engage to adopt as the basis for their commercial relations, pending the conclusion of a new treaty of commerce and navigation on the basis of the treaty which was in force previous to the present war, the system of reciprocal treatment on the footing of the most favored nation, in which are included import and export duties, customs formalities, transit and tonnage dues, and the admission and treatment of agents, subjects and vessels of one country in the territories of the other.

Article XIII. As soon as possible after the present Treaty comes into force, all prisoners of war shall be reciprocally restored. The Imperial Governments of Japan and Russia shall each appoint a special Commissioner to take charge of prisoners. All prisoners in the hands of one Government shall be delivered to and received by the Commissioner of the other Government or by his duly authorized representative, in such convenient numbers and at such convenient ports of the delivering State as such delivering State shall notify in advance to the Commissioner of the receiving State.

The Governments of Japan and Russia shall present to each other, as soon as possible after the delivery of prisoners has been completed, a statement of the direct expenditures respectively incurred by them for the care and maintenance of the prisoners from the date of capture or surrender and up to the time of death or delivery. Russia engages to repay Japan, as soon as possible after the exchange of the statements as above provided, the difference between the actual amount so expended by Japan and the actual amount similarly disbursed by Russia.

Article XIV. The present treaty shall be ratified by their Majesties, the Emperor of Japan and the Emperor of all the Russias. Such ratification shall, with as little delay as possible, and in any case not later than fifty days from the date of the signature of the Treaty, be announced to the Imperial Governments of Japan and Russia respectively through the French Minister at Tokio and the Ambassador of the United States in St. Petersburg, and from the date of the later of such announcements this treaty shall in all its parts come into full force.

The formal exchange of ratifications shall take place at Washington as soon as possible.

Article XV. The present treaty shall be signed in duplicate in both the English and French languages. The texts are in absolute conformity, but in case of a discrepancy in interpretation, the French text shall prevail.

Additional Articles. In conformity with the provisions of Articles III and IX of the Treaty of Peace between Japan and Russia of this date, the undersigned plenipotentiaries have concluded the following additional Articles:

To *Article III.* The Imperial Governments of Japan and Russia mutually engage to commence the withdrawal of their military forces from the territory of Manchuria simultaneously and immediately after the Treaty of Peace comes into operation, and within a period of eighteen months from that date, the Armies of the two countries shall be completely withdrawn from Manchuria, except from the leased territory of the Liao-tung Peninsula.

The forces of the two countries occupying the front positions shall be first withdrawn.

The High Contracting Parties reserve to themselves the right to maintain guards to protect their respective railway lines in Manchuria. The number of such guards shall not exceed fifteen per kilometer, and within that maximum number, the Commanders of the Japanese and Russian armies shall, by common accord, fix the number of such guards to be employed as small as possible while having in view the actual requirements.

The Commanders of the Japanese and Russian forces in Manchuria shall agree upon the details of the evacuation in conformity with the above principles, and shall take by common accord the measures necessary to carry out the evacuation as soon as possible, and in any case not later than the period of eighteen months.

To *Article IX.* As soon as possible after the present Treaty comes into force, a Commission of Delimitation, composed of an equal number of members to be appointed, respectively, by the two High Contracting Parties, shall on the spot, mark in a permanent manner the exact boundary between the Japanese and Russian possessions on the island of Saghalien. The Commission shall be bound, so far as topographical considerations permit, to follow the fiftieth parallel of north latitude as the boundary line, and in case any deflections from that line at any points are found to be necessary, compensation will be made by correlative deflections at other points. It shall also be the duty of said Commission to prepare a list and a description of the adjacent islands included in the cession, and, finally, the Commission shall prepare and sign maps showing the boundaries of the ceded territory. The work of the Commission shall be subject to the approval of the High Contracting Parties. The foregoing additional articles are to be considered as ratified with the ratification of the treaty of peace to which they are annexed.

Portsmouth, the 5th day of the 9th month of the 38th year of Meiji, corresponding to the 23rd August,
5th September, 1905.

No. 11. Treaty of Alliance between Korea and Japan, August 26, 1894[11]

In view of the fact that on the 25th of July, 1894, the Korean Government entrusted His Imperial Majesty's Envoy Extraordinary and Minister Plenipotentiary at Söul, Korea, with the expulsion, on their behalf, of Chinese soldiers from Korean territory, the Governments of Japan and Korea have been placed in a situation to give mutual assistance both offensive and defensive. Consequently, the undersigned Plenipotentiaries, duly authorized by their respective Governments, have, with a view of defining the fact and of securing in the premises concerted action on the part of the two countries, agreed to the following Articles:—

Article I. The object of the alliance is to maintain the independence of Korea on a firm footing and to promote the respective interests of both Japan and Korea by expelling Chinese soldiers from Korean territory.

Article II. Japan will undertake all warlike operations against China, both offensive and defensive, while Korea will undertake to give every possible facility to Japanese soldiers regarding their movements and supply of provisions.

Article III. This treaty shall cease and determine at the conclusion of a treaty of peace with China.

No. 12. Protocol Concluded between Japan and Korea on February 23, 1904, regarding the Situation of Korea[12]

Article I. For the purposes of maintaining a permanent and solid friendship between Japan and Korea and firmly establishing peace in the Far East, the Imperial Government of Korea shall place full confidence in the Imperial Government of Japan and adopt the advice of the latter in regard to improvements in administration.

Article II. The Imperial Government of Japan shall in a spirit of firm friendship ensure the safety and repose of the Imperial House of Korea.

Article III. The Imperial Government of Japan definitively guarantee the independence and territorial integrity of the Korean Empire.

Article IV. In case the welfare of the Imperial House of Korea or the territorial integrity of Korea is endangered by aggression of a third Power or by internal disturbances, the Imperial Government of Japan shall immediately take such necessary measures as the circumstances require, and in such cases the Imperial Government of Korea shall give full facilities to promote the action of the Imperial Japanese Government.

The Imperial Government of Japan may, for the attainment of the above-mentioned objects, occupy, when the circumstances require it, such places as may be necessary from strategical points of view.

Article V. The Governments of the two countries shall not in future, without mutual consent, conclude with a third Power such an arrangement as may be contrary to the principles of the present protocol.

Article VI. Details in connection with the present Protocol shall be arranged, as the circumstances may require, between the Representative of Japan and the Minister of State for Foreign Affairs of Korea.

No.13. Treaty of Annexation (Signed on August 22, 1910 Promulgated on the 29th of August) [13]

His Majesty the Emperor of Japan and His Majesty the Emperor of Korea, having in view the special and close relations between Their respective countries, desiring to promote the common weal of the two nations and to assure permanent peace in the Extreme East, and being convinced that these objects can be best attained by the annexation of Korea to the Empire of Japan, have resolved to conclude a Treaty of such annexation, and have for that purpose appointed as Their Plenipotentiaries, that is to say:

His Majesty the Emperor of Japan, Viscount Masakata Terauchi, His Resident-General;

And His Majesty the Emperor of Korea, Yi Wan Yong, His Minister President of State;

Who, upon mutual conferences and deliberation, have agreed to the following Articles:

Article I. His Majesty the Emperor of Korea makes complete and permanent cession to His Majesty the Emperor of Japan of all rights of sovereignty over the whole of Korea.

Article II. His Majesty the Emperor of Japan accepts the cession mentioned in the preceding Article, and consents to the complete annexation of Korea to the Empire of Japan.

Article III. His Majesty the Emperor of Japan will accord to Their Majesties the Emperor and ex-Emperor and His Imperial Highness the Crown Prince of Korea and Their Consorts and Heirs such titles, dignity and honour as are appropriate to Their respective ranks, and sufficient annual grants will be made for the maintenance of such titles, dignity and honour.

Article IV. His Majesty the Emperor of Japan will also accord appropriate honour and treatment to the members of the Imperial House of Korea and their heirs, other than those mentioned in the preceding Article, and the funds necessary for the maintenance of such honour and treatment will be granted.

Article V. His Majesty the Emperor of Japan will confer peerages and monetary grants upon those Koreans who, on account of meritorious services, are regarded as deserving recognition.

Article VI. In consequence of the aforesaid annexation, the Government of Japan assume the entire government and administration of Korea and undertake to afford full protection for the persons and property to Koreans obeying the laws there in force, and to promote the welfare of all such Koreans.

Article VII. The Government of Japan will, so far as circumstances permit, employ in the public service of Japan in Korea those Koreans who accept the new *regime* loyally and in good faith and who are duly qualified for such service.

Article VIII. This Treaty, having been approved by his Majesty the Emperor of Japan and His Majesty the Emperor of Korea, shall take effect from the date of its promulgation.

In faith whereof, the respective Plenipotentiaries have signed this Treaty, and have affixed thereto their seals.

[Signatures]

2

THE FIRST WORLD WAR
AND ITS AFTERMATH: 1914-25

Little fighting took place in the Far East during the First World War. Yet new tensions were created among all the world powers by problems resulting from or intensified by the war. Perhaps most notable in this respect was the worsening of relations between the United States and Japan who, though allied against a common enemy after the United States entry into the war, found themselves increasingly rivals in the Far East.

The limited military action in the Shantung Peninsula, resulting in the Japanese ejection of Germany from its position there, not only gave Japan satisfaction for the German role in the Three-Power Intervention twenty years earlier, but created a fresh area of tension in Chinese-Japanese relations. The immediate and major consequence was the Japanese presentation of the Twenty-one Demands on China in 1915. The demands were a clear demonstration of the extent of Japanese ambitions in China and foreshadowed the Japanese course of action on the continent during the next three decades.

United States reaction to the demands marked the change from a minor conflict on policy to a major one. Japan, taking advantage of the concentration of European attention on the war, had planned to achieve secretly the acceptance of the demands and confront the world with a *fait accompli*. However, the United States prevented the Japanese government from doing that. The letter of Secretary of State Bryan to the Japanese Ambassador not only clearly stated United States policy at the time, but also forecast what it would be fifteen years later when Japanese aggression against China went into high gear. The doctrine of nonrecognition associated almost exclusively with United States policy toward Japanese aggression in Manchuria was clearly stated in the Bryan note to the Japanese and Chinese governments in 1915.

26

The peace settlement at Versailles did not deal conclusively with any of the Far Eastern ramifications of the First World War, the confirmation of the Japanese succession to German rights in Shantung not even settling Chinese-Japanese disputes over the peninsula. The Washington Conference of 1921-22 was a well-intentioned, but ill-fated attempt to solve the problems left untouched at Versailles. The Four-Power Pact was an American diplomatic victory, for it resulted in the ending of the Anglo-Japanese Alliance which had created concern in the United States as American-Japanese tension had mounted. However, this treaty never contributed to an easing of subsequent tensions in the Pacific area, as it had been intended to do.

The Five-Power Treaty was regarded as a major step toward the elimination of the threat of war in the Pacific. It was based on the erroneous assumption that mere mechanical limitation of the capacity of the three major (and two minor) naval powers to wage war on the sea would be sufficient to guarantee against the outbreak of war.

The Nine-Power Pact was a serious attempt to help China solve its basic problems and thus to eliminate it as a source of tension in the Far East in general and in American-Japanese relations in particular. Had each signatory lived up to its commitments there is no reason to doubt that China could eventually have solved its internal problems as anticipated and thus have ceased to be the scene of international rivalry and consequently of international tension. However, because of developments largely unforeseen—or at least not taken into account in the Washington settlement—Japan increasingly felt that it could not continue to be bound by the treaty. Its abandonment of the treaty was the real start of Japanese aggression a decade later. The Shantung treaty between China and Japan settled only temporarily the dispute arising from Japan's seizure of German rights there.

Of minor military but major political significance was the peculiar Siberian Intervention which began in the closing months of the war. The leaders of Russia's then revolutionary government deeply resented the intervention; they regarded it as a conclusive demonstration of the current and subsequent ill will of the "capitalistic, aggressive" powers—both the West and Japan—toward them and their government. However slight a threat this may have been in actual fact was of little consequence compared with what they imagined it to be. Also during the course of the intervention the relations between American and Japanese forces in Siberia were bad and this in turn had an adverse effect on the relations between Washington and Tokyo, not exactly smooth since the Twenty-one Demands.

The diplomatic correspondence over the intervention clearly out-
lines the incompatibility of the American and Japanese policies on
the venture, the former being as reluctant as the latter was eager.
The establishment of diplomatic relations between China and Japan on the one hand and Russia on the other signalized the emergence of the Soviet Union into Far Eastern international relations.
The conventions with China and Japan reveal, first, the weakness
of Russia's position vis-a-vis Japan and, second, the manner in
which it was attempting at the time to win China to its side. This
Russian tactic of trying to offset the pressure of Japanese power
through alliance with China was to be typical of Russian policy for
the next twenty years, though circumstances forced occasional modifications.

No. 1. Japanese Ultimatum to Germany, August 15, 1914[1]

We consider it highly important and necessary in the present
situation to take measures to remove the causes of all disturbance
of the peace in the Far East and to safeguard general interests as
contemplated in the agreement of alliance between Japan and Great
Britain. In order to secure firm and enduring peace in Eastern Asia
the establishment of which is the aim of the said agreement, the
Imperial Japanese Government sincerely believes it to be its duty
to give advice to the Imperial German Government to carry out the
following two propositions:

1. To withdraw immediately from Japanese and Chinese waters
the German men-of-war and armed vessels of all kinds, and to dis-
arm at once those which cannot be withdrawn.

2. To deliver on a date not later than September 15 to the Imperial Japanese authorities, without condition or compensation, the
entire leased territory of Kiaochau with a view to the eventual restoration of the same to China.

The Imperial Japanese Government announces at the same time
that, in the event of its not receiving by noon of August 23 an answer
from the Imperial German Government signifying unconditional acceptance of the above advice offered by the Imperial Japanese Government, Japan will be compelled to take such action as it may
deem necessary to meet the situation.

No. 2. British Official Announcement regarding Japanese Participation in the War, August 18, 1914[2]

The Governments of Great Britain and Japan having been in communication with each other, are of opinion that it is necessary for

each to take action to protect the general interest in the Far East contemplated by the Anglo-Japanese Alliance, keeping specially in view the independence and integrity of China, and provided for in that Agreement.

It is understood that the action of Japan will not extend to the Pacific Ocean beyond the China Seas except in so far as it may be necessary to protect Japanese shipping lines in the Pacific, nor beyond Asiatic waters westward of the China Seas, nor to any foreign territory except territory in German occupation on the Continent of Eastern Asia.

No. 3. Imperial Rescript Making a Declaration of War against Germany, August 23, 1914[3]

We, by the Grace of Heaven, Emperor of Japan, on the throne occupied by the same Dynasty from time immemorial, do hereby make the following proclamation to all Our loyal and brave subjects:

We, hereby, declare war against Germany and We command Our Army and Navy to carry on hostilities against that Empire with all their strength, and We also command all Our competent authorities to make every effort in pursuance of their respective duties to attain the national aim within the limit of the law of nations.

Since the outbreak of the present war in Europe, the calamitous effect of which We view with grave concern, We, on our part, have entertained hopes of preserving the peace of the Far East by the maintenance of strict neutrality but the action of Germany has at length compelled Great Britain, Our Ally, to open hostilities against that country, and Germany is at Kiaochau, its leased territory in China, busy with warlike preparations, while her armed vessels, cruising the seas of Eastern Asia, are threatening Our commerce and that of Our Ally. The peace of the Far East is thus in jeopardy.

Accordingly, Our Government, and that of His Britannic Majesty, after a full and frank communication with each other, agreed to take such measures as may be necessary for the protection of the general interests contemplated in the Agreement of Alliance, and We on Our part, being desirous to attain that object by peaceful means, commanded Our Government to offer, with sincerity, an advice to the Imperial German Government. By the last day appointed for the purpose, however, Our Government failed to receive an answer accepting their advice.

It is with profound regret that We, in spite of Our ardent devotion to the cause of peace, are thus compelled to declare war, especially at this early period of Our reign and while we are still in mourning for Our lamented Mother.

It is Our earnest wish, that, by the loyalty and valour of Our faithful subjects, peace may soon be restored and the glory of the Empire be enhanced.

No. 4. Treaty of Peace between the Allied and Associate Powers and Germany, June 28, 1919[1]

Article 156. Germany renounces in favour of Japan, all her rights, title and privileges—particularly those concerning the territory of Kiaochow, railways, mines and submarine cables—which she acquired in virtue of the Treaty concluded by her with China on March 6, 1898, and of all other arrangements relative to the Province of Shantung.

All German rights in the Tsingtao-Tsinanfu Railway, including its branch lines, together with its subsidiary property of all kinds, stations, shops, fixed and rolling stock, mines, plants and material for the exploitation of the mines, are and remain acquired by Japan, together with all rights and privileges attaching thereto.

The German State submarine cables from Tsingtao to Shanghai and from Tsingtao to Chefoo, with all the rights, privileges and properties attaching thereto, are similarly acquired by Japan, free and clear of all charges and encumbrances.

Article 157. The movable and immovable property owned by the German State in the territory of Kiaochow, as well as all the rights which Germany might claim in consequence of the works or improvements made or of the expenses incurred by her, directly or indirectly, in connection with this territory, are and remain acquired by Japan, free and clear of all charges and encumbrances.

Article 158. Germany shall hand over to Japan within three months from the coming into force of the present Treaty the archives, registers, plans, title deeds, and documents of every kind, whatever they may be, relating to the administration, whether civil, military, financial, judicial or other, of the territory of Kiaochow.

Within the same period Germany shall give particulars to Japan of all treaties, arrangements or agreements relating to the rights, title or privileges referred to in the two preceding Articles.

No. 5. The Twenty-one Demands: Instructions Given by Baron Kato, to Mr. Hioki (Presented, Tokyo, December 3, 1914)[5]

In order to provide for the readjustment of affairs consequent on the Japan-German war and for the purpose of ensuring a lasting peace in the Far East by strengthening the position of the Empire, the Imperial Government have resolved to approach the Chinese

Government with a view to conclude treaties and agreements mainly along the lines laid down in the first four groups of appended proposals. Of these, the first group relates to the settlement of the Shantung question, while the second group has for its chief aim the defining of Japan's position in South Manchuria and Eastern Inner Mongolia, that is to say, securing at this time from the Chinese Government full recognition of Japan's natural position in these regions, absence of which had hitherto been the cause for various questions tending to estrange the feelings of the two peoples towards each other. The object of the third group is to safeguard the best interest of the Han-yeh-ping Company, with which Japanese capitalists are closely identified. It will thus be seen that there is nothing especially new in our proposals embodied in the foregoing three groups, while as regards the fourth group, it is only intended to emphasize the principle of China's territorial integrity, which has so often been declared by the Imperial Government.

Believing it absolutely essential, for strengthening Japan's position in Eastern Asia as well as for preservation of the general interests of that region, to secure China's adherence to the foregoing proposals, the Imperial Government are determined to attain this end by all means within their power. You are, therefore, requested to use your best endeavor in the conduct of the negotiations, which are hereby placed in your hands.

As regards the proposals contained in the fifth group, they are presented as the wishes of the Imperial Government. The matters which are dealt with under this category are entirely different in character from those which are included in the first four groups. An adjustment, at this time, of these matters, some of which have been pending between the two countries, being nevertheless highly desirable for the advancement of the friendly relations between Japan and China as well as for safeguarding their common interests, you are also requested to exercise your best efforts to have our wishes carried out.

It is very likely that in the course of these negotiations the Chinese Government desire to find out the attitude of the Imperial Government on the question of the disposition of the leased territory of Kiaochou Bay. If the Chinese Government will accept our proposals as above stated, the Imperial Government may, with due regard to the principle of China's territorial integrity and in the interest of the friendship of the two countries, well consider the question with a view to restoring the said territory to China, in the event of Japan's being given free hand in the disposition thereof as the result of the coming peace conference between Japan and Germany.

As, however, it will be absolutely necessary, in restoring the said territory to China, to lay certain conditions such as the opening of the territory for foreign trade, establishment of a Japanese settlement, etc., you will ask for further instructions when you propose to declare to the Chinese government the willingness of the Imperial Government to consider the question. I avail, &c.

No. 6. The Twenty-one Demands[6]

Group I. The Japanese Government and the Chinese Government, being desirous to maintain the general peace in the Far East and to strengthen the relations of amity and good neighborhood existing between the two countries, agree to the following articles:

Article I. The Chinese Government engage to give full assent to all matters that the Japanese Government may hereafter agree with the German Government respecting the disposition of all the rights, interests and concessions, which, in virtue of treaties or otherwise, Germany possesses *vis-à-vis* China in relation to the Province of Shantung.

Article II. The Chinese Government engage that, within the Province of Shantung or along its coast, no territory or island will be ceded or leased to any other Power, under any pretext whatever.

Article III. The Chinese Government agree to Japan's building a railway connecting Chefoo or Lungkow with the Kiaochou-Tsinanfu Railway.

Article IV. The Chinese Government engage to open of their own accord, as soon as possible, certain important cities and towns in the Province of Shantung for the residence and commerce of foreigners. The place to be so opened shall be decided upon in a separate agreement.

Group II. The Japanese Government and the Chinese Government, in view of the fact that the Chinese Government has always recognized the predominant position of Japan in South Manchuria and Eastern Inner Mongolia, agree to the following articles:

Article I. The two contracting parties mutually agree that the term of the lease of Port Arthur and Dairen and the term respecting the South Manchuria Railway and the Antung-Mukden Railway shall be extended to a further period of 99 years respectively.

Article II. The Japanese subjects shall be permitted in South Manchuria and Eastern Inner Mongolia to lease or own land required either for erecting buildings for various commercial and industrial uses or for farming.

Article III. The Japanese subjects shall have liberty to enter, reside and travel in South Manchuria and Eastern Inner Mongolia, and to carry on business of various kinds—commercial, industrial and otherwise.

Article IV. The Chinese Government grant to the Japanese subjects the right of mining in South Manchuria and Eastern Inner Mongolia. As regards the mines to be worked, they shall be decided upon in a separate agreement.

Article V. The Chinese Government agree that the consent of the Japanese Government shall be obtained in advance, (1) whenever it is proposed to grant to other nationals the right of constructing a railway or to obtain from other nationals the supply of funds for constructing a railway in South Manchuria and Eastern Inner Mongolia, and (2) whenever a loan is to be made with any other Power, under security of the taxes of South Manchuria and Eastern Inner Mongolia.

Article VI. The Chinese Government engage that whenever the Chinese Government need the service of political, financial or military advisers or instructors in South Manchuria or Eastern Inner Mongolia, Japan shall first be consulted.

Article VII. The Chinese Government agree that the control and management of the Kirin-Changchun Railway shall be handed over to Japan for a term of 99 years dating from the signing of this Treaty.

Group III. The Japanese Government and the Chinese Government, having regard to the close relations existing between Japanese capitalists and the Han-yeh-ping Company and desiring to promote the common interests of the two nations, agree to the following articles:

Article I. The two Contracting Parties mutually agree that when the opportune moment arrives the Han-yeh-ping Company shall be made a joint concern of the two nations, and that, without the consent of the Japanese Government, the Chinese Government shall not dispose or permit the Company to dispose of any right or property of the Company.

Article II. The Chinese Government engage that, as a necessary measure for protection of the invested interests of Japanese capitalists, no mines in the neighborhood of those owned by the Han-yeh-ping Company shall be permitted, without the consent of the said company, to be worked by anyone other than the said company; and further that whenever it is proposed to take any other measure which may likely affect the interests of the said company directly or indirectly, the consent of the said company shall first be obtained.

Group IV. The Japanese Government and the Chinese Government, with the object of effectively preserving the territorial integrity of China, agree to the following article:

The Chinese Government engage not to cede or lease to any other Power any harbor or bay or any island along the coast of China.

Group V. 1. The Chinese Central Government to engage influential Japanese as political, financial and military advisers;

2. The Chinese Government to grant the Japanese hospitals, temples and schools in the interior of China the right to own land;

3. In the face of many police disputes which have hitherto arisen between Japan and China, causing no little annoyance, the police in localities (in China), where such arrangements are necessary, to be placed under joint Japanese and Chinese administration, or Japanese to be employed in police offices in such localities, so as to help at the same time the improvement of the Chinese police service;

4. China to obtain from Japan supply of a certain quantity of arms, or to establish an arsenal in China under joint Japanese and Chinese management and to be supplied with experts and materials from Japan;

5. In order to help the development of the Nanchang-Kiukiang Railway, with which Japanese capitalists are so closely identified, and with due regard to the negotiations which have for years been pending between Japan and China in relation to the railway question in South China, China to agree to give to Japan the right of constructing a railway to connect Wuchang with the Kiukiang-Nanchang line, and also the railways between Nanchang and Hangchou and between Nanchang and Chaochou.

6. In view of the relations between the Province of Fukien and Formosa and of the agreement respecting the nonalienation of that province, Japan to be consulted first whenever foreign capital is needed in connection with the railways, mines and harbour works (including dockyards) in the Province of Fukien.

7. China to grant to Japanese subjects the right of preaching in China.

Mr. Hioki, the Japanese Minister, handed these to President Yuan Shih-k'ai on January 18, 1915.

No. 7. The Twenty-one Demands: The Secretary of State to the Japanese Ambassador [Chinda][7]

Department of State
Washington, March 13, 1915

Excellency:

On February 8 last your excellency left with me at the Department a memorandum setting forth the demands which the Imperial Japanese Government felt obliged to make upon China, and on the 22nd of the same month your excellency delivered to me an additional memorandum presenting certain "requests" affecting the relations between the two countries which the Imperial Government has urged China to consider.

The American Government is glad to learn from these two communications of the Imperial Government that the "requests" were not presented to China as "demands" but that they were but "wishes" for which "friendly consideration" was asked on the part of China. The American Government understands from this distinction between the "demands" and the "requests" that the latter are not to be pressed if the Chinese Government should decline to consider them.

Inasmuch as these requests appear to have a bearing upon the traditional attitude of both the United States and Japan towards China, I desire to present to your excellency the following considerations of the Government of the United States relative to the effect which, it is thought, these demands and requests may have upon the relations of the United States with the Chinese Republic. . . .

The United States . . . believes that it may rely upon the often repeated assurances of your excellency's Government relative to the independence, integrity and commerce of China, and that no steps will be taken contrary to the spirit of those assurances.

For two generations American missionaries and teachers have made sacrifices in behalf of religious and educational work in China. American capital has been invested and industries have been established in certain regions. The activity of Americans has never been political, but on the contrary has been primarily commercial with no afterthought as to their effect upon the governmental policy of China. As an outgrowth of these two interests Americans have become concerned in the legitimate participation in the economic development of China along broader lines. Many projects which in other countries are left to private enterprise are in China conducted necessarily under government direction. United States citizens and capital are thus engaged in certain public improvements such as the Huai River conservancy, and Hukuang Railway project, etc. A fourth matter of great moment to the United States is its broad and extensive treaty rights with China. These in general relate to commercial privileges and to the protection of Americans in China. In view of these treaty rights and its increasing economic interests in China, this Government has noted with grave concern certain of the suggestions which Japan has, in the present critical stage of the growth and development of the new Republic, considered it advisable to lay before the Chinese Government. While on principle and under the treaties of 1844, 1858, 1868 and 1903 with China the United States has grounds on which to base objections to the Japanese "demands" relative to Shantung, South Manchuria and East Mongolia, nevertheless the United States frankly recognizes that territorial contiguity creates special relations between Japan and these districts. This Government, therefore, is disposed to raise no question, at this time, as to Articles I and II of the Japanese proposals. Further, as to Article IV and Article V, paragraphs 2, 5 and 7, this Government perceives no special menace to the existing rights and interests of the United States or of its citizens in China. On the other hand Article V, paragraph 4, restricting the purchase of arms and ammunition to purchases from Japan, and paragraph 6 contemplating a monopoly on the development of the province of Fukien, the United States Government considers, would, if they should become operative, be violations of the principle of equal opportunity for the commerce and industries of other nations. American citizens may claim a right to share in the commercial development not only in Fukien but in other provinces as well. The United States is not unmindful that many serious disadvantages would result to its commercial and industrial enterprises if special preference is given one nation in the matter of concessions. An example is shown in the operation of the South Manchuria Railway whereby discriminations have been made for some time against freight brought into Manchuria in other than Japanese vessels. This case indicates the embarrassing results of concessions of a broad preference or option. The United States, as well as every other nation, has the right to have its citizens free to make contracts with the Central and Provincial Governments without having the exercise of their rights interrupted or regarded as unfriendly by a third power; for each American enterprise in China is treated on its own merits as to its usefulness and prospective benefit, and without any regard to the possible effect it might have on China's future political status in the Orient.

The rights and privileges which are set forth in these two paragraphs and which Japan seeks to obtain from China, are in conflict with rights of Americans secured by treaties between the United States and China. . . . It remains to call attention to Article III forbidding the alienation or lease of any port, harbor or island on the Coast of China, and to Article V, paragraph 1, requiring China to employ competent Japanese subjects and advisors for conducting administrative, financial and military affairs and paragraph 3 suggesting the joint policing of China, "where it is deemed necessary."

With reference to the first of these three proposals, Baron Kato has explained to the American Ambassador at Tokyo that Japan has no desire for a naval station on the coast of China, either at Tsingtau, or south of that point, as it would be valueless to her, but that it would however object to another nation having such a station. With reference to the employment of advisers the United States believes it may be assumed that the Chinese Government will not discriminate unfairly in their selection, although it should be pointed out that this Government understands that Japan has six out of twenty-five advisors to the Republic representing eight nations. In respect to the proposed joint policing of certain places where there has been some friction between Japanese and Chinese, this Government feels apprehensive that this plan, instead of tending to lessen such friction might create greater difficulties than those which it is desired to remove.

But what is more important is the fact that these proposals, if accepted by China, while not infringing the territorial integrity of the Republic, are clearly derogatory to the political independence and administrative entity of that country. The same is in a measure true of Paragraph 4 of Article V relative to the purchase of arms. It is difficult for the United States, therefore, to reconcile these requests with the maintenance of the unimpaired sovereignty of China, which Japan, together with the United States and the Great Powers of Europe, has reaffirmed from time to time during the past decade and a half in formal declarations, treaties and exchanges of diplomatic notes. The United States, therefore, could not regard with indifference the assumption of political, military or economic domination over China by a foreign Power, and hopes that your excellency's Government will find it consonant with their interests to refrain from pressing upon China an acceptance of proposals which would, if accepted, exclude Americans from equal participation in the economic and industrial development of China and would limit the political independence of that country.

The United States is convinced that an attempt to coerce China to submit to these proposals would result in engendering resentment on the part of the Chinese and opposition by other interested Powers, thereby creating a situation which this Government confidently believes the Imperial Government do not desire.

The United States Government embraces this opportunity to make known that it has viewed the aspirations of Japan in the Far East with that friendship and esteem which have characterized the relations of the two nations in the past. This Government cannot too earnestly impress upon your excellency's Government that the United States is not jealous of the prominence of Japan in the East or of the intimate cooperation of China and Japan for their mutual benefit. Nor has the United States any intention of obstructing or embarrassing Japan, or of influencing China in opposition to Japan. On the contrary the policy of the United States, as set forth in this note, is directed to the maintenance of the independence, integrity, and commercial freedom of China and the preservation of legitimate American rights and interests in that Republic.

Accept [etc.],

W. J. Bryan

No. 8. The Twenty-one Demands: The Secretary of State to Ambassador Guthrie[8]

Department of State
Washington, May 11, 1915

Please call upon the Minister for Foreign Affairs and present to him a note textually as follows:

In view of the circumstances of the negotiations which have taken place and which are now pending between the Government of Japan and the Government of China, and of the agreements which have been reached as a result thereof, the Government of the United States has the honor to notify the Imperial Japanese Government that it cannot recognize any agreement or undertaking which has been entered into or which may be entered into between the Governments of Japan and China, impairing the treaty rights of the United States and its citizens in China, the political or territorial integrity of the Republic of China, or the international policy relative to China commonly known as the open door policy. An identical note has been transmitted to the Government of the Chinese Republic.

Bryan

No. 9. Treaty respecting the Province of Shantung (Signed at Peking, May 25, 1915)[9]

Article I. The Chinese Government engage to recognize all matters that may be agreed upon between the Japanese Government and the German Government respecting the disposition of all the rights, interests and concessions, which, in virtue of treaties or otherwise, Germany possesses *vis-à-vis* China in relation to the Province of Shantung.

Article II. The Chinese Government engage that, in case they undertake the construction of a railway connecting Chefoo or Lungkou with the Kiaochou-Tsinan Railway, they shall, in the event of Germany's surrendering her right of providing capital for the Chefoo-Weihsien railway line, enter into negotiations with Japanese capitalists for the purpose of financing the said undertaking.

Article III. The Chinese Government engage to open, of their own accord, as early as possible, suitable cities and towns in the Province of Shantung for the residence and trade of foreigners.

Article IV. The present Treaty shall take effect on the day of its signature.

No. 10. Note [to the Japanese Minister] respecting Shantung[10]

Peking
May 25, 1915

Monsieur le Ministre: In the name of the Chinese Government I have the honour to make the following declaration to your excellency's Government:

The Chinese Government will never lease or alienate, under any designation whatever, to any foreign Power any territory within or along the coast of the Province of Shantung or any island lying near the said coast.

I avail, &c.,

(Signed) Lu Tseng-tsiang
(Minister of Foreign Affairs)

No. 11. Treaty respecting South Manchuria and Eastern Inner Mongolia (Signed at Peking, May 25, 1915)[11]

Article I. The High Contracting Parties mutually agree to extend the terms of the lease of Port Arthur and Dairen, and the terms relating to the South Manchurian Railway and to the Antung-Mukden Railway, to a period of ninety-nine years respectively.

Article II. The subjects of Japan shall be permitted in South Manchuria to lease land necessary either for erecting buildings for various commercial and industrial uses or for agricultural purposes.

Article III. The subjects of Japan shall have liberty to enter, travel and reside in South Manchuria and to carry on business of various kinds—commerical, industrial and otherwise.

Article IV. The Government of China shall permit joint undertakings, in Eastern Inner Mongolia, of the subjects of Japan and citizens of China, in agriculture and industries auxiliary thereto.

No. 12. The Siberian Intervention: Declaration of the American Government against Intervention, March 5, 1918[12]

The Acting Secretary of State to the Ambassador in Japan (Morris)

Washington, March 5, 1918,
4 p.m.

At your earliest opportunity you will please read to the Japanese Government the following message but leave no copy unless they request you to do so:

The Government of the United States has been giving the most careful and anxious consideration to the conditions now prevailing in Siberia and their possible remedy. It realizes the extreme danger of anarchy to which the Siberian provinces are exposed and the imminent risk also of German invasion and domination. It shares with the governments of the Entente the view that, if intervention is deemed wise, the Government of Japan is in the best situation to undertake it and could accomplish it most efficiently. It has, moreover, the utmost confidence in the Japanese Government and would be entirely willing, so far as its own feelings towards that Government are concerned, to intrust the enterprise to it. But it is bound in frankness to say that the wisdom of intervention seems to it most questionable. If it were undertaken the Government of the United States assumes that the most explicit assurances would be given that it was undertaken by Japan as an ally of Russia, in Russia's interest, and with the sole view of holding it safe against Germany and at the absolute disposal of the final peace conference. Otherwise the Central Powers could and would make it appear that Japan was doing in the East exactly what Germany is doing in the West and so seek to counter the condemnation which all the world must pronounce against Germany's invasion of Russia, which she attempts to justify on the pretext of restoring order. And it is the judgment of the Government of the United States, uttered with the utmost respect, that, even with such assurances given, they would in the same way be discredited by those whose interest it was to discredit them; that a hot resentment would be generated in Russia itself, and that the whole action might play into the hands of the enemies of Russia, and particularly of the enemies of the Russian revolution, for which the Government of the United States entertains the greatest sympathy, in spite of all the unhappiness and misfortune which has for the time being sprung out of it. The Government of the United States begs once more to express to the Government of Japan its warmest friendship and confidence and once more begs it to accept these expressions of judgment as uttered only in the frankness of friendship.

Polk.

No. 13. Memorandum of the Secretary of State of a Conference at the White House in Reference to the Siberian Situation[13]

July 6, 1918.

Present: The President, the Secretary of State, the Secretary of War, the Secretary of the Navy, General March, and Admiral Benson.

After debating the whole subject of the present conditions in Siberia as affected by the taking of Vladivostok by the Czecho-Slovaks, the landing of American, British, French, and Japanese forces from the naval vessels in that port, and the occupation of the railroad through western Siberia by other Czecho-Slovaks with the reported taking of Irkutsk by these troops; and after reading and discussing the communication of the Supreme War Council favoring an attempt to restore an eastern front against the Central powers, and also a memorandum by the Secretary of State—

The following propositions and program were decided upon:

(1) That the establishment of an eastern front through a military

expedition, even if it was wise to employ a large Japanese force, is physically impossible though the front was established east of the Ural Mountains; (2) That under present conditions any advance westward of Irkutsk does not seem possible and needs no further consideration; (3) That the present situation of the Czecho-Slovaks requires this Government and other Governments to make an effort to aid those at Vladivostok in forming a junction with their compatriots in Western Siberia; and that this Government on sentimental grounds and because of the effect on friendly Slavs everywhere would be subject to criticism if it did not make this effort and would doubtless be held responsible if they were defeated by lack of such effort; (4) That in view of the inability of the United States to furnish any considerable force within a short time to assist the Czecho-Slovaks, the following plan of operations should be adopted, provided the Japanese Government agrees to cooperate; (a) The furnishing of small arms, machine guns, and ammunition to the Czecho-Slovaks at Vladivostok by the Japanese Government; this Government to share the expense and to supplement the supplies as rapidly as possible; (b) The assembling of a military force at Vladivostok composed of approximately 7,000 Americans and 7,000 Japanese to guard the line of communication of the Czecho-Slovaks preceeding toward Irkutsk; the Japanese to send troops at once; (c) The landing of available forces from the American and Allied naval vessels to hold possession of Vladivostok and cooperate with the Czecho-Slovaks; (d) The public announcement by this and Japanese Governments that the purpose of landing troops is to aid Czecho-Slovaks against German and Austrian prisoners, that there is no purpose to interfere with internal affairs of Russia, and that they guarantee not to impair the political or territorial sovereignty of Russia; and (e) To await further developments before taking further steps.

No. 14. The Siberian Intervention: The Japanese Ambassador [Ishii] to the Acting Secretary of State[14]

Memorandum
    The Japanese Government, actuated by the sentiment of sincere friendship towards the Russian people, have always entertained the most sanguine hopes of the speedy reestablishment of order in

Russia and a healthy and untrammeled development of her national life. Abundant proof, however, is now afforded to show that the Central European Empires, taking advantage of the chaotic and defenseless condition in which Russia has momentarily been placed, are consolidating their hold on that country and are steadily extending their activities to the Russian far eastern possessions. They have persistently interfered with the passage of the Czecho-Slovak troops through Siberia. In the forces now opposing these valiant troops the German and Austro-Hungarian prisoners are freely enlisted and they practically assume the position of command. The Czecho-Slovak troops, aspiring to secure a free and independent existence for their race and loyally espousing the common cause of the Allies, justly command every sympathy and consideration from the cobelligerents to whom their destiny is a matter of deep and abiding concern. In the presence of danger to which the Czecho-Slovak troops are actually exposed in Siberia at the hands of the Germans and Austro-Hungarians, the Allies have naturally felt themselves unable to view with indifference the untoward course of events and a certain number of their troops have already been ordered to proceed to Vladivostok. The Government of the United States, equally sensible of the gravity of the situation, recently approached the Japanese Government with proposals for an early dispatch of troops to relieve pressure now weighing upon the Czecho-Slovak forces.

The Japanese Government, being anxious to fall in with the desires of the American Government and also to act in harmony with the Allies in this expedition, have decided to proceed at once to dispatch suitable forces for the proposed mission. A certain number of these troops will be sent forthwith to Vladivostok. In adopting this course, the Japanese Government remain unshaken in their constant desire to promote relations of enduring friendship with Russia and the Russian people and reaffirm their avowed policy of respecting the territorial integrity of Russia and of abstaining from all interference in her internal politics. They further declare that upon the realization of the objects above indicated they will immediately withdraw all Japanese troops from Russian territory and will leave wholly unimpaired the sovereignty of Russia in all its phases whether political or military.

Washington, undated
[Received August 2, 1918]

No. 15. The Siberian Intervention: The Acting Secretary of State to the Ambassador [Morris] in Japan (Telegram)[15]

Washington, August 3, 1918,
4 p. m.

Copy of following statement has been handed to Japanese Ambassador and given to the press:

In the judgment of the Government of the United States, a judgment arrived at after repeated and very searching considerations of the whole situation, military intervention in Russia would be more likely to add to the present sad confusion there than to cure it, and would injure Russia rather than help her out of her distresses.

Such military intervention as has been most frequently proposed, even supposing it to be efficacious in its immediate object of delivering an attack upon Germany from the east, would in its judgment be more likely to turn out to be merely a method of making use of Russia than to be a method of serving her. Her people, if they profited by it at all, could not profit by it in time to deliver them from their present desperate difficulties, and their substance would meantime be used to maintain foreign armies, not reconstitute their own or to feed their own men, women, and children. We are bending all our energies now to the purpose, the resolute and confident purpose, of winning on the western front, and it would in the judgment of the Government of the United States be most unwise to divide or dissipate our forces.

As the Government of the United States sees the present circumstances, therefore, military action is admissible in Russia now only to render such protection and help as is possible to the Czecho-Slovaks against the armed Austrian and German prisoners who are attacking them and to steady any efforts at self-government or self-defense in which the Russians themselves may be willing to accept assistance. Whether from Vladivostok or from Murmansk and Archangel, the only present object for which American troops will be employed will be to guard military stores which may subsequently be needed by Russian forces and to render such aid as may be acceptable to the Russians in the organization of their own self-defense.

With such objects in view the Government of the United States is now cooperating with the Governments of France and Great Britian in the neighborhood of Murmansk and Archangel. The United States and Japan are the only powers which are just now in a position to act in Siberia in sufficient force to accomplish even such modest objects as those that have been outlined. The Government of the United States has, therefore, proposed to the Government of Japan that each of the two governments send a force of a few thousand men to Vladivostok, with the purpose of cooperating as a single force in the occupation of Vladivostok and in safeguarding, so far as it may, the country to the rear of the westward-moving Czecho-Slovaks; and the Japanese Government has consented.

In taking this action the Government of the United States wishes to announce to the people of Russia in the most public and solemn manner that it contemplates no interference with the political sovereignty of Russia, no intervention in her internal affairs—not even in the local affairs of the limited areas which her military force may be obliged to occupy—and no impairment of her territorial integrity, either now or hereafter, but that what we are about to do has as its single and only object the rendering of such aid as shall be acceptable to the Russian people themselves in their endeavors to regain control of their own affairs, their own territory, and their own destiny. The Japanese Government, it is understood, will issue a similar assurance.

These plans and purposes of the Government of the United States have been communicated to the Governments of Great Britain, France, and Italy, and those Governments have advised the Department of State that they assent to them in principle. No conclusion that the Government of the United States has arrived at in this important matter is intended, however, as an effort to restrict the actions or interfere with the independent judgment of the Governments with which we are now associated in the War.

It is also the hope and purpose of the Government of the United States to take advantage of the earliest opportunity to send to Siberia a commission of merchants, agricultural experts, labor advisers, Red Cross representatives, and agents of the Young Men's Christian Association accustomed to organizing the best methods of spreading useful information and rendering educational help of a modest kind in order in some systematic way to relieve the immediate economic necessities of the people there in every way for which an opportunity may open. The execution of this plan will follow and will not be permitted to embarrass the military assistance rendered to the Czecho-Slovaks.

It is the hope and expectation of the Government of the United

States that the Governments with which it is associated will, wherever necessary or possible, lend their active aid in the execution of these military and economic plans.

Polk.

No. 16. The Washington Conference: The Four-Power Pact[16]

The United States of America, the British Empire, France, and Japan,

With a view to the preservation of the general peace and the maintenance of their rights in relation to their insular possessions and insular dominions in the region of the Pacific Ocean,

Have determined to conclude a treaty to this effect. . . .

I. The High Contracting Parties agree as between themselves to respect their rights in relation to their insular possessions and insular dominions in the region of the Pacific Ocean.

If there should develop between any of the High Contracting Parties a controversy arising out of any Pacific question and involving their said rights which is not satisfactorily settled by diplomacy and is likely to affect the harmonious accord now happily subsisting between them, they shall invite the other High Contracting Parties to a joint conference to which the whole subject will be referred for consideration and adjustment.

II. If the said rights are threatened by the aggressive action of any other Power, the High Contracting Parties shall communicate with one another fully and frankly in order to arrive at an understanding as to the most efficient measures to be taken, jointly or separately, to meet the exigencies of the particular situation.

III. This Treaty shall remain in force for ten years from the time it shall take effect, and after the expiration of said period it shall continue in force subject to the right of any of the High Contracting Parties to terminate it upon twelve months' notice.

IV. This Treaty shall be ratified as soon as possible in accordance with the constitutional methods of the High Contracting Parties and shall take effect on the deposit of ratifications, which shall take place at Washington, and thereupon the agreement between Great Britain and Japan, which was concluded at London, July 13, 1911, shall terminate. The Government of the United States will transmit to all the Signatory Powers a certified copy of the *proces-verbal* of the deposit of ratification. . . .

Done at the City of Washington, the thirteenth day of December, One Thousand Nine Hundred and Twenty-one.

No. 17. The Washington Conference: The Five-Power
Pact[17]

Chapter I.
General Provisions Relating to the
Limitation of Armament

Article I. The Contracting Powers agree to limit their respective naval armament as provided in the present Treaty.

Article II. The Contracting Parties may retain respectively the capital ships which are specified in Chapter II, Part 1. On the coming into force of the present Treaty, but subject to the following provisions of this Article, all other capital ships, built or building, of the United States, the British Empire and Japan shall be disposed of as prescribed in Chapter II, Part 2.

In addition to the capital ships specified in Chapter II, Part 1, the United States may complete and retain two ships of the *West Vir-·ginia* class now under construction. On the completion of these two ships, the *North Dakota* and *Delaware* shall be disposed of as prescribed in Chapter II, Part 2.

The British Empire may, in accordance with the replacement table in Chapter II, Part 3, construct two new capital ships not exceeding 35,000 tons (35,560 metric tons) standard displacement each. On the completion of the said two ships the *Thunderer, King George V, Ajax* and *Centurion* shall be disposed of as prescribed in Chapter II, Part 2.

Article III. Subject to the provisions of Article II, the Contracting Powers shall abandon their respective capital ship-building programmes, and no new capital ships shall be constructed or acquired by any of the Contracting Powers except replacement tonnage which may be constructed or acquired as specified in Chapter II, Part 3.

Ships which are replaced in accordance with Chapter II, Part 3, shall be disposed of as prescribed in Part 2 of that Chapter.

Article IV. The total capital ship replacement tonnage of each of the Contracting Powers shall not exceed in standard displacement: for the United States 525,000 tons (533,400 metric tons); for the British Empire 525,000 tons (533,400 metric tons); for France 175,000 tons (177,800 metric tons); for Italy 175,000 tons (177,800 metric tons); for Japan 315,000 tons (320,040 metric tons.)

Article V. No capital ship exceeding 35,000 tons (35,560 metric tons) standard displacement shall be acquired by, or constructed by, for, or within the jurisdiction of, any of the Contracting Powers.

Article VI. No capital ship of any of the Contracting Powers shall carry a gun with a calibre in excess of 16 inches (406 milli-metres.)

Article VII. The total tonnage for aircraft-carriers of each of the Contracting Powers shall not exceed in standard displacement: for the United States 135,000 (137,160 metric tons); for the British Empire 135,000 tons (137,160 metric tons); for France 60,000 tons (60,960 metric tons); for Italy 60,000 tons (60,960 metric tons); for Japan 81,000 tons (82,296 metric tons.)

Article VIII. The replacement of aircraft-carriers shall be effected only as prescribed in Chapter II, Part 3, provided, however, that all aircraft carrier tonnage in existence or building on November 12, 1921, shall be considered experimental, and may be replaced, within the total tonnage limit prescribed in Article VII, without regard to its age.

Article IX. No aircraft-carrier exceeding 27,000 tons (27,432 metric tons) standard displacement shall be acquired by, or constructed by, for or within the jurisdiction of, any of the Contracting Powers.

However, any of the Contracting Powers may, provided that its total tonnage allowance of aircraft-carriers is not thereby exceeded, build not more than two aircraft-carriers, each of a tonnage of not more than 33,000 tons (33,528 metric tons) standard displacement, and in order to effect economy any of the Contracting Powers may use for this purpose any two of their ships, whether constructed or in course of construction, which would otherwise be scrapped under the provisions of Article II. The armament of any aircraft carriers exceeding 27,000 tons (27,432 metric tons) standard displacement shall be in accordance with the requirements of Article X, except that the total number of guns to be carried in case any of such guns be of a calibre exceeding 6 inches (152 millimetres), except anti-aircraft guns and guns not exceeding 5 inches (127 millimetres), shall not exceed eight.

Article X. No aircraft carrier of any of the Contracting Powers shall carry a gun with a calibre in excess of 8 inches (203 milli-metres). Without prejudice to the Provisions of Article IX, if the armament carried includes guns exceeding 6 inches (152 milli-metres) in calibre the total number of guns carried, except anti-aircraft guns and guns not exceeding 5 inches (127 millimetres) shall not exceed ten. If alternatively the armament contains no guns exceeding 6 inches (152 millimetres) in calibre, the number of guns is not limited. In either case the number of anti-aircraft guns and of guns not exceeding 5 inches (127 millimetres) is not limited.

Article XI. No vessel of war exceeding 10,000 tons (10,160 metric tons) standard displacement, other than a capital ship or aircraft carrier, shall be acquired by, or constructed by, for, or within the jurisdiction of, any of the Contracting Powers. Vessels not specifically built as fighting ships nor taken in the time of peace under Government control for fighting purposes, which are employed on fleet duties or as troop transports or in some other way for the purpose of assisting in the prosecution of hostilities otherwise than as fighting ships, shall not be within the limitations of this Article.

Article XII. No vessels of war of any of the Contracting Powers, hereafter laid down, other than a capital ship, shall carry a gun with a calibre in excess of 8 inches (203 millimetres).

Article XIII. Except as provided in Article IX, no ship designated in the present Treaty to be scrapped may be reconverted into a vessel of war.

Article XIV. No preparations shall be made in merchant ships in time of peace for the installation of warlike armaments for the purpose of converting such ships into vessels of war, other than the necessary stiffening of decks for the mounting of guns not exceeding 6 inches (152 millimetres) calibre.

Article XV. No vessel of war constructed within the jurisdiction of any of the Contracting Powers for a non-Contracting Power shall exceed the limitations as to displacement and armament prescribed by the present Treaty for vessels of a similar type which may be constructed by or for any of the Contracting Powers; provided, however, that the displacement for aircraft-carriers constructed for a non-Contracting Power shall in no case exceed 27,000 tons (27,432 metric tons) standard displacement.

Article XVI. If the construction of any vessel of war for a non-Contracting Power is undertaken within the jurisdiction of any of the Contracting Powers, such Power shall promptly inform the other Contracting Powers of the date of the signing of the contract and the date on which the keel of the ship is laid, and shall also communicate to them the particulars relating to the ship prescribed in Chapter II, Part 3, Section 1 (b), (4) and (5).

Article XVII. In the event of a Contracting Power being engaged in war, such Power shall not use as a vessel of war any vessel of war which may be under construction within its jurisdiction for any other Power, or which may have been constructed within its jurisdiction for another Power and not delivered.

Article XVIII. Each of the Contracting Powers undertakes not to dispose by gift, sale or any mode of transfer of any vessel of war in such a manner that such vessel may become a vessel of war in the Navy of any foreign Power.

Article XIX. The United States, the British Empire and Japan agree that the *status quo* at the time of the signing of the present Treaty, with regard to fortifications and naval bases, shall be maintained in their respective territories and possessions specified hereunder:

(1) The insular possessions which the United States now holds or may hereafter acquire in the Pacific Ocean, except *(a)* those adjacent to the coast of the United States, Alaska and the Panama Canal Zone, not including the Aleutian Islands, and *(b)* the Hawaiian Islands;

(2) Hong-Kong and the insular possessions which the British Empire now holds or may hereafter acquire in the Pacific Ocean, east of the meridian of 110° east longitude, except *(a)* those adjacent to the coast of Canada, *(b)* the Commonwealth of Australia and its territories, and *(c)* New Zealand;

(3) The following insular territories and possessions of Japan in the Pacific Ocean, to wit: the Kurile Islands, the Bonin Islands, Amami-Oshima, the Loochoo Islands, Formosa and the Pescadores, and any insular territories or possessions in the Pacific Ocean which Japan may hereafter acquire.

The maintenance of the *status quo* under the foregoing provisions implies that no new fortifications or naval bases shall be established in the territories and possessions specified; that no measures shall be taken to increase the existing naval facilities for the repair and maintenance of naval forces, and that no increase shall be made in the coast defences of the territories and possessions above specified. This restriction, however, does not preclude such repair and replacement of worn-out weapons and equipment as is customary in naval and military establishments in time of peace.

[*Article XX.* Omitted.]

[Chapter II. Rules Relating to the Execution of the Treaty–Definition of Terms. This chapter is omitted. It consists of extremely detailed provisions for the implementation of the Treaty. Its nature can be judged by the titles of the Parts: Part 1. Capital Ships Which May be Retained by the Contracting Powers. Part 2. Rules for Scrapping Vessels of War. Part 3. Replacement. Part 4. Definitions.]

CHAPTER III.
MISCELLANEOUS PROVISIONS

Article XXI. If during the term of the present Treaty the requirements of the national security of any Contracting Power in respect of naval defence are, in the opinion of that Power, materially affected by any change of circumstances, the Contracting Powers will, at the request of such Power, meet in conference with a view to the reconsideration of the provisions of the Treaty and its amendment by mutual agreement.

In view of possible technical and scientific developments, the United States, after consultation with the other Contracting Powers, shall arrange for a conference of all the Contracting Powers which shall convene as soon as possible after the expiration of eight years from the coming into force of the present Treaty to consider what changes, if any, in the Treaty may be necessary to meet such developments.

Article XXII. Whenever any Contracting Power shall become engaged in a war which in its opinion affects the naval defence of its national security, such Power may after notice to the other Contracting Powers suspend for the period of hostilities its obligations under the present Treaty other than those under Articles XIII and XVII, provided that such Power shall notify the other Contracting Powers that the emergency is of such a character as to require such suspension. . . .

[*Article XXIII* specifies that the treaty should remain in force until December 31st, 1936, and describes the way in which it could be terminated.]

[*Article XXIV* deals with ratification.]

Done at the City of Washington the sixth day of February, One Thousand Nine Hundred and Twenty-two.

No.18. The Washington Conference: The Nine-Power Pact, a Treaty Relating to Principles and Policies to Be Followed in Matters concerning China (Signed at Washington, February 6, 1922)[18]

The United States of America, Belgium, the British Empire, China, France, Italy, Japan, the Netherlands and Portugal:

Desiring to adopt a policy designed to stabilize conditions in the Far East, to safeguard the rights and interests of China, and to promote intercourse between China and the other Powers upon the basis of equality of opportunity;

Have resolved to conclude a treaty for that purpose and to that end have appointed as their respective Plenipotentiaries: [Here follows a long list of the representatives of the powers involved.]

Who, having communicated to each other their full powers, found to be in good and due form, have agreed as follows:

Article I. The Contracting Powers, other than China, agree:
(1) To respect the sovereignty, the independence, and the territorial and administrative integrity of China;

(2) To provide the fullest and most unembarrassed opportunity to China to develop and maintain for herself an effective and stable government;

(3) To use their influence for the purpose of effectually establishing and maintaining the principle of equal opportunity for the commerce and industry of all nations throughout the territory of China;

(4) To refrain from taking advantage of conditions in China in order to seek special rights or privileges which would abridge the rights of subjects or citizens of friendly States, and from countenancing action inimical to the security of such States.

Article II. The Contracting Powers agree not to enter into any treaty, agreement, arrangement, or understanding either with one another, or, individually or collectively with any Power or Powers, which would infringe or impair the principles stated in Article I.

Article III. With a view to applying more effectually the principles of the Open Door or equality of opportunity in China for the trade and industry of all nations, the Contracting Powers, other than China, agree that they will not seek, nor support their respective nationals in seeking:

(a) any arrangement which might purport to establish in favour of their interests any general superiority of rights with respect to commercial or economic development in any designated region of China;

(b) any such monopoly or preference as would deprive the nationals of any other Power of the right of undertaking any legitimate trade or industry in China or of participating with the Chinese Government, or with any local authority, in any category of public enterprise, or which by reason of its scope, duration or geographical extent is calculated to frustrate the practical application of the principle of equal opportunity.

It is understood that the foregoing stipulations of this article are not to be so construed as to prohibit the acquisition of such properties or rights as may be necessary to the conduct of a particular commercial, industrial, or financial undertaking or to the encouragement of invention and research.

China undertakes to be guided by the principles stated in the foregoing stipulations of this article in dealing with applications for economic rights and privileges from Governments and nationals of all foreign countries, whether Parties to the present Treaty or not

Article IV. The Contracting Powers agree not to support any agreements by their respective nationals with each other designed to create Spheres of Influence or to provide for the enjoyment of mutually exclusive opportunities in designated parts of Chinese territory.

Article V. China agrees that, throughout the whole of the railways in China, she will not exercise or permit unfair discrimination of any kind. In particular there shall be no discrimination whatever, direct or indirect, in respect of charges or of facilities on the ground of the nationality of passengers or the countries from which or to which they are proceeding, or the origin or ownership of goods or the country from which or to which they are consigned, or the nationality or ownership of the ship or other means of conveying such passengers or goods before or after their transport on the Chinese Railways.

The Contracting Powers, other than China, assume a corresponding obligation in respect of any of the aforesaid railways over which they or their nationals are in a position to exercise any control in virtue of any concession, special agreement or otherwise.

Article VI. The Contracting Powers, other than China, agree fully to respect China's rights as a neutral in time of war to which China is not a Party; and China declares that when she is a neutral she will observe the obligations of neutrality.

Article VII. The Contracting Powers agree that, whenever a situation arises which in the opinion of any one of them involves the application of the stipulations of the present Treaty, and renders desirable discussion of such application, there shall be full and frank communication between the Contracting Powers concerned.

Article VIII. Powers not signatory to the present Treaty, which have Governments recognized by the Signatory Powers and which have treaty relations with China, shall be invited to adhere to the present Treaty. To this end the Government of the United States will make the necessary communications to non-signatory Powers and will inform the Contracting Powers of the replies received. Adherence by any Power shall become effective on receipt of notice thereof by the Government of the United States.

Article IX. The present Treaty shall be ratified by the Contracting Powers in accordance with their respective constitutional methods and shall take effect on the date of the deposit of all the ratifications, which shall take place at Washington as soon as possible. The Government of the United States will transmit to the other Contracting Powers a certified copy of the proces-verbal of the deposit of ratifications.

The present Treaty, of which the French and English texts are

both authentic, shall remain deposited in the archives of the Government of the United States, and duly certified copies thereof shall be transmitted by that Government to the other Contracting Powers.
  In faith whereof the above-named Plenipotentiaries have signed the present Treaty.
  Done at the City of Washington the Sixth day of February One Thousand Nine Hundred and Twenty-two.

[Signatures]

No. 19. Treaty between Japan and China for the Settlement of Outstanding Questions Relative to Shantung (Signed at Washington, February 4, 1922)[19]

Article I. Japan shall restore to China the former German Leased Territory of Kiaochow. [Article III specified that the transfer should be completed within six months after the treaty went into force.]
  Article IX. The Japanese troops, including gendarmes, now stationed along the Tsingtao-Tsinanfu Railway and its branches, shall be withdrawn as soon as the Chinese police or military force shall have been sent to take over the protection of the Railway. [Article X stipulated that the withdrawal be completed within three months, if possible, but no later than six months after the signature of the treaty.]
  Article XIV. Japan shall transfer to China the Tsingtao-Tsinanfu Railway and its branches, together with all other properties appurtenant thereto, including wharves, warehouses and other similar properties. [Article XV called for China to reimburse Japan for the value of the railway property, amounting to 53,406,141 gold Marks as the assessed value of the railway property as left by the Germans, plus "the amount which Japan, during her administration of the Railway, has actually expended for permanent improvements on or additions to the said properties," less depreciation.]
  Article XXIII. The Government of Japan declares that it will not seek the establishment of an exclusive Japanese settlement, or of an international settlement, in the former German Leased Territory of Kiaochow. . . .

No. 20. Agreement on General Principles for the Settlement of the Questions between the Republic of China and the Union of Soviet Socialist Republics (Signed at Peking, May 31, 1924)[20]

Article I. Immediately upon the signing of the present Agreement

he normal diplomatic and consular relations between the two Con-
racting Parties shall be re-established.

The Government of the Republic of China agrees to take the
necessary steps to transfer to the Government of the Union of Soviet
Socialist Republics the Legation and Consular buildings formerly
belonging to the Tsarist Government.

Article II. The Governments of the two Contracting Parties agree
to hold, within one month after the signing of the present Agreement, a Conference which shall conclude and carry out detailed
arrangements relative to the questions in accordance with the principles as provided in the following articles.

Such detailed arrangements shall be completed as soon as possible and, in any case, not later than six months from the date of
he opening of the Conference provided in the preceding paragraph.

Article III. The Governments of the two Contracting Parties agree
to annul at the Conference, as provided in the preceding article, all
Conventions, Treaties, Agreements, Protocols, Contracts, etc.,
concluded between the Government of China and the Tsarist Government and to replace them with new treaties, agreements, etc., on
he basis of equality, reciprocity, and justice, as well as the spirit
of the Declarations of the Soviet Government of the years of 1919
and 1920.

Article IV. The Government of the Union of Soviet Socialist Republics, in accordance with its policy and Declarations of 1919 and 1920.
declares that all Treaties, Agreements, etc., concluded between
the former Tsarist Government and any third Party or Parties affecting the sovereign rights or interests of China are null and void.

The Governments of both Contracting Parties declare that in
future neither Government will conclude any treaties or agreements
which prejudice the sovereign rights or interests of either Contracting Party.

Article V. The Government of the Union of Soviet Socialist Republics recognizes that Outer Mongolia is an integral part of the
Republic of China and respects China's sovereignty therein.

The Government of the Union of Soviet Socialist Republics declares that, as soon as the questions for the withdrawal of all the
troops of the Union of Soviet Socialist Republics from Outer Mongolia—namely, as to the time-limit of the withdrawal of such troops
and the measures to be adopted in the interests of the safety of the
frontiers—are agreed upon at the Conference as provided in Article
II of the present Agreement, it will effect the complete withdrawal
of all the troops of the Union of Soviet Socialist Republics from
Outer Mongolia.

Article VI. The Governments of the two Contracting Parties mutually pledge themselves not to permit, within their respective territories, the existence and or activities of any organizations or groups whose aim is to struggle by acts of violence against the Governments of either Contracting Party.

The Governments of the two Contracting Parties further pledge themselves not to engage in propaganda directed against the political and social systems of either Contracting Party.

Article VII. The Governments of the two Contracting Parties agree to redemarcate their national boundaries at the Conference as provided in Article II of the present Agreement, and, pending such redemarcation, to maintain the present boundaries.

Article VIII. The Governments of the two Contracting Parties agree to regulate at the aforementioned Conference the questions relating to the navigation of rivers, lakes and other bodies of water which are common to their respective frontiers, on the basis of equality and reciprocity.

Article IX. The Governments of the two Contracting Parties agree to settle at the aforementioned Conference the questions of the Chinese Eastern Railway in conformity with the principles as hereinafter provided:

(1) The Governments of the two Contracting Parties declare that the Chinese Eastern Railway is a purely commercial enterprise

The Governments of the two Contracting Parties declare that, with the exception of matters pertaining to the business operations which are under the direct control of the Chinese Eastern Railway, all other matters affecting the rights of the National and the Local Governments of the Republic of China—such as judicial matters, matters relating to civil administration, military administration, police, municipal government, taxation and landed property (with the exception of land required by the said Railway)—shall be administered by the Chinese Authorities.

(2) The Government of the Union of Soviet Socialist Republics agrees to the redemption by the Government of the Republic of China, with Chinese capital, of the Chinese Eastern Railway, as well as all appurtenant properties, and to the transfer to China of all shares and bonds of the said Railway.

(3) The Governments of the two Contracting Parties shall settle at the Conference, as provided in Article II of the present Agreement, the amount and conditions governing the redemption as well as the procedure for the transfer of the Chinese Eastern Railway.

(4) The Government of the Union of Soviet Socialist Republics agrees to be responsible for the entire claims of the shareholders,

bondholders and creditors of the Chinese Eastern Railway incurred prior to the Revolution of March 9, 1917.

(5) The Governments of the two Contracting Parties mutually agree that the future of the Chinese Eastern Railway shall be determined by the Republic of China and the Union of Soviet Socialist Republics to the exclusion of any third Party or Parties.

(6) The Governments of the two Contracting Parties agree to draw up an arrangement for the provisional management of the Chinese Eastern Railway pending the settlement of the questions as provided under Section (3) of the present article.

(7) Until the various questions relating to the Chinese Eastern Railway are settled at the Conference as provided in Article II of the present agreement, the rights of the two Governments arising out of the Contract of August 27/ September 8, 1896, for the construction and operation of the Chinese Eastern Railway, which do not conflict with the present Agreement and the Agreement for the Provisional Management of the said Railway and which do not prejudice China's rights of sovereignty, shall be maintained.

Article X. The Government of the Union of Soviet Socialist Republics agrees to renounce the special rights and privileges relating to all Concessions in any part of China acquired by the Tsarist Government under various Conventions, Treaties, Agreements, etc.

Article XI. The Government of the Union of Soviet Socialist Republics agrees to renounce the Russian portion of the Boxer Indemnity.

Article XII. The Government of the Union of Soviet Socialist Republics agrees to relinquish the rights of extra-territoriality and consular jurisdiction.

Article XIII. The Governments of the two Contracting Parties agree to draw up simultaneously with the conclusion of a Commercial Treaty and the Conference as provided in Article II of the present Agreement, a Custom Tariff for the two Contracting Parties in accordance with the principles of equality and reciprocity.

Article XIV. The Governments of the two Contracting Parties agree to discuss at the aforementioned conference the questions relating to the claims for compensation of losses.

Article XV. The present agreement shall come into effect from the date of signature.

No. 21. Convention Embodying Basic Rules of the Relations between Japan and the Union of Soviet Socialist Republics (Signed at Peking, January 20, 1925)[21]

Article I. The High Contracting Powers agree that, with the coming into force of the present Convention, diplomatic and consular relations shall be established between them.

Article II. The Union of Soviet Socialist Republics agrees that the Treaty of Portsmouth of September 5th, 1905, shall remain in full force.

It is agreed that the Treaties, Conventions and Agreements, other than the said Treaty of Portsmouth, which were concluded between Japan and Russia prior to November 7, 1917, shall be reexamined at a Conference to be subsequently held between the Governments of the High Contracting Parties and are liable to revision or annulment as altered circumstances may require.

Article III. The Governments of the High Contracting Parties agree that, upon the coming into force of the present Convention, they shall proceed to the revision of the Fishery Convention of 1907, taking into consideration such changes as may have taken place in the general conditions since the conclusion of the said Fishery Convention.

Pending the conclusion of a convention so revised, the Government of the Union of Soviet Socialist Republics shall maintain the practices established in 1924 relating to the lease of fishery lots to Japanese subjects.

Article IV. The Governments of the High Contracting Parties agree that, upon the coming into force of the present Convention, they shall proceed to the conclusion of a treaty of commerce and navigation in conformity with the principles hereunder mentioned, and that, pending the conclusion of such a treaty, the general intercourse between the two countries shall be regulated by those principles.

(1) The subjects or citizens of each of the High Contracting Parties shall, in accordance with the laws of the country: (a) have full liberty to enter, travel and reside in the territories of the other, and (b) enjoy constant and complete protection for the safety of their lives and property.

(2) Each of the High Contracting Parties shall, in accordance with the laws of the country, accord in its territories to the subjects or citizens of the other, to the widest possible extent and on condition of reciprocity, the right of private ownership and the liberty to engage in commerce, navigation, industries and other peaceful pursuits.

(3) Without prejudice to the right of each Contracting Party to regulate by its own laws the system of international trade in that country, it is understood that neither Contracting Party shall apply in discrimination against the other Party any measure of pro

hibition, restriction or impost which may serve to hamper the growth of the intercourse, economic or otherwise, between the two countries, it being the intention of both Parties to place the commerce, navigation and industry of each country, as far as possible, on the footing of the most favoured nation.

The Governments of the High Contracting Parties further agree that they shall enter into negotiations, from time to time as circumstances may require, for the conclusion of special arrangements relative to commerce and navigation to adjust and to promote economic relations between the two countries.

Article V. The High Contracting Parties solemnly affirm their desire and intention to live in peace and amity with each other, scrupulously to respect the undoubted right of a State to order its own life within its own jurisdiction in its own way, to refrain and restrain all persons in any governmental service for them, and all organizations in receipt of any financial assistance from them, from any act overt or covert liable in any way whatever to endanger the order and security in any part of the territories of Japan or the Union of Soviet Socialist Republics.

It is further agreed that neither Contracting Party shall permit the presence in the territories under its jurisdiction:

(a) of organizations or groups pretending to be the Government for any part of the territories of the other Party, or

(b) of alien subjects or citizens who may be found to be actually carrying on political activities for such organizations or groups.

Article VI. In the interest of promoting economic relations between the two countries, and taking into consideration the needs of Japan with regard to natural resources, the Government of the Union of Soviet Socialist Republics is willing to grant to Japanese subjects, companies and associations concessions for the exploitation of minerals, forests and other natural resources in all the territories of the Union of Soviet Socialist Republics.

Article VII. The present Convention shall be ratified.

Such ratification by each of the High Contracting Parties shall, with as little delay as possible, be communicated, through its diplomatic representative at Peking to the Government of the other Party, and from the date of the later of such communications this Convention shall come into full force.

The formal exchange of the ratifications shall take place at Peking as soon as possible.

In witness whereof the respective Plenipotentiaries have signed the present Convention in duplicate in the English language, and have affixed thereto their seals.

Done at Peking, this twentieth day of January, one thousand nine hundred and twenty-five.

[Signatures]

No.22. Protocol (A) (On Japanese Troops in Saghalien)[22]

Article III. In view of climatic conditions in Northern Saghalien preventing the immediate homeward transportation of Japanese troops now stationed there, these troops shall be completely withdrawn from the said region by May 15, 1925.

Such withdrawal shall be commenced as soon as climatic conditions will permit and any and all districts in Northern Saghalien so evacuated by Japanese troops shall immediately thereupon be restored in full sovereignty to the proper authorities of the Union of Soviet Socialist Republics. . . .

Article IV. The High Contracting Parties mutually declare that there actually exists no treaty or agreement of military alliance nor any other secret agreement which either of them has entered into with any third Party and which constitutes an infringement upon, or a menace to, the sovereignty, territorial rights or national safety of the other Contracting Party.

No.23. Protocol (B) (On Saghalien Concessions)[23]

The High Contracting Parties have agreed upon the following as the basis for the Concession Contracts to be concluded within five months from the date of the complete evacuation of Northern Saghalien by Japanese troops, as provided for in Article 3 of Protocol (A), signed this day between the Plenipotentiaries of Japan and of the Union of Soviet Socialist Republics.

(1) The Government of the Union of Soviet Socialist Republics agrees to grant to Japanese concerns recommended by the Government of Japan the concession for the exploitation of 50 per cent, in area, of each of the oilfields in Northern Saghalien which are mentioned in the Memorandum submitted to the Representatives of the Union by the Japanese Representative on August 29, 1924. For the purpose of determining the area to be leased to the Japanese concerns for such exploitation, each of the said oilfields shall be divided into checker-board squares of from fifteen to forty dessiatines each, and a number of these squares, representing 50 per cent of the whole area, shall be allotted to the Japanese, it being understood that the squares to be so leased to the Japanese are, as a rule, to be non-contiguous to one another, but shall include all the wells now being drilled or worked by the Japanese. With regard to

the remaining unleased lots of the oilfields mentioned in the said Memorandum, it is agreed that, should the Government of the Union of Soviet Socialist Republics decide to offer such lots, wholly or in part for foreign concession, Japanese concerns shall be afforded equal opportunity in the matter of such concession.

(2) The Government of the Union of Soviet Socialist Republics also agrees to authorize Japanese concerns recommended by the Government of Japan to prospect oilfields, for a period of from five to ten years, on the Eastern coast of Northern Saghalien over an area of one thousand square versts to be selected within one year after the conclusion of the Concession Contracts, and in case oilfields shall have been established in consequence of such prospecting by the Japanese, the concession for the exploitation of 50 per cent, in area, of the oilfields so established shall be granted to the Japanese.

(3) The Government of the Union of Soviet Socialist Republics agrees to grant to Japanese concerns recommended by the Government of Japan the concession for the exploitation of coal fields on the western coast of Northern Saghalien over a specific area which shall be determined in the Concession Contracts. The Government of the Union of Soviet Socialist Republics further agrees to grant to such Japanese concerns the concession regarding coal fields in the Doue district over a specific area to be determined in the Concession Contracts. With regard to the coal fields outside the specific area mentioned in the preceding two paragraphs, it is also agreed that, should the Government of the Union of Soviet Socialist Republics decide to offer them for foreign concession, Japanese concerns shall be afforded equal opportunity in the matter of such concession.

(4) The period of the concessions for the exploitation of oil and coal fields stipulated in the preceding paragraphs shall be from forty to fifty years.

(5) As royalty for the said concessions, the Japanese concessionaries shall make over annually to the Government of the Union of Soviet Socialist Republics, in case of coal fields, from 5 to 8 per cent of their gross output, and, in case of oilfields, from 5 to 15 per cent of their gross output: provided that in the cases of a gusher, the royalty may be raised up to 45 per cent of its gross output. . . . .

3

THE MANCHURIAN CRISIS: 1931-35

The Manchurian Crisis was one of the decisive developments in world affairs in the first half of the twentieth century. For Japan it began fourteen years of authoritarian government, dominated by the military, and simultaneously a period of major war and aggression, marked successively by brilliant military victories, great military losses, and, finally, crushing defeat. For China it meant the loss of Manchuria, an area of vital economic importance, and the beginning of foreign aggression that not only prevented the Nationalist Government from addressing itself to vital political, economic, administrative, and social problems, but also created conditions of chaos which proved to be an ideal breeding ground for the communism that eventually took over control of the country. In United States-Japanese relations it brought intensified disagreement which was to grow to a point at which it could be resolved only by war. In Soviet-Japanese relations it created a long land frontier that was the scene of constant, though mainly minor, military tension which also eventuated in war. In general world affairs it dealt a mortal blow to the League of Nations as the existing international organization designed to maintain world peace and security.

The crisis was initiated by the Mukden Incident. On the evening of September 18, 1931, a minor bomb explosion, apparently the work of the Japanese themselves, occurred on the main line of the South Manchurian Railway, just outside the city of Mukden. Using the explosion as a pretext, the Kwantung Army, the powerful element of the Imperial Japanese Army stationed in the Kwantung Leased Territory and responsible for the guarding of the South Manchurian Railway, began military operations which resulted in the occupation of all Manchuria and the eventual creation of the puppet state of "Manchoukuo." Kwantung Army success in Manchuria plus its political and diplomatic repercussions in Tokyo contributed significantly to the accession to power in government of the Japanese military.

China's government, powerless to offer effective military resistance to the Kwantung Army, resorted to the only other means of defense available to it, appeal to the League of Nations. The League in its investigation found against Japan; and consequently, although its recommendations for a general settlement of the Manchurian issue were eminently reasonable, Japan refused to accept them, denounced the League, and withdrew from it. These events clearly demonstrated the inherent weakness of the League which was subsequently defied also by Hitler's Germany and Mussolini's Italy. Thus, Japanese actions in Manchuria crippled the League, rendering it incapable of acting effectively to prevent the Second World War.

The United States, standing outside the League, co-operated with it to the greatest extent possible under the circumstances, but was also unsuccessful in getting the Japanese government to honor its commitments under the Nine-Power Pact and to withdraw from Manchuria. This was the beginning of ten years of struggle over Japanese policy and actions in China that was ended only by the attack on Pearl Harbor.

The purchase of the Russian interest in the Chinese Eastern Railway by the puppet state of Manchoukuo eliminated the Soviet Union from the area and consequently the possibility of an open clash there. However, the powerful forces of the Kwantung Army all along the 1,500-mile frontier between Manchuria and the Soviet Union were confronted by a similar Soviet military force with the result that tension was increased between Japan and the Soviet Union, a tension which was also released in war.

Thus, the Manchurian Crisis not only demonstrated the strength of the Japanese military in both military and political affairs and resulted in a resounding strategic, economic, and diplomatic victory for Japan, but was also a direct cause of the Second World War.

No. 1. Statement Issued [by Japanese Government] after Extraordinary Cabinet Meeting, September 24, 1931[1]

(1) The Japanese Government has constantly been exercising honest endeavors in pursuance of its settled policy to foster friendly relations between Japan and China and to promote the common prosperity and well-being of the two countries. Unfortunately, the conduct of officials and individuals of China, for some years past,

has been such that our national sentiment has frequently been irritated. In particular, unpleasant incidents have taken place one after another in regions of Manchuria and Mongolia in which Japan is interested in especial degree until an impression has gained strength in the minds of the Japanese people that Japan's fair and friendly attitude is not being reciprocated by China in like spirit. Amidst an atmosphere of perturbation and anxiety thus created a detachment of Chinese troops destroyed tracks of the South Manchurian Railway in the vicinity of Mukden and attacked our railway guards at midnight of September 18. A clash between Japanese and Chinese troops then took place.

(2) The situation became critical as the number of Japanese guards stationed along the entire railway did not then exceed ten thousand four hundred while there were in juxtaposition some two hundred twenty thousand Chinese soldiers. Moreover, hundreds of thousands of Japanese residents were placed in jeopardy. In order to forestall imminent disaster the Japanese army had to act swiftly. The Chinese soldiers, garrisoned in neighboring localities, were disarmed and the duty of maintaining peace and order was left in the hands of the local Chinese organizations under the supervision of Japanese troops.

(3) These measures having been taken, our soldiers were mostly withdrawn within the railway zone. There still remain some detachments in Mukden and Kirin and a small number of men in a few other places. But nowhere does a state of military occupation as such exist. Reports that Japanese authorities have seized customs or salt gabelle office at Yingkou or that they have taken control of Chinese railways between Supingkai and Chengchiatun or between Mukden and Sinmintun are entirely untrue, nor has the story of our troops having ever been sent north of Changchun or into Chientao any foundation in fact.

(4) The Japanese Government at a special cabinet meeting September 19th took decision that all possible efforts should be made to prevent aggravation of the situation and instructions to that effect were given to the commander of the Manchurian garrison. It is true that a detachment was despatched from Changchun to Kirin September 21st, but it was not with a view to military occupation but only for the purpose of removing the menace to the South Manchurian Railway on one flank. As soon as that object has been attained the bulk of our detachment will be withdrawn. It may be added that while a mixed brigade of four thousand men was sent from Korea to join the Manchurian garrison the total number of men in the garrison at present still remains within the limit set by the

treaty and that fact cannot therefore be regarded as having in any way added to the seriousness of the international situation.

(5) It may be superfluous to repeat that the Japanese Government harbors no territorial designs in Manchuria. What we desire is that Japanese subjects shall be enabled to safely engage in various peaceful pursuits and be given an opportunity for participating in the development of that land by means of capital and labor. It is the proper duty of a government to protect the rights and interests legitimately enjoyed by the nation or individuals. The endeavors of the Japanese Government to guard the South Manchurian Railway against wanton attacks would be viewed in no other light. The Japanese Government, true to established policy, is prepared to cooperate with the Chinese Government in order to prevent the present incident from developing into a disastrous situation between the two countries and to work out such constructive plans as will once for all eradicate causes for future friction. The Japanese Government would be more than gratified if the present difficulty could be brought to a solution which will give a new turn to mutual relations of the two countries.

No. 2. The Stimson Doctrine. The Secretary of State to the Ambassador to Japan [Forbes] [2]

Washington, January 7, 1932—noon

Please deliver to the Foreign Office on behalf of your Government as soon as possible the following note:

With the recent military operations about Chinchow, the last remaining administrative authority of the Government of the Chinese Republic in South Manchuria, as it existed prior to September 18th, 1931, has been destroyed. The American Government continues confident that the work of the neutral commission recently authorized by the Council of the League of Nations will facilitate an ultimate solution of the difficulties now existing between China and Japan. But in view of the present situation and of its own rights and obligations therein, the American Government deems it to be its duty to notify both the Imperial Japanese Government and the Government of the Chinese Republic that it cannot admit the legality of any situation *de facto* nor does it intend to recognize any treaty or agreement entered into between those Governments, or agents thereof, which may impair the treaty rights of the United States or its citizens in China, including those which relate to the sovereignty, the independence, or the territorial and administrative integrity of the Republic of China, or to the international policy relative to China, commonly known as the open door policy; and that it does not intend to recognize any situation, treaty or agreement which may be brought about by means contrary to the covenants and obligations of the Pact of Paris of August 27, 1928, to which Treaty both China and Japan, as well as the United States, are parties.

State that an identical note is being sent to the Chinese government.

Stimson

No. 3. Japan-Manchoukuo Protocol (Signed September 15, 1932)[3]

Whereas Japan has recognized the fact that Manchoukuo, in accordance with the free will of its inhabitants, has organized and established itself as an independent State [Note: "Manchoukuo" was established on March 1, 1932.]; and

Whereas Manchoukuo has declared its intention of abiding by all international engagements entered into by China in so far as they are applicable to Manchoukuo;

Now the Governments of Japan and Manchoukuo have, for the purpose of establishing a perpetual relationship of good neighbourhood between Japan and Manchoukuo, each respecting the territorial rights of the other, and also in order to secure the peace of the Far East, agreed as follows:—

1. Manchoukuo shall confirm and respect, in so far as no agreement to the contrary shall be made between Japan and Manchoukuo in the future, all rights and interests possessed by Japan or her subjects within the territory of Manchoukuo by virtue of Sino-Japanese treaties, agreements or other arrangements or of Sino-Japanese contracts, private as well as public;

2. Japan and Manchoukuo, recognizing that any threat to the territory or to the peace and order of either of the High Contracting Parties constitutes at the same time a threat to the safety and existence of the other, agree to co-operate in the maintenance of their national security; it being understood that such Japanese forces as may be necessary for this purpose shall be stationed in Manchoukuo.

The present Protocol shall come into effect from the date of its signature.

The present Protocol has been drawn up in Japanese and Chinese, two identical copies being made in each language. Should any difference arise in regard to interpretation between the Japanese and the Chinese texts, Japanese shall prevail.

In witness whereof the undersigned, duly authorized by their respective Governments have signed the present Protocol and have affixed their seals thereto.

Done at Hsinking, this fifteenth day of the Ninth month of the Seventh year of Showa, corresponding to the fifteenth day of the Ninth month of the First year of Tatung.

> (L. S.) Nobuyoshi Muto
> Ambassador Extraordinary
> and Plenipotentiary of
> His Majesty the Emperor of Japan

> (L. S.) Cheng Hsiao-hsu
> Prime Minister of Manchoukuo

No. 4. Report of the Commission of Enquiry (Lytton Commission Report)[4]

1. Opinion of the Commission concerning "the so-called incident of September 18th":

Appreciating the tense situation and high feeling which had preceded this incident, and realizing the discrepancies which are bound to occur in accounts of interested persons, especially with regard to an event which took place at night, the Commission, during its stay in the Far East, interviewed as many as possible of the representative foreigners who had been in Mukden at the time of the occurrences or soon after, including newspaper correspondents and other persons who had visited the scene of conflict shortly after the event, and to whom the first official Japanese account had been given. After a thorough consideration of such opinions, as well as of the accounts of the interested parties, and after a mature study of the considerable quantity of written material and a careful weighing of the great mass of evidence which was presented or collected, the Commission has come to the following conclusions:

Tense feeling undoubtedly existed between the Japanese and Chinese military forces. The Japanese, as was explained to the Commission in evidence, had a carefully prepared plan to meet the case of possible hostilities between themselves and the Chinese. On the night of September 18th-19th, this plan was put into operation with swiftness and precision. The Chinese, in accordance with the instructions referred to on page 69, had no plan of attacking the Japanese troops, or of endangering the lives or property of Japanese nationals at this particular time or place. They made no concerted or authorized attack on the Japanese forces and were surprised by the Japanese attack and subsequent operations. **An explosion un-**

doubtedly occurred on or near the railroad between 10 and 10:30 p. m. on September 18th, but the damage, if any, to the railroad did not in fact prevent the punctual arrival of the southbound train from Changchun, and was not in itself sufficient to justify military action. The military operations of the Japanese troops during this night, which have been described above, cannot be regarded as measures of legitimate self-defence. In saying this, the Commission does not exclude the hypothesis that the officers on the spot may have thought they were acting in self-defence. [pp. 70-71.]

2. Conclusion of the Commission regarding the establishment of "Manchukuo."

Since September 18th, 1931, the activities of the Japanese military authorities, in civil as well as military matters, were marked by essentially political considerations. The progressive military occupation of the Three Eastern Provinces removed in succession from the control of the Chinese authorities the towns of Tsitsihar, Chinchow and Harbin, finally all the important towns of Manchuria; and following each occupation, the civil administration was reorganized. It is clear that the Independence Movement, which had never been heard of in Manchuria before September 1931, was only made possible by the presence of the Japanese troops.

A group of Japanese civil and military officials, both active and retired, who were in close touch with the new political movement in Japan . . . conceived, organized and carried through this movement, as a solution to the situation in Manchuria as it existed after events of September 18th.

With this object, they made use of the names and actions of certain Chinese individuals, and took advantage of certain minorities among the inhabitants, who had grievances against the former administration.

It is also clear that the Japanese General Staff realized from the start, or at least in a short time, the use which could be made of such an autonomy movement. In consequence, they provided assistance and gave direction to the organizers of the movement. The evidence received from all sources has satisfied the Commission that, while there were a number of factors which contributed to the creation of "Manchukuo," the two which, in combination, were most effective, and without which, in our judgment, the new State could not have been formed, were the presence of Japanese troups and the activities of Japanese officials, both civil and military.

For this reason, the present regime cannot be considered to have been called into existence by a genuine and spontaneous independence movement. [p. 97.]

3. Comments of the Commission on the Government of "Manchukuo."

As regards the "Government" and the public services, although the titular heads of the Departments are Chinese residents in Manchuria, the main political and administrative power rests in the hands of Japanese officials and advisers. The political and administrative organization of the "Government" is such as to give to these officials and advisers opportunities, not merely of giving technical advice, but also of actually controlling and directing the administration. They are doubtless not under the orders of the Tokyo Government, and their policy has not always coincided with the official policy either of the Japanese Government or of the Headquarters of the Kwantung Army. But in the case of all-important problems, these officials and advisers, some of whom were able to act more or less independently in the first days of the new organization, have been constrained more and more to follow the direction of Japanese official authority. This authority, in fact, by reason of the occupation of the country by its troops, by the dependence of the "Manchukuo Government" on those troops for the maintenance of its authority both internally and externally, in consequence, too, of the more and more important role entrusted to the South Manchuria Railway Company in the management of the railways under the jurisdiction of the "Manchukuo Government," and finally by the presence of its consuls, as liaison agents, in the most important urban centres, possesses in every contingency the means of exercising an irresistible pressure. The liaison between the "Manchukuo Government" and Japanese official authority is still further emphasized by the recent appointment of a special ambassador, not officially accredited, but resident in the capital of Manchuria, exercising in his capacity of Governor-General of the Kwantung Leased Territory a control over the South Manchuria Railway Company and concentrating in the same office the authority of a diplomatic representative, the head of the Consular Service, and Commander-in-chief of the Army of Occupation. [p. 106.]

4. Conclusions of the Commission concerning the opinion of residents of Manchuria. Such are the opinions of the local population conveyed to us during our tour in Manchuria. After careful study of the evidence presented to us in public and private interviews, in letters and written statements, we have come to the conclusion that there is no general Chinese support for the "Manchukuo Govern-

ment, " which is regarded by the local Chinese as an instrument of the Japanese. [p. 111.]

5. General Principles to which any satisfactory solution should conform.

1. Compatibility with the interests of both China and Japan. Both countries are Members of the League and each is entitled to claim the same consideration from the League. A solution from which both did not derive benefit would not be a gain to the cause of peace.

2. Consideration for the interests of the U.S.S.R. To make peace between two of the neighbouring countries without regard for the interests of the third would be neither just nor wise, nor in the interests of peace.

3. Conformity with existing multilateral treaties. Any solution should conform to the provisions of the Covenant of the League of Nations, the Pact of Paris, and the Nine-Power Treaty of Washington.

4. Recognition of Japan's interests in Manchuria. The rights and interests of Japan in Manchuria are facts which cannot be ignored, and any solution which failed to recognize them and to take into account also the historical associations of Japan with that country would not be satisfactory.

5. The establishment of new treaty relations between China and Japan. A restatement of the respective rights, interests and responsibilities of both countries in Manchuria in new treaties, which shall be part of the settlement by agreement, is desirable if future friction is to be avoided and mutual confidence and co-operation are to be restored.

6. Effective provision for the settlement of future disputes. As a corollary to the above, it is necessary that provision should be made for facilitating the prompt settlement of minor disputes as they arise.

7. Manchurian autonomy. The government in Manchuria should be modified in such a way as to secure, consistently with the sovereignty and administrative integrity of China, a large measure of autonomy designed to meet the local conditions and special characteristics of the Three Provinces. The new civil regime must be so constituted and conducted as to satisfy the essential requirements of good government.

8. Internal order and security against external aggression. The internal order of the country should be secured by an ef-

fective local gendarmerie force, and security against external aggression should be provided by the withdrawal of all armed forces other than gendarmerie, and by the conclusion of a treaty of non-aggression between the countries interested.

9. Encouragement of an economic rapprochement between China and Japan.

For this purpose, a new commercial treaty between the two countries is desirable. Such a treaty should aim at placing on an equitable basis the commercial relations between the two countries and bringing them into conformity with their improved political relations.

10. International co-operation in Chinese reconstruction.

Since the present political instability in China is an obstacle to friendship with Japan and an anxiety to the rest of the world (as the maintenance of peace in the Far East is a matter of international concern), and since the conditions enumerated above cannot be fulfilled without a strong Central Government in China, the final requisite for a satisfactory solution is temporary international co-operation in the internal reconstruction of China, as suggested by the late Dr. Sun Yat-sen. [pp. 130-31.]

6. Suggestions for a final solution.

We suggest, in the first place, that the Council of the League should invite the Governments of China and Japan to discuss a solution of their disputes on the lines indicated in the last chapter. [See "General Principles" above.]

If the invitation is accepted, the next step would be the summoning as soon as possible of an Advisory Conference, to discuss and to recommend detailed proposals for the constitution of a special regime for the administration of the Three Eastern Provinces.

Such conference, it is suggested, might be composed of representatives of the Chinese and Japanese Governments and of two delegations representing the local population, one selected in a manner to be prescribed by the Chinese Government, and one selected in a manner to be prescribed by the Japanese Government. If agreed to by the parties, the assistance of neutral observers might be secured.

If the conference were unable to reach agreement on any particular point, it would submit to the Council the point of difference and the Council would then attempt to secure an agreed settlement on these points.

Simultaneously with the sitting of the Advisory Conference, the matters at issue between Japan and China relating to respective rights and interests should be discussed separately, in this case also, if so agreed, with the help of neutral observers.

Finally, we suggest that the results of these discussions and negotiations should be embodied in four separate instruments:

1. A Declaration by the Government of China constituting a special administration for the Three Eastern Provinces, in the terms recommended by the Advisory Conference.
2. A Sino-Japanese Treaty dealing with Japanese interests.
3. A Sino-Japanese Treaty of Conciliation and Arbitration, Non-Aggression and Mutual Assistance.
4. A Sino-Japanese Commercial Treaty. [pp. 132-33.]

7. Suggestions Concerning Treaty dealing with Japanese Interests. The aims of this treaty should be:

1. The free participation of Japan in the economic development of Manchuria, which would not carry with it a right to control the country either economically or politically.
2. The continuance in the Province of Jehol of such rights as Japan now enjoys there.
3. An extension to the whole of Manchuria of the right to settle and lease land, coupled with some modification of the principle of extra-territoriality.
4. An agreement regarding the operation of the railways. [p. 135.]

No. 5. Notification by the Japanese Government of Its Intention to Withdraw from the League of Nations[5]

Telegram from the Minister for Foreign Affairs of Japan to the Secretary-General.

Tokio, March 27th, 1933

The Japanese Government believe that the national policy of Japan, which has for its aim to ensure the peace of the Orient and thereby to contribute to the cause of peace throughout the world, is identical in spirit with the mission of the League of Nations, which is to achieve international peace and security. It has always been with pleasure, therefore, that this country has for thirteen years past, as an original Member of the League and a permanent Member of its Council, extended a full measure of co-operation with her fellow-Members towards the attainment of its high purpose. It is, indeed, a matter of historical fact that Japan has continuously participated in the various activities of the League with a zeal not inferior to that exhibited by any other nation. At the same time, it is and has always been the conviction of the Japanese Government that, in order to render possible the maintenance of peace in various regions of the world, it is necessary in existing circumstances to allow the operation of the Covenant of the League to vary in accordance with the actual conditions prevailing in each of those regions. Only by acting on this just and equitable principle can the League fulfill its mission and increase its influence.

Acting on this conviction, the Japanese Government, ever since the Sino-Japanese dispute was, in September, 1931, submitted to the League, have, at meetings of the League and on other occasions, continually set forward a consistent view. This was that, if the League was to settle the issue fairly and equitably, and to make a real contribution to the promotion of peace in the Orient, and thus enhance its prestige, it should acquire a complete grasp of the actual conditions in this quarter of the globe and apply the Covenant of the League in accordance with these conditions. They have repeatedly emphasized and insisted upon the absolute necessity of taking into consideration the fact that China is not an organized State; that its internal conditions and external relations are characterized by extreme confusion and complexity and by many abnormal and exceptional features; and that, accordingly, the general principles and usages of international law which govern the ordinary relations between nations are found to be considerably modified in their operation so far as China is concerned, resulting in the quite abnormal and unique international practices which actually prevail in that country.

However, the majority of the Members of the League evinced, in the course of its deliberations during the past seventeen months, a failure either to grasp these realities or else to face them and take them into proper account. Moreover, it has frequently been made manifest in these deliberations that there exist serious differences of opinion between Japan and these Powers concerning the application and even the interpretation of various international engagements and obligations, including the Covenant of the League and the principles of international law. As a result, the report adopted by the Assembly at the special session of February 24th last, entirely misapprehending the spirit of Japan, pervaded as it is by no other desire than the maintenance of peace in the Orient, contains gross errors both in the ascertainment of facts and in the conclusions deduced. In asserting that the action of the Japanese army at the time of the incident of September 18th and subsequently did not fall within the just limits of self-defence, the report assigned no reasons and came to an arbitrary conclusion, and in ignoring alike the state

of tension which preceded, and the various aggravations which suc-
ceeded, the incident–for all of which the full responsibility is incumbent upon China–the report creates a source of fresh conflict
in the political arena of the Orient. By refusing to acknowledge the
actual circumstances that led to the foundation of Manchukuo, and by
attempting to challenge the position taken up by Japan in recognizing
the new State, it cuts away the ground for the stabilization of the
Far-Eastern situation. Nor can the terms laid down in its recommendations–as was fully explained in the statement issued by this
Government on February 25th last–ever be of any possible service
in securing enduring peace in these regions.

The conclusion must be that, in seeking a solution of the question,
the majority of the League have attached greater importance to up-
holding inapplicable formulas than to the real task of assuring
peace, and higher value to the vindication of academic theses than
to the eradication of the sources of future conflict. For these reasons, and because of the profound differences of opinion existing
between Japan and the majority of the League in their interpretation
of the Covenant and of other treaties, the Japanese Government
have been led to realize the existence of an irreconcilable divergence of views, dividing Japan and the League on policies of peace,
and especially as regards the fundamental principles to be followed
in the establishment of a durable peace in the Far East. The Japanese Government, believing that, in these circumstances, there
remains no room for further co-operation, hereby gives notice, in
accordance with the provisions of Article I, paragraph 3, of the
Covenant, of the intention of Japan to withdraw from the League of
Nations.

> (Signed) Count Yasuya Uchida
> Minister for Foreign Affairs
> of Japan

*No. 6. Agreement between Manchoukuo and the Union of
Soviet Socialist Republics for the Cession to
Manchoukuo of the Rights of the Union of Soviet
Socialist Republics concerning the North Manchuria
Railway [Chinese Eastern Railway] (Signed
at Tokyo, March 23, 1935)* [6]

Article I. The Government of the Union of Soviet Socialist Republics shall cede to the Government of Manchoukuo all the rights they
possess concerning the North Manchuria Railway (Chinese Eastern

Railway), in consideration of which the Government of Manchoukuo shall pay to the Government of the Union of Soviet Socialist Republics the sum of one hundred and forty million (140, 000, 000) yen in Japanese currency.

Article II. All the rights of the Government of the Union of Soviet Socialist Republics concerning the North Manchuria Railway (Chinese Eastern Railway), shall pass to the Government of Manchoukuo upon the coming into force of the present Agreement, and at the same time the North Manchuria Railway (Chinese Eastern Railway) shall be placed under the complete occupation and the sole management of the Government of Manchoukuo.

Article VII. Out of the sum of one hundred and forty million (140, 000, 000) yen in Japanese currency referred to in Article I of the present Agreement, the sum of forty-six million seven hundred thousand (46, 700, 000) yen shall be paid in cash in accordance with the provisions of Article VIII of the present Agreement, and the settlement for the remaining sum of ninety-three million three hundred thousand (93, 300, 000) yen shall be effected in the form of payments made by the Government of Manchoukuo for goods delivered to the Government of the Union of Soviet Socialist Republics in accordance with the provisions of Article IX of the present Agreement.

Article VIII. Out of the sum of forty-six million seven hundred thousand (46, 700, 000) yen to be paid in cash in accordance with the provisions of Article VII of the present Agreement, the sum of twenty-three million three hundred thousand (23, 300, 000) yen shall be paid simultaneously with the signing of the present Agreement.

Article XII. It is understood that the term "North Manchuria Railway (Chinese Eastern Railway)" includes all the rights, enterprises and properties appurtenant thereto.

Article XIII. The Governments of Manchoukuo and the Union of Soviet Socialist Republics, with a view to promote and facilitate the intercourse and traffic between the two countries, shall conclude, within three months from the coming into force of the present Agreement, a separate agreement which will provide for the settlement of questions concerning the conveyance of passengers, luggage and goods in transit, direct service for passengers, luggage and goods between railway stations of the Union of Soviet Socialist Republics and those of the North Manchuria Railway (Chinese Eastern Railway), and also, technical conditions permitting, direct services without reloading of goods between the Ussuri Railway and the North Manchuria Railway (Chinese Eastern Railway) via the station of Suifenho.

Within the period of the said three months, the two Governments shall conclude another separate agreement which will provide for telegraphic connection between the telegraphic lines hitherto operated by the North Manchuria Railway (Chinese Eastern Railway) and those of the Union of Soviet Socialist Republics.

No. 7. Note from Japanese Foreign Minister to Soviet Ambassador[7]

In view of the close and special relations existing between Japan and Manchoukuo, the Japanese Government undertakes to guarantee the exact fulfilment by the Government of Manchoukuo, within the respective limits of time set forth by the above-mentioned Agreement, of all the obligations of payment, in money as well as goods, which the Government of Manchoukuo are under in favour of the Government of the Union of Soviet Socialist Republics as the result of such cession in accordance with Article VII of the said Agreement. . . .

In case any difficulties should arise in connection with the execution of payments on the part of the Government of Manchoukuo, the Japanese Government will make every effort necessary under the given circumstances in order that the Government of the Union of Soviet Socialist Republics may receive all the payments due them from the Government of Manchoukuo wholly and within the respective limits of time prescribed by the said Agreement, so that the Government of the Union of Soviet Socialist Republics may suffer absolutely no loss in connection with the said difficulties.

4

THE SECOND WORLD WAR IN THE
FAR EAST: FIRST PHASE, 1937-41

Japan's attack on Chinese forces near Peiping on July 7, 1937, began the active Far Eastern phase of the Second World War, although the preliminary shots had been fired at Mukden almost six years earlier. For more than four years, until just after the Japanese attack on Pearl Harbor, the Sino-Japanese conflict was an undeclared war. This chapter deals not only with the specific issues involved in the struggle between China and Japan, but also with the broader developments that resulted in the involvement of Japan's Axis partners, the United States, and the Soviet Union, in that struggle and that eventually made the Far East into a major military theater of the Second World War.

The statements by the Japanese government, Prince Konoye, and Generalissimo Chiang Kai-shek outline the issues over which the two governments then declared that their conflict was being waged. The Yonai statement and the treaty between Japan and its puppet government in occupied China reveal the political devices that the Japanese resorted to in an unsuccessful attempt to win a war that they had been unable to win on the field of battle.

The Soviet treaties with China and Japan were the Soviet reaction to the direct and indirect threats that the Japanese attack on China and the Japanese alliance with the Soviet Union's European enemies posed for that government. The neutrality pact between the Soviet Union and Japan remained one of the most important diplomatic facts of the Far Eastern phase of the Second World War, because it was the means by which the Soviet Union hoped, successfully—as events turned out—to avoid a military involvement with the Japanese enemy until the most favorable conditions developed, i.e., a victorious end to the war in Europe and a greatly weakened military position for Japan.

The Rome-Berlin-Tokyo alliance was regarded as a major threat to the rest of the world because it was a powerful coalition among what were temporarily the two greatest military powers, Germany and Japan, and an Italy, not as strong but by no means militarily insignificant, between 1937 and 1942. However, distance, the extent of German and Japanese military operations which were never co-ordinated effectively, and the lack of any real basis for close co-operation made the military potential of the alliance a threat rather than a reality. Nevertheless, the threat was one which posed an extremely difficult strategic problem for the Allies; and the diplomatic, political, and propaganda significance of the alliance was great.

The negotiations between the United States and Japan in 1941, preceding the attack on Pearl Harbor, revealed that it was as impossible for Japan to yield to American demands to withdraw from China and to sever its relations with the European end of the Axis as it was for the United States to yield to Japanese demands to accept the Japanese position in China and the Axis alliance.

The significance of the events between 1937 and 1941 lay not simply in the fact that the Far East was being drawn into the vortex of the Second World War, but that it was becoming far more firmly integrated into the whole web of world affairs than had ever been the case previously. During and after the Second World War the problems of the Far East became not the problems of a region but those of a complex new world.

No. 1. Statement by the Japanese Government, November 3, 1938[1]

By the august virtue of His Majesty, our naval and military forces have captured Canton and the three cities of Wuhan; and all the vital areas of China have thus fallen into our hands. The Kuomintang Government exists no longer except as a mere local regime. However, so long as it persists in its anti-Japanese and pro-communist policy our country will not lay down its arms—never until that regime is crushed.

What Japan seeks is the establishment of a new order which will insure the permanent stability of East Asia. In this lies the ultimate purpose of our present military campaign.

This new order has for its foundation a tripartite relationship of mutual aid and co-ordination between Japan, Manchoukuo and China in political, economic, cultural and other fields. Its object is to secure international justice, to perfect the joint defence against

Communism, and to create a new culture and realize a close economic cohesion throughout East Asia. This indeed is the way to contribute toward the stabilization of East Asia and the progress of the world.

What Japan desires of China is that that country will share in the task of bringing about this new order in East Asia. She confidently expects that the people of China will fully comprehend her true intentions and that they will respond to the call of Japan for their cooperation. Even the participation of the Kuomintang Government would not be rejected, if, repudiating the policy which has guided it in the past and remolding its personnel, so as to translate its re-birth into fact, it were to come forward to join in the establishment of the new order.

Japan is confident that other Powers will on their part correctly appreciate her aims and policy and adapt their attitude to the new conditions prevailing in East Asia. For the cordiality hitherto manifested by the nations which are in sympathy with us, Japan wishes to express her profound gratitude.

The establishment of a new order in East Asia is in complete conformity with the very spirit in which the Empire was founded; to achieve such a task is the exalted responsibility with which our present generation is entrusted. It is, therefore, imperative to carry out all necessary internal reforms, and with a full development of the aggregate national strength, material as well as moral, fulfill at all costs this duty incumbent upon our nation.

Such the Government declare to be the immutable policy and determination of Japan.

No. 2. Statement by the Japanese Prime Minister [Prince Konoye] December 22, 1938[2]

The Japanese Government are resolved to carry on the military operations for the complete extermination of the anti-Japanese Kuomintang Government, and at the same time to proceed with the work of establishing a new order in East Asia together with those far-sighted Chinese who share in our ideals and aspirations.

The spirit of renaissance is now sweeping over all parts of China and enthusiasm for reconstruction is mounting ever higher. The Japanese Government desire to make public their basic policy for adjusting the relations between Japan and China, in order that their intentions may be thoroughly understood both at home and abroad.

Japan, China and Manchoukuo will be united by the common aim of establishing the new order in East Asia and of realizing a relationship of neighborly amity, common defence against Communism, and economic co-operation. For that purpose it is necessary first of all that China should cast aside all narrow and prejudiced views belonging to the past and do away with folly of anti-Japanism, and resentment regarding Manchoukuo. In other words, Japan frankly desires China to enter of her own will into complete diplomatic relations with Manchoukuo.

The existence of the Comintern influence in East Asia cannot be tolerated. Japan therefore considers it an essential condition of the adjustment of Sino-Japanese relations that there should be concluded an anti-Comintern Agreement between the two countries in consonance with the spirit of the anti-Comintern Agreement between Japan, Germany and Italy, and in order to ensure the full accomplishment of her purpose, Japan demands, in view of the actual circumstances prevailing in China, that Japanese troops be stationed, as an anti-Communist measure, at specified points during the time the said agreement is in force, and also that the Inner Mongolian region be designated as a special anti-Communist area.

As regards economic relations between the two countries, Japan does not intend to exercise economic monopoly in China, nor does she intend to demand of China to limit the interests of those Third Powers, who grasp the meaning of the new East Asia and are willing to act accordingly. Japan only seeks to render effective the co-operation and collaboration between the two countries. That is to say, Japan demands that China, in accordance with the principle of equality between the two countries, should recognize the freedom of residence and trade on the part of Japanese subjects in the interior of China, with a view to promoting the economic interests of both peoples; and that, in the light of the historical and economic relations between the two nations, China should extend to Japan facilities for the development of China's natural resources, especially in the regions of North China and Inner Mongolia.

The above gives the general lines of what Japan demands of China. If the true object of Japan in conducting the present vast military campaign be fully understood, it will be plain that what she seeks is neither territory nor indemnity for the costs of military operations. Japan demands only the minimum guarantee needed for the execution by China of her function as a participant in the establishment of the new order.

Japan not only respects the sovereignty of China, but she is prepared to give positive consideration to the questions of the abolition of extra-territoriality and of the rendition of concessions and settlements—matters which are necessary for the full independence of China.

No. 3. Statement by Generalissimo Chiang Kai-shek, December 26, 1938[3]

. . . All our men in service are aware that the present war is fought because Japan wants to conquer China and China wants to save herself from extinction. To attain this end, efforts are being redoubled in military training. Likewise, the general public has fully realized that Japan's ultimate aim is to subjugate our country and that there will be no other way out, if we do not fight for existence. For this reason, the determination of both Chinese soldiers and civilians to fight to the end has been growing firmer and firmer despite hardships and sufferings. The growth of nationalism and the consolidation of national unity enhance our confidence in the ultimate victory.

Because of our firm determination and national solidarity, the enemy has been using the tactics of threats and inducements besides military action. Following the statement made by the Japanese Government on November 3, a number of illogical and absurd utterances have successively been made by the Japanese Premier and Ministers of War, Navy and Foreign Affairs. These kaleidoscopic and paradoxical statements were apparently intended to hoodwink their own people and the world at large. What is more, these sugar-coated words were expected to produce intoxicating effects on the Chinese people. In the meanwhile, inspired public opinion in Japan has been clamoring support to these official views. . . .

The following is an analysis of the Japanese official and private views regarding their intrigues in the Far East, with Prince Konoye's statement on December 22 as the basis:

1. Creation of a new order in East Asia has been the most favorite slogan of the Japanese. A new order in East Asia, as referred to by Mr. Arita, Japanese Foreign Minister in his statement on December 19, means political, economic and cultural co-operation between Japan, Manchoukuo and China, suppression of Communism, protection of Oriental culture, breaking down of economic walls, promotion of the status of China from a semi-colonial State to full statehood, and stabilization of the Far East. Prince Konoye, in a press interview of December 14, said that the end of the China incident does not only lie in military success but also in the rebirth of China and the creation of a new order in East Asia. The founda-

tion of the new order will be laid after the rebirth of China and co-operation between Japan, Manchoukuo and China.

We must understand that the rebirth of China is taken by the Japanese to mean destruction of an independent China and creation of an enslaved China. The so-called new order is to be created after China has been reduced to a slave nation and linked up with made-in-Japan Manchoukuo. The aim of the Japanese is to control China militarily under the pretext of anti-Communism, to eliminate Chinese culture under the cloak of protection of Oriental culture and to expel European and American influences from the Far East under the pretext of breaking down economic walls. The formation of the "tripartite economic unit" or "economic bloc" is a tool to control the economic lifeline of China. In other words, creation of a new order in Asia means destruction of international order in the Far East, enslavement of China and domination of the Pacific and the whole world.

2. The so-called "East Asia Bloc" co-operation between Japan, China, Manchoukuo and the mutual and inseparable tie binding Japan, China and Manchoukuo, have been the favorite slogans of Japanese official and public quarters during the past few months. These slogans are even broader in sense than the "economic unit, " or "economic bloc, " that has been advocated before. Under the cloak of these slogans the Japanese attempted to devour the North-eastern Provinces and the whole of China and make them an integral unit. Japanese magazines openly advocated that Japan, Manchoukuo and China under the "East Asia Bloc" should form a patriarchal system with Japan as the patriarch and Manchoukuo and China as his children. In other words, the former will be the governor and the latter the governed slaves. . . .

3. The so-called "economic unit" or "economic bloc" has been advocated in Japan for many years and is now being actively carried out. It is the most important point of the "East Asia Bloc" and is sometimes called "economic assistance" or "economic co-opera-tion." The formation of the "economic bloc" is not only intended to control China's customs and currency but also her production and trade in order to dominate the Far East. When this policy is pushed further, they will be able to control the livelihood of every Chinese citizen, thus gradually subjugating the Chinese race.

4. The recent establishment of the "Asia Development Board" marked the settlement of a long dispute among Japanese leaders over the creation of an organ to take charge of China affairs. A "China Affairs Bureau" was proposed some time ago, but it was later changed into the "Asia Development Board." As the "China

Affairs Bureau" is already an insult to the Chinese, the establishment of the present "Asia Development Board" is apparently a greater insult to all the Asiatics. This is not only designed to dismember and conquer China, but also to threaten the whole of Asia. . . .

A careful study of the statement made by Prince Konoye on December 22 will enable us to grasp the true significance of Japan's policy. In the first place, he again asserted the creation of a new order in East Asia through the co-operation of Japan, Manchoukuo and China. As this statement was intended for international consumption, the Japanese Premier had apparently exercised due care in choosing words and phrases that tend to conceal Japan's sinister aims. Therefore, on the surface the statement made no territorial claims nor demand for indemnities, and, what is more, it revealed that Japan is considering the relinquishment of her extraterritorial rights and retrocession of her concessions to China. Such sugar-coated words may, therefore, fool those people who are not aware of the true meaning of the so-called "new order, " but to us, the motives behind their plans in China are as clear as daylight.

Secondly, the aim of the anti-Communist co-operation between China and Japan, suggested by Prince Konoye, is to station Japanese troops in North China and to demarcate Inner Mongolia as a Communist-suppression area. It is absurd to suggest that China, organized under the Three People's Principles, should fight Communism. It may be said that Japan's ultimate objective is to take advantage of the anti-Communist bugaboo in order to control the military, political, cultural, and even diplomatic affairs of China.

The failure to realize this aim long before the outbreak of the hostilities has been the deep-rooted cause for Japan's hostile attitude toward this country. It was because we did not want to fall into the Japanese trap that we put up armed resistance against tremendous odds. If the proposal for anti-Communist co-operation were acceptable we would have accepted it long ago. In reality, the proposed anti-Communism co-operation is not aimed against the Comintern, nor against Soviet Russia, but against China. If this is really aimed against Soviet Russia, why was it that Japan yielded to the Soviet forces during the Changkufeng Incident? It is therefore apparent that anti-Communism is only a means to pull the wool over the eyes of the world and to fulfill their object of stationing troops in North China and Inner Mongolia. Had China agreed to the stationing of Japanese on Chinese soil, the present war of resistance would not have occurred at all. If China were really afraid of Japan

and let the latter station troops in the North, she would have annexed the whole of North China and Inner Mongolia to Japan during
the Tsinan Incident when Japanese forces attempted to block the
advance of the National troops in their Northern Expedition.

Thirdly, the demand for the special privilege of developing North
China and Inner Mongolia, made in Prince Konoye's statement, is
in fact an attempt to dominate China economically and to control
Chinese economic life. In addition, a claim was made for freedom
of residence and trade for Japanese nationals in the interior. This
reminds us of the Japanese special service sections and *ronin,* Jap-
anese-sponsored drug traffic, white slavery, arms smuggling, manufacturing of traitors, and other atrocities that tend to undermine
the morality of our people and the peace and order of this country. . . .

Fourthly, Prince Konoye, in his statement, further stated that
Japan seeks only to render effective co-operation and collaboration
between the two countries. Of course, it is only logical and proper
that all nations should maintain cordial relations with each other,
but the real motive behind Japan's overtures for "co-operation,"
"collaboration," and the "formation of an East Asian Bloc" is to
undermine China's independence. . . .

Judging from Prince Konoye's statement, we can conclude that
the real aim of Japan is to devour China and subjugate the Chinese
race. The so-called co-operation between China and Japan is only
a matter of formality. Territory and indemnity are not wanted by
Japan, simply because she is desirous of something more remuner-
ative. In plain words, the "economic bloc" proposed by Japan is
aimed to attain complete control over China's finances and economic resources, which is far better than indemnity. Japan's demand
for the stationing of troops in North China and Inner Mongolia and
for freedom of residence and trade in the interior is apparently
prompted by her desire to control Chinese territory and enslave
the Chinese people. Japan conquered Korea under the pretext of
"Japanese-Korean co-operation" and now she has coined new high-
sounding terms, such as "East Asia Bloc." In other words, these
terms are smoke-screens for annexing China and establishing a
"Continental Empire of Japan."

In conclusion, to Japan the present war is an act of violence that
represents the collapse of morality; but to China it is a sacred
struggle for international justice. Japanese militarists have run
amuck regardless of human civilization and welfare. Nations which
are responsible for the maintenance of the sanctity of international

treaties are in duty bound to checkmate the aggressor, but they have thus far hesitated to take up the responsibility. Regardless of any sacrifice, China is now fighting alone for international justice. In the present war of resistance, we are not only fighting for our national independence, and complete realization of our revolutionary task, but also for the sanctity of international treaties and restoration of world order. The current war is a struggle between evil and good, right and wrong, might and right, law and disorder, and justice and violence. We believe justice will triumph. All the right-thinking peoples of the world will co-operate with us for the sake of justice. The final victory will be ours if we continue to struggle resolutely despite hardships and sufferings.

No. 4. Statement of Premier Admiral Mitsumasa Yonai on Establishment of the New Central Government of China, March 13, 1940[4]

To free the world from contentions and conflicts and to make peace and goodwill prevail among mankind is an aim consonant with the great idea upon which our Empire was founded. It is to that end that a new order in East Asia is contemplated. Every country should be enabled to find its proper place of peace and contentment; there should be amity and harmony among neighbors, and there should be mutual respect for one another's natural endowments, and common prosperity and progress for all.

In the performance of the sacred task of reconstructing East Asia, the first step to be taken is to create and insure a new international relationship between Japan, Manchoukuo and China. Needless to say, this new relationship should of necessity conform to the ideal underlying the construction of the new order in East Asia. That is why neighborly amity and good will, common defense against the Comintern, and economic co-operation were advocated in the statement of Premier Prince Fumimaro Konoye.

Our goal is plain as day. The concrete program for the construction of the new order which the Japanese Government proposes to accomplish in concert with the new Central Government of China is formulated on that very statement. It is devoted to no other purpose than that the nations concerned shall respect one another's racial and national endowment, and shall cultivate friendly relations of mutual aid and good fellowship, stand guard against the menace of Communism so as to insure the peace of East Asia, and practice the principle of ministering to one another's need by setting up a reciprocal economic system. That Japan will respect China's independence and freedom has been made clear in the successive statements issued by our Government, and it will be proved in fact as the present disturbances subside.

Although Japan and China are now engaged in hostilities, the two people retain in their hearts, the spirit of mutual sympathy and tolerance. The longer the hostilities last, the greater will be the sacrifice imposed upon East Asia. But certainly the great timeless mission of our Empire cannot be abandoned simply because of the sacrifices of this conflict. The determination of our Government and people is firm as ever, and the strength of our nation has been replenished according to plan, so that we are ready to carry on our campaign, no matter how long, until the eyes of China's anti-Japanese and pro-Communist regime are finally opened.

Far-sighted men are not lacking among the four hundred million people of China. Some enlightened leaders have long advocated peace and national salvation. In order to rescue their nation from suffering and distress, they are fearlessly standing for right and dedicating their lives to their cause. These men who share in the same solicitudes toward the general welfare of East Asia are our comrades. We cannot but admire them for their high purpose and their unselfish enterprise.

Mr. Wang Ching-wei is an outstanding figure of this group. He could not endure to see the actual state of affairs by which his people were needlessly plunged into the depth of misery owing to the mistaken policy of the Chungking regime, which in the last analysis only hastened the sovietization of his country. He came out for national salvation through opposition to Communism and conclusion of peace with Japan. In the face of all manners of pressure and persecution by Chungking, he pursued the path of his conviction, bringing light to his people lost in darkness.

Thus has he won the confidence and the following of his nation. His peace and national salvation movement as well as the preparation for a new Central Government have made rapid headway since the Sixth Kuomintang National Congress which was held in Shanghai in August last year (1939).

For the sake of the peace of East Asia we are truly gratified to know that the Central Political Council is to meet soon, and a new Central Government will be brought into being with the united support and co-operation of both regimes at Peking and Nanking and also of many leaders representing the various political groups and the various sections of society. Japan will, of course, render whole-hearted assistance toward the formation of the new Govern-

₁ent and is prepared speedily to extend recognition following its
stablishment.
In this connection I should like to add that I am deeply impressed
y the fact that in full accord with Mr. Wang, those leading states-
₁en in the Peking and Nanking Governments, who have for the past
wo and a half years devoted every ounce of their energy to the re-
onstruction and rehabilitation of their respective areas, are now
oing forward with the work of restoring peace and building up a
ew China.
On the eve of the establishment of a new central Government of
₁hina I express my ardent hope that Mr. Wang and all those other
₁en of vision and leadership, united in purpose and resolute in
ction, will proceed with the great task for the regeneration of
sia. I am convinced that their earnest endeavors will meet with
opular approval and support, both in and out of China, and that
₁e misfortune brought on by the present Sino-Japanese conflict
vill be turned into an eternal blessing.

*No. 5. Treaty concerning the Basic Relations between
Japan and China, between Japan and the Wang
Ching-wei Regime in Japanese-occupied China
(Signed at Nanking, November 30, 1940)*[5]

The Imperial Government of Japan and the National Government
f the Republic of China:
Being desirous that these two countries should respect their in-
erent characteristics and closely co-operate with each other as
ood neighbors under their common ideal of establishing a new
rder in East Asia on an ethical basis, establishing thereby a per-
₁anent peace in East Asia, and with this as a nucleus contributing
oward the peace of the world in general, and
Desiring for this purpose to establish fundamental principles to
egulate the relations between the two countries, have agreed as
ollows:
Article I. The Governments of the two countries shall, in order
o maintain permanently good neighbourly and amicable relations
₁etween the two countries, mutually respect their sovereignty and
erritories and at the same time take mutually helpful and friendly
₁easures, political, economic and cultural and otherwise.
The Governments of the two countries agree to eliminate, and
o prohibit in the future, such measures and causes as are destructive of the amity between the two countries in politics, diplo-

macy, education, propaganda and trade and commerce, and other spheres.

Article II. The Governments of the two countries shall closely co-operate for cultural harmony, creation and development.

Article III. The Governments of the two countries agree to engage in joint defense against all destructive operations of communistic nature that jeopardize the peace and welfare of their countries.

The Governments of the two countries shall in order to accomplish the purpose mentioned in the preceding paragraph, eliminate communistic elements and organizations in their respective territories, and at the same time co-operate closely concerning information and propaganda with reference to the defense against communistic activities.

Japan shall, in order to carry out the defense against communistic activities through collaboration of the two countries, station required forces in specified areas of Mengchiang [Inner Mongolian provinces of Chahar, Suiyuan, and Ninghsia. Note in original.] and of North China for the necessary duration, in accordance with the terms to be agreed upon separately.

Article IV. The Governments of the two countries undertake to co-operate closely for the maintenance of common peace and order until the Japanese forces sent to China complete their evacuation in accordance with the terms as provided for separately.

The areas for stationing Japanese forces for the period requiring the maintenance of common peace and order and other matters pertaining thereto shall be determined as agreed separately between the two countries.

Article V. The Government of the Republic of China shall recognize that Japan may, in accordance with previous practices or in order to preserve the common interests of the two countries, station for a required duration its naval units and vessels in specified areas within the territory of the Republic of China, in accordance with the terms to be agreed upon separately between the two countries.

Article VI. The Governments of the two countries shall effect close economic co-operation between the two countries in conformance with the spirit of complementing each other and ministering to each other's needs, as well as in accordance with the principles of equality and reciprocity.

With reference to specific resources in North China and Mengchiang, especially mineral resources required for national defense, the Government of the Republic of China undertake that they shall be developed through close co-operation of the two countries. With reference to the development of specific resources in other areas which are required for national defense, the Government of the Republic of China shall afford necessary facilities to Japan and Japanese subjects.

With regard to the utilization of the resources referred to in the preceding paragraph, while considering the requirements of China, the Government of the Republic of China shall afford positive and full facilities to Japan and Japanese subjects.

The Governments of the two countries shall take all the necessary measures to promote trade in general and to facilitate and rationalize the demand and supply of goods between the two countries. The Governments of the two countries shall extend specially close cooperation with respect to the promotion of trade and commerce in the lower basin of the Yangtze River and the rationalization of the demand and supply of goods between Japan on the one hand and North China and Mengchiang on the other.

The Government of Japan shall, with respect to the rehabilitation and development of industries, finance, transportation and communication in China, extend necessary assistance and co-operation to China through consultation between the two countries.

Article VII. According to the development of the new relations between Japan and China under the present Treaty, the Government of Japan shall abolish extra-territorial rights possessed by Japan in China and render to the latter its concessions; and the Government of China shall open its territory for domicile and business of Japanese subjects.

Article VIII. The Governments of the two countries shall conclude separate agreements regarding specific items which are necessary to accomplish the object of the present treaty.

[Note: Article IX is omitted. The treaty was signed by General Nobuyuki Abe for Japan and by Wang Ching-wei. In Article IV of an annexed protocol it was provided that: "The Government of the Republic of China shall compensate the damages to rights and interests suffered by Japanese subjects in China on account of the China Affair since its outbreak."]

No. 6. Joint Declaration by the Governments of Japan, "Manchukuo,"and the Wang Ching-wei Regime in Japanese-occupied China (Signed at Nanking, November 30, 1940)[6]

The Imperial Government of Japan; the Imperial Government of Manchoukuo; and the National Government of the Republic of China:

Being desirous that the three countries should respect one another's inherent characteristics and closely co-operate with one another as good neighbors under their common ideal of establishing a new order in East Asia on an ethical basis, constituting thereby the mainstay of a permanent peace in East Asia, and with this as a nucleus contributing toward the peace of the world in general, declare as follows:

1. Japan, Manchoukuo and China will respect mutually their sovereignty and territories.

2. Japan, Manchoukuo and China will bring about general co-operation on a reciprocal basis among the three countries, especially a good neighbourly friendship, common defense against communistic activities, and economic co-operation, and for that purpose will take all the necessary measures in every direction.

3. Japan, Manchoukuo and China will promptly conclude agreements in accordance with the present declaration.

No. 7. Treaty of Nonaggression between the Union of Soviet Socialist Republics and the Republic of China, August 21, 1937 [7]

Article I. The two High Contracting Parties solemnly reaffirm that they condemn recourse to war for the solution of international controversies and that they renounce it as an instrument of national policy in their relations with each other, and in pursuance of this pledge, they undertake to refrain from any aggression against each other either individually or jointly with one or more other Powers.

Article II. In the event that either of the High Contracting Parties should be subjected to aggression on the part of one or more third Powers, the other High Contracting Party obligates itself not to render assistance of any kind, either directly or indirectly to such third Power or Powers at any time during the entire conflict, and also to refrain from taking any action or entering into any agreement which may be used by the aggressor or aggressors to the disadvantage of the Party subjected to aggression.

Article III. The provisions of the present Treaty shall not be so interpreted as to affect or modify the rights and obligations arising, in respect of the High Contracting Parties, out of bilateral or multilateral treaties or agreements of which both High Contracting Parties are signatories and which were concluded prior to the entering into force of the present Treaty.

Article IV. The present Treaty is drawn up in duplicate in English. It comes into force on the day of signature by the above-mentioned plenipotentiaries and shall remain in force for a period of five years. Either of the High Contracting Parties may notify the other, six months before the expiration of the period, of its desire to terminate the Treaty. In case both Parties fail to do so in time, the Treaty shall be considered as being automatically extended for a period of two years after the expiration of the first period. Should neither of the High Contracting Parties notify the other, six months before the expiration of the two year period, of its desire to terminate the Treaty, it shall continue in force for another period of two years, and so on successively.

No. 8. Agreement and Supplementary Protocol between Japan and Germany (Signed at Berlin, November 25, 1936)[s]

The Imperial Government of Japan and the Government of Germany,

In cognizance of the fact that the object of the Communistic International (the so-called Comintern) is the disintegration of, and the commission of violence against, existing States by the exercise of all means at its command,

Believing that the toleration of interference by the Communistic International in the internal affairs of nations not only endangers their internal peace and social welfare, but threatens the general peace of the world,

Desiring to co-operate for defence against communistic disintegration, have agreed as follows:

Article I. The High Contracting States agree that they will mutually keep each other informed concerning the activities of the Communistic International, will confer upon the necessary measures of defence, and will carry out such measures in close co-operation.

Article II. The High Contracting States will jointly invite third States whose internal peace is menaced by the disintegrating work of the Communistic International, to adopt defensive measures in the spirit of the present Agreement or to participate in the present Agreement.

Article III. The Japanese and German texts are each valid as the original text of this Agreement. The Agreement shall come into force on the day of its signature and shall remain in force for the term of five years. The High Contracting States will, in a reasonable time before the expiration of the said term, come to an understanding upon the further manner of their co-operation.

In witness whereof the undersigned, duly authorized by their respective Governments, have affixed hereto their seals and signatures.

Done in duplicate at Berlin, November 25th, 11th year of Showa, corresponding to November 25th, 1936.

(Signed) Viscount Kintomo Mushakoji
Imperial Japanese Ambassador Extraordinary and Plenipotentiary

(Signed) Joachim von Ribbentrop
German Ambassador Extraordinary and Plenipotentiary

Supplementary Protocol to the Agreement Guarding against the Communistic International

On the occasion of the signature this day of the Agreement guarding against the Communistic International the undersigned plenipotentiaries have agreed as follows:

(a) The competent authorities of both High Contracting States will closely co-operate in the exchange of reports on the activities of the Communistic International and on measures of information and defence against the Communistic International.

(b) The competent authorities of both High Contracting States will, within the framework of the existing law, take stringent measures against those who at home or abroad work on direct or indirect duty of the Communistic International or assist its disintegrating activities.

(c) To facilitate the co-operation of the competent authorities of the two High Contracting States as set out in (a) above, a standing committee shall be established. By this committee the further measures to be adopted in order to counter the disintegrating activities of the Communistic International shall be considered and conferred upon.

[Dates and signatures.]

No. 9. Secret Additional Agreement to the Agreement against the Communist International[9]

The Government of the German Reich and the Imperial Japanese Government, recognizing that the Government of the Union of the [sic] Soviet Socialist Republics is working toward a realization of the aims of the Communist International, and intends to employ its army for this purpose; convinced that this fact threatens not only the existence of the High Contracting States, but endangers world peace most seriously; in order to safeguard their common interests have agreed as follows:

Article I. Should one of the High Contracting States become the object of an unprovoked attack or threat of attack by the Union of Soviet Socialist Republics, the other High Contracting State obligates itself to take no measures which would tend to ease the situation of the Union of Soviet Socialist Republics.

Should the case described in paragraph 1 occur, the High Contracting States will immediately consult on what measures to take to safeguard their common interests.

Article II. For the duration of the present Agreement, the High Contracting States will conclude no political treaties with the Union of Soviet Socialist Republics contrary to the spirit of this Agreement without mutual consent.

[Article III omitted because it involves only minor technical details.]

No.10. Protocol Concluded by Italy, Germany, and Japan at Rome, November 6, 1937[10]

The Italian Government, the Government of the German Reich, and the Imperial Government of Japan,

Considering that the Communist International continues constantly to imperil the civilized world in the Occident and Orient, disturbing and destroying peace and order,

Considering that only close collaboration looking to the maintenance of peace and order can limit and remove that peril,

Considering that Italy—who with the advent of the Fascist regime has with inflexible determination combated that peril and rid her territory of the Communist International—has decided to align herself against the common enemy along with Germany and Japan, who for their part are animated by like determination to defend themselves against the Communist International,

Have in conformity with Article 2 of the Agreement against the Communist International concluded at Berlin on November 25, 1936, by Germany and Japan, agreed upon the following:

Article I. Italy becomes a party to the Agreement against the Communist International and to the Supplementary Protocol concluded on November 25, 1936, between Germany and Japan, the text of which is included in the annex to the present Protocol.

Article II. The three powers signatory to the present Protocol agree that Italy will be considered as an original signatory to the Agreement and Supplementary Protocol mentioned in the preceding article, the signing of the present Protocol being equivalent to the signature of the original text of the aforesaid Agreement and Supplementary Protocol.

Article III. The present Protocol shall constitute an integral part of the above-mentioned agreement and Supplementary Protocol.

Article IV. The present Protocol is drawn up in Italian, Japanese, and German, each text being considered authentic. It shall enter into effect on the date of signature.

In testimony whereof, etc. . . . .

Ciano—Von Ribbentrop—Hotta

No. 11. *Mutual Assistance Pact among Japan, Germany, and Italy (Signed at Berlin, September 27, 1940)*[11]

The Governments of Germany, Italy and Japan, considering it as a condition precedent of any lasting peace that all nations of the world be given each its own proper place, have decided to stand by and co-operate with one another in regard to their efforts in Greater East Asia and the regions of Europe respectively wherein it is their prime purpose to establish and maintain a new order of things calculated to promote the mutual prosperity and welfare of the people concerned.

Furthermore, it is the desire of the three Governments to extend cooperation to such nations in other spheres of the world as may be inclined to put forth endeavours along lines similar to their own, in order that their ultimate aspirations for world peace may thus be realized.

Accordingly, the Governments of Germany, Italy and Japan have agreed as follows:

I. Japan recognizes and respects the leadership of Germany and Italy in the establishment of a new order in Europe.

II. Germany and Italy recognize and respect the leadership of Japan in the establishment of a new order in Greater East Asia.

III. Germany, Italy and Japan agree to co-operate in their efforts on the aforesaid lines. They further undertake to assist one another with all political, economic and military means when one of the three contracting Powers is attacked by a Power at present not involved in the European war or in the Chinese-Japanese conflict.

IV. With a view to implementing the present Pact, joint technical commissions the members of which are to be appointed by the respective Governments of Germany, Italy and Japan will meet without delay.

V. Germany, Italy and Japan affirm that the aforesaid terms do not in any way affect the political status which exists at present as between each of the three contracting parties and Soviet Russia.

VI. The present Pact shall come into effect immediately upon signature and shall remain in force for ten years from the date of its coming into force. At proper time before the expiration of the said term the high contracting parties shall at the request of any one of them enter into negotiations for its renewal.

No. 12. Neutrality Pact between Japan and the Union of Soviet Socialist Republics[12]

Article 1. Both contracting parties undertake to maintain peaceful and friendly relations between themselves and mutually to respect the territorial integrity and inviolability of the other contracting party.

Article 2. Should one of the Contracting Parties become the object of hostilities on the part of one or several third Powers, the other contracting power will observe neutrality throughout the entire duration of the conflict.

Article 3. The present pact comes into force from the day of its ratification by both contracting parties and shall remain valid for five years. Should neither of the contracting parties denounce the pact one year before the expiration of that term, it will be considered automatically prolonged for the following five years.

Article 4. The present pact is subject to ratification as soon as possible. The instruments of ratification shall be exchanged at Tokyo, also as soon as possible. . . .

Done in Moscow, 13 April 1941, which corresponds to the 13th day of the fourth month of the 16th year of Showa.

No. 13. Outline of Proposed Basis for Agreement between the United States and Japan[13]

Document handed by the Secretary of State [Hull] to the Japanese Ambassador (Nomura) on November 26, 1941

Strictly Confidential   Washington, November 26, 1941.
Tentative and Without
Commitment.

Section I.

Draft Mutual Declaration of Policy

The Government of the United States and the Government of Japan both being solicitous for the peace of the Pacific affirm that their national policies are directed toward lasting and extensive peace throughout the Pacific area, that they have no territorial designs in that area, that they have no intention of threatening other countries or of using military force aggressively against any neighboring nation, and that, accordingly, in their national policies they will actively support and give practical application to the following fundamental principles upon which their relations with each other and all other governments are based:

(1) The principle of inviolability of territorial integrity and sovereignty of each and all nations.

(2) The principle of non-interference in the internal affairs of other countries.

(3) The principle of equality, including equality of commercial opportunity and treatment.

(4) The principle of reliance upon international cooperation and conciliation for the prevention and pacific settlement of controversies and for improvement of international conditions by peaceful methods and processes.

The Government of Japan and the Government of the United States have agreed that toward eliminating chronic political instability, preventing recurrent economic collapse, and providing a basis for peace, they will actively support and practically apply the following principles in their economic relations with each other and with other nations and peoples:

(1) The principle of non-discrimination in international commercial relations.

(2) The principle of international economic cooperation and abolition of extreme nationalism as expressed in excessive trade restrictions.

(3) The principle of non-discriminatory access by all nations to raw material supplies.

(4) The principle of full protection of the interests of consuming countries and populations as regards the operation of international commodity agreements.

(5) The principle of establishment of such institutions and arrangements of international finance as may lend aid to the essential enterprises and the continuous development of all countries and may permit payments through processes of trade consonant with the welfare of all countries.

Section II.

Steps to be Taken by the Government of the United States and by the Government of Japan

The Government of the United States and the Government of Japan propose to take steps as follows:

1. The Government of the United States and the Government of Japan will endeavor to conclude a multilateral non-aggression pact among the British Empire, China, Japan, the Netherlands, the Soviet Union, Thailand and the United States.

2. Both Governments will endeavor to conclude among the American, British, Chinese, Japanese, the Netherland and Thai Governments an agreement whereunder each of the Governments would pledge itself to respect the territorial integrity of French Indochina and, in the event that there should develop a threat to the territorial integrity of Indochina, to enter into immediate consultation with a view to taking such measures as may be deemed necessary and advisable to meet the threat in question. Such agreement would provide also that each of the Governments party to the agreement would not seek or accept preferential treatment in its trade or economic relations with Indochina and would use its influence to obtain for each of the signatories equality of treatment in trade and commerce with French Indochina.

3. The Government of Japan will withdraw all military, naval, air and police forces from China and from Indochina.

4. The Government of the United States and the Government of Japan will not support—militarily, politically, economically—any government or regime in China other than the National Government of the Republic of China with capital temporarily at Chungking.

5. Both Governments will give up all extraterritorial rights in China, including rights and interests in and with regard to international settlements and concessions, and rights under the Boxer Protocol of 1901.

Both Governments will endeavor to obtain the agreement of the British and other governments to give up extraterritorial rights in China, including rights in international settlements and in concessions and under the Boxer Protocol of 1901.

6. The Government of the United States and the Government of Japan will enter into negotiations for the conclusion between the United States and Japan of a trade agreement, based upon reciprocal most-favored-nation treatment and reduction of trade barriers by both countries, including an undertaking by the United States to bind raw silk on the free list.

7. The Government of the United States and the Government of Japan will, respectively, remove the freezing restrictions on Japanese funds in the United States and on American funds in Japan.

8. Both Governments will agree upon a plan for the stabilization of the dollar-yen rate, with the allocation of funds adequate for this purpose, half to be supplied by Japan and half by the United States.

9. Both Governments will agree that no agreement which either has concluded with any third power or powers shall be interpreted by it in such a way as to conflict with the fundamental purpose of this agreement, the establishment and preservation of peace throughout the Pacific area.

10. Both Governments will use their influence to cause other governments to adhere to and give practical application to the basic political and economic principles set forth in this agreement.

No. 14. Memorandum Handed by the Japanese Ambassador [Nomura] to the Secretary of State at 1:00 P.M. on December 7, 1941[14]

[Note: On finishing reading the following document Mr. Cordell Hull, the Secretary of State, then made the following remarks. "I must say that in all my conversations with you (the Japanese Ambassador) during the last nine months I have never uttered one word of untruth. This is borne out absolutely by the record. In all my fifty years of public service I have never seen a document that was more crowded with infamous falsehoods and distortions—infamous falsehoods and distortions on a scale so huge that I never imagined until today that any Government on the planet was capable of uttering them."]

1. The Government of Japan, prompted by a genuine desire to come to an amicable understanding with the Government of the United States in order that the two countries by their joint efforts may secure the peace of the Pacific Area and thereby contribute toward the realization of world peace, has continued negotiations with the utmost sincerity since April last with the Government of the United States regarding the adjustment and advancement of Japanese-American relations and the stabilization of the Pacific Area.

The Japanese Government has the honor to state frankly its view concerning the claims the American Government has persistently maintained as well as the measures the United States and Great Britain have taken toward Japan during these eight months.

2. It is the immutable policy of the Japanese Government to insure the stability of East Asia and to promote world peace and

thereby to enable all nations to find each its proper place in the world.

Ever since the China Affair broke out owing to the failure on the part of China to comprehend Japan's true intentions, the Japanese Government has striven for the restoration of peace and it has consistently exerted its best efforts to prevent the extension of warlike disturbances. It was also to that end that in September last year Japan concluded the Tripartite Pact with Germany and Italy.

However, both the United States and Great Britain have resorted to every possible measure to assist the Chungking regime so as to obstruct the establishment of a general peace between Japan and China, interfering with Japan's constructive endeavors toward the stabilization of East Asia. Exerting pressure on the Netherlands East Indies, or menacing French Indochina, they have attempted to frustrate Japan's aspiration to the ideal of common prosperity in cooperation with these regions. Furthermore, when Japan in accordance with its protocol with France took measures of joint defence of French Indochina, both American and British Governments, wilfully misinterpreting it as a threat to their own possessions, and inducing the Netherlands Government to follow suit, they enforced the assets freezing order, thus severing economic relations with Japan. While manifesting thus an obviously hostile attitude, these countries have strengthened their military preparations perfecting an encirclement of Japan, and have brought about a situation which endangers the very existence of the Empire.

Nevertheless, to facilitate a speedy settlement, the Premier of Japan proposed, in August last, to meet the President of the United States for a discussion of important problems between the two countries covering the entire Pacific area. However, the American Government, while accepting in principle the Japanese proposal, insisted that the meeting should take place after an agreement of view has been reached on fundamental and essential questions.

3. Subsequently, on September 25th the Japanese Government submitted a proposal based on the formula proposed by the American Government, taking fully into consideration past American claims and also incorporating Japanese views. Repeated discussions proved of no avail in producing readily an agreement of view. The present cabinet, therefore, submitted a revised proposal, moderating still further the Japanese claims regarding the principal points of difficulty in the negotiation and endeavored strenuously to reach a settlement. But the American Government, adhering steadfastly to its original assertions, failed to display in the slightest degree a spirit of conciliation. The negotiation made no progress.

Therefore, the Japanese Government, with a view to doing its utmost for averting a crisis in Japanese-American relations, submitted on November 20th still another proposal in order to arrive at an equitable solution of the more essential and urgent questions which, simplifying its previous proposal, stipulated the following points:

(1) The Governments of Japan and the United States undertake not to dispatch armed forces into any of the regions, excepting French Indochina, in the Southeastern Asia and the Southern Pacific area.

(2) Both Governments shall cooperate with the view to securing the acquisition in the Netherlands East Indies of those goods and commodities of which the two countries are in need.

(3) Both Governments mutually undertake to restore commercial relations to those prevailing prior to the freezing of assets.

The Government of the United States shall supply Japan the required quantity of oil.

(4) The Government of the United States undertakes not to resort to measures and actions prejudicial to the endeavors for the restoration of general peace between Japan and China.

(5) The Japanese Government undertakes to withdraw troops now stationed in French Indochina upon either the restoration of peace between Japan and China or the establishment of an equitable peace in the Pacific Area; and it is prepared to remove the Japanese troops in the southern part of French Indochina to the northern part upon the conclusion of the present agreement.

As regards China, the Japanese Government, while expressing its readiness to accept the offer of the President of the United States to act as "introducer" of peace between Japan and China as was previously suggested, asked for an undertaking on the part of the United States to do nothing prejudicial to the restoration of Sino-Japanese peace when the two parties have commenced direct negotiations.

The American Government not only rejected the above-mentioned new proposal, but made known its intention to continue its aid to Chiang Kai-shek; and in spite of its suggestion mentioned above, withdrew the offer of the President to act as so-called "introducer" of peace between Japan and China, pleading that time was not yet ripe for it. Finally on November 26th, in an attitude to impose upon the Japanese Government those principles it has persistently maintained, the American Government made a proposal totally ignoring Japanese claims, which is a source of profound regret to the Japanese Government.

4. From the beginning of the present negotiation the Japanese Government has always maintained an attitude of fairness and moderation, and did its best to reach a settlement, for which it made all possible concessions often in spite of great difficulties. As for the China question which constituted an important subject of the negotiation, the Japanese Government showed a most conciliatory attitude. As for the principle of non-discrimination in international commerce, advocated by the American Government, the Japanese Government expressed its desire to see the said principle applied throughout the world, and declared that along with the actual practice of this principle in the world, the Japanese Government would endeavour to apply the same in the Pacific Area, including China, and made it clear that Japan had no intention of excluding from China economic activities of third powers pursued on an equitable basis. Furthermore, as regards the question of withdrawing troops from French Indochina, the Japanese Government even volunteered, as mentioned above, to carry out an immediate evacuation of troops from Southern French Indochina as a measure of easing the situation.

It is presumed that the spirit of conciliation exhibited to the utmost degree by the Japanese Government in all these matters is fully appreciated by the American Government.

On the other hand, the American Government, always holding fast to theories in disregard of realities, and refusing to yield an inch on its impractical principles, caused undue delay in the negotiation. It is difficult to understand this attitude of the American Government and the Japanese Government desires to call the attention of the American Government especially to the following points:

1. The American Government advocates in the name of world peace those principles favorable to it and urges upon the Japanese Government the acceptance thereof. The peace of the world may be brought about only by discovering a mutually acceptable formula through recognition of the reality of the situation and mutual appreciation of one another's position. An attitude such as ignores realities and imposes one's selfish views upon others will scarcely serve the purpose of facilitating the consummation of negotiations.

Of the various principles put forward by the American Government as a basis of the Japanese-American Agreement, there are some which the Japanese Government is ready to accept in principle, but in view of the world's actual conditions, it seems only a utopian ideal on the part of the American Government to attempt to force their immediate adoption.

Again, the proposal to conclude a multilateral non-aggression pact between Japan, United States, Great Britain, China, the Soviet Union, the Netherlands and Thailand, which is patterned after the old concept of collective security, is far removed from the realities of East Asia.

2. The American proposal contained a stipulation which states – "Both Governments will agree that no agreement, which either has concluded with any third power or powers, shall be interpreted by it in such a way as to conflict with the fundamental purpose of this agreement, the establishment and preservation of peace throughout the Pacific Area." It is presumed that the above provision has been proposed with a view to restrain Japan from fulfilling its obligations under the Tripartite Pact when the United States participates in the War in Europe, and, as such, it cannot be accepted by the Japanese Government.

The American Government, obsessed with its own views and opinions, may be said to be scheming for the extension of the war. While it seeks, on the one hand, to secure its rear by stabilizing the Pacific Area, it is engaged, on the other hand, in aiding Great Britain and preparing to attack, in the name of self-defense, Germany and Italy, two Powers that are striving to establish a new order in Europe. Such a policy is totally at variance with the many principles upon which the American Government proposes to found the stability of the Pacific Area through peaceful means.

3. Whereas, the American Government, under the principles it rigidly upholds, objects to settle international issues through military pressure, it is exercising in conjunction with Great Britain and other nations pressure by economic power. Recourse to such pressure as a means of dealing with international relations should be condemned as it is at times more inhumane than military pressure.

4. It is impossible not to reach the conclusion that the American Government desires to maintain and strengthen, in coalition with Great Britain and other Powers, its dominant position it has hitherto occupied not only in China but in other areas of East Asia. It is a fact of history that the countries of East Asia for the past hundred years or more have been compelled to observe the *status quo* under the Anglo-American policy of imperialistic exploitation and to sacrifice themselves to the prosperity of the two nations. The Japanese Government cannot tolerate the perpetuation of such a situation since it directly runs counter to Japan's fundamental policy to enable all nations to enjoy each its proper place in the world.

The stipulation proposed by the American Government relative to French Indochina is a good exemplification of the above-mentioned American policy. Thus, the six countries–Japan, the United

States, Great Britain, the Netherlands, China and Thailand—excepting France, should undertake among themselves to respect the territorial integrity and sovereignty of French Indochina and equality in trade and commerce would be tantamount to placing that territory under the joint guarantee of the Governments of those six countries. Apart from the fact that such a proposal totally ignores the position of France, it is unacceptable to the Japanese Government in that such an arrangement cannot but be considered as an extension to French Indochina of a system similar to the Nine Power Treaty structure which is the chief factor responsible for the present predicament of East Asia.

5. All the items demanded of Japan by the American Government regarding China such as wholesale evacuation of troops or unconditional application of the principles of non-discrimination in international commerce ignored the actual conditions of China, and are calculated to destroy Japan's position as the stabilizing factor of East Asia. The attitude of the American Government in demanding Japan not to support militarily, politically or economically any regime other than the regime at Chungking, disregarding thereby the existence of the Nanking Government, shatters the very basis of the present negotiations. This demand of the American Government falling, as it does, in line with its above-mentioned refusal to cease from aiding the Chungking regime, demonstrates the intention of the American Government to obstruct the restoration of normal relations between Japan and China and the return of peace to East Asia.

5. In brief, the American proposal contains certain acceptable items such as those concerning commerce, including the conclusion of a trade agreement, mutual removing of the freezing restrictions, and stabilization of yen and dollar exchange, or the abolition of extraterritorial rights in China. On the other hand, however, the proposal in question ignores Japan's sacrifices in the four years of the China Affair, menaces the Empire's existence itself and disparages its honour and prestige. Therefore, viewed in its entirety, the Japanese Government regrets that it cannot accept the proposal as a basis of negotiation.

6. The Japanese Government, in its desire for an early conclusion of the negotiation, proposed simultaneously with the conclusion of the Japanese-American negotiation, agreements to be signed with Great Britain and other interested countries. The proposal was accepted by the American Government. However, since the American Government made the proposal of November 26th as a result of frequent consultation with Great Britain, Australia,

the Netherlands and Chungking, and presumably by catering to the wishes of the Chungking regime in the questions of China, it must be concluded that all these countries are at one with the United States in ignoring Japan's position.

7. Obviously it is the intention of the American Government to conspire with Great Britain and other countries to obstruct Japan's efforts toward the establishment of peace through the creation of a new order in East Asia, and especially to preserve Anglo-American rights and interests by keeping Japan and China at war. This intention has been revealed clearly during the course of the present negotiation. Thus, the earnest hope of the Japanese Government to adjust Japanese-American relations and to preserve and promote the peace of the Pacific through co-operation with the American Government has finally been lost.

The Japanese Government regrets to have to notify hereby the American Government that in view of the attitude of the American Government it cannot but consider that it is impossible to reach an agreement through further negotiations.

December 7, 1941.

No. 15. The Imperial Rescript Declaring War on United States of America and Britain[15]

We, by grace of heaven, Emperor of Japan, seated on the Throne of a line unbroken for ages eternal, enjoin upon ye, Our loyal and brave subjects:

We hereby declare war on the United States of America and the British Empire. The men and officers of Our army and navy shall do their utmost in prosecuting the war. Our public servants of various departments shall perform faithfully and diligently their appointed tasks, and all other subjects of Ours shall pursue their respective duties; the entire nation with a united will shall mobilize their total strength so that nothing will miscarry in the attainment of our war aims.

To insure the stability of East Asia and to contribute to world peace is the farsighted policy which was formulated by Our Great Illustrious Imperial Grandsire and Our Great Imperial Sire succeeding Him, and which We lay constantly to heart.

To cultivate friendship among nations and to enjoy prosperity in common with all nations has always been the guiding principle of Our Empire's foreign policy. It has been truly unavoidable and far from Our wishes that Our Empire has now been brought to cross swords with America and Britain.

More than four years have passed since China, failing to comprehend the true intentions of Our Empire, and recklessly courting trouble, disturbed the peace of East Asia and compelled Our Empire to take up arms. Although there has been re-established the National Government of China, with which Japan had effected neighborly intercourse and co-operation, the regime which has survived at Chungking, relying upon American and British protection, still continues its fratricidal opposition.

Eager for the realization of their inordinate ambition to dominate the Orient, both America and Britain, giving support to the Chungking regime, have aggravated the disturbances in East Asia.

Moreover, these two Powers, inducing other countries to follow suit, increased military preparations on all sides of Our Empire to challenge us. They have obstructed by every means our peaceful commerce, and finally resorted to a direct severance of economic relations, menacing gravely the existence of Our Empire.

Patiently have We waited and long have We endured in the hope that Our Government might retrieve the situation in peace, but Our adversaries showing not the least spirit of conciliation, have unduly delayed a settlement; and in the meantime, they have intensified the economic and political pressure to compel thereby Our Empire to submission.

This trend of affairs would, if left unchecked, not only nullify Our Empire's efforts of many years for the sake of the stabilization of East Asia, but also endanger the very existence of Our nation. The situation being such as it is, Our Empire for its existence and self-defense has no other recourse but to appeal to arms and to crush every obstacle in its path.

The hallowed spirits of Our Imperial Ancestors guarding Us from above, We rely upon the loyalty and courage of Our subjects in Our confident expectation that the task bequeathed by Our Forefathers will be carried forward, and that the source of evil will be speedily eradicated and an enduring peace immutably established in East Asia, preserving thereby the glory of Our Empire.

5

JAPAN'S WARTIME DIPLOMACY: 1941-45

The early, brilliant success and the extent of Japanese military operations in the Second World War obscured the diplomatic moves that Japan undertook, both as a preliminary to its military campaigns and as an attempt to consolidate what it hoped were the favorable political consequences of its victories, especially those subsequent to Pearl Harbor.

The agreements between Japan and France respecting Indochina were not only a necessary preliminary to the Japanese military operations in Southeast Asia but also, as the preceding chapter shows, a vital issue in the American-Japanese negotiations of 1941. The Japanese action of March, 1945, of removing the French authorities reflected the worsening of Japan's military position, but it also contributed to the confusion, chaos, and conflict that developed in Indochina immediately after the war.

The treaties between Japan and Burma and the Philippines reveal the manner in which the Japanese government dealt with those colonial countries to which it gave independence. Japan never granted independence to Malaya and Indonesia and consequently had no formal treaty relations with them. Japan, of course, recognized Thailand's independence.

The two documents dealing with Greater East Asia, although they contain the essence of the ambitious program that Japan envisaged for the Asia that it had conquered, only hint at the manner in which the Japanese used the GEA concept as the basis of their wartime diplomacy in Asia and as a central theme of massive domestic and foreign propaganda during the war. The 1943 declaration was made when the tide of war had only recently turned against Japan, the 1945 declaration when its military position was already desperate and when the San Francisco conference that was to result in the creation of the United Nations was about to open.

Although the Japanese government made a great fuss over its grants of "independence" to both Burma and the Philippines and devoted major efforts to the dissemination of its Greater East Asia propaganda, the true impact of the Japanese on the colonial areas assumed a far different form. In the first place, the ejection of the colonial powers from their colonies by military means was of far greater importance, for it not only demonstrated that their military strength which was at least one basis for their control was non-existent, but it also broke for a period of only a few years the continuity of colonial rule. Both made it impossible for the colonial powers to return to their colonies and automatically resume their administration after the Japanese defeat.

However specious Japanese-granted independence may have been and however hollow the promise of a Greater East Asia Co-prosperity Sphere, Japanese occupation also meant more than three years of uninterrupted anti-colonial propaganda—carried out not only by the Japanese, but more significantly by local leaders—and more than three years of power, prestige, and influence which, although definitely circumscribed by the Japanese military occupations, was nevertheless far more than anything which had been previously allowed or enjoyed by the new leaders of new independence movements. This is what largely filled the vacuum created by military defeat and the interruption of colonial rule and provided the positive barrier to the reinstitution of colonial rule.

Soviet relations with Japan in 1944 and 1945 reveal that well before its declaration of war against Japan the Soviet government was taking diplomatic advantage of Japan's worsening military situation. It should be noted that the Soviet Union in 1944 regained in large measure what it had been forced to give up in 1925 in order to obtain diplomatic recognition from Japan.

No. 1. Protocol between France and Japan concerning Security and Political Understanding[1]

Signed at Tokyo, May 9, 1941.
Ratifications exchanged at Tokyo, July 5, 1941.
Entered into force, July 5, 1941.
Promulgated, July 9, 1941.

The French Government and the Japanese Government equally desirous of maintaining peace in the Far East . . .
Have agreed as follows:
1. The Japanese Government guarantees to the French Govern-

ment the definitive and irrevocable character of the settlement of the conflict between France and Thailand, which has resulted, as a consequence of the mediation of the Japanese Government, in the Convention of Peace entered into between France and Thailand on May 9, 1941, and the documents annexed thereto.

2. The French Government accepts the above-mentioned guarantee of the Japanese Government. It will set itself to the maintenance of peace in the Far East and in particular to the establishment of the friendly relations of good neighborhood as well as the development of firm economic relations between French Indochina and Japan.

The French Government declares in addition that it does not intend to conclude with respect to French Indochina any agreement or understanding with a third Power, envisaging political, economic, or military cooperation of a nature opposed, directly or indirectly, to Japan.

3. The present Protocol will be ratified and ratifications will be exchanged in Tokyo in the second month following the date of its signature. The French Government can, should the occasion arise, substitute for its instrument of ratification, a written notification of ratification; in that case, the French Government will send its instrument of ratification to the Japanese Government as soon as it is able to do so.

The present Protocol will enter into force on the day of the exchange of ratifications.

No. 2. Protocol between France and the Empire of Japan concerning the Common Defense of French Indochina[2]

Signed at Vichy, July 29, 1941.
Entered into force, July 29, 1941.
Promulgated, August 1, 1941.

The French Government and the Imperial Government of Japan,
Taking into consideration the present international situation,
Recognizing that in consequence, in case the security of Indochina would be menaced, Japan would be forced to consider that the general stability of East Asia and its own security would be endangered;
Renewing on this occasion the engagements taken, on the one side, by Japan to respect the rights and interests of France in the Far East and especially the territorial integrity of French Indochina and

the sovereign rights of France over all parts of the Indochinese Union, and on the other side by France in not concluding in regard to Indochina any agreement or understanding with a third Power envisaging political, economic, or military cooperation of a nature opposed directly or indirectly to Japan;

Have agreed to the following provisions:

1) The two Governments are to cooperate militarily for the common defense of French Indochina.

2) The measures to be taken in view of this cooperation will be the object of special arrangements.

3) The above provisions will remain in force only as long as the circumstances motivating their adoption continue.

No. 3. Japanese Removal of French Authorities in Indochina, March 10, 1945[3]

In accordance with the agreement entered into with France, concerning the common defense of Indochina, Nippon has consistently co-operated with the French civil and military authorities in Indochina for the defense of this region. More recently however, with the development of the war situation, a gradual change has taken place in the attitude of the local French authorities, and they have failed to translate into action the spirit of common defense in the face of attacks upon Indochina by America, Britain and others.

The Nippon representative has from time to time urged reconsideration upon them, but to no avail, so that Nippon forces now find themselves obliged to defend Indochina singly against the enemy who is pressing close upon the region. It means that for the defense of Indochina, Nippon forces have resolved to attain their objective by rejecting those who are of enemy character, and, by extending assistance to such local authorities as will co-operate with Nippon. The above is a measure Nippon, much against her desire, has been compelled to adopt by military necessity, and its application shall be limited to a minimum extent.

It goes without saying that, regarding Indochina, Nippon entertains no territorial designs and the Nippon Government desires to declare that it is prepared to render all possible assistance to the inhabitants of Indochina engaged in the defense of their homeland against the invaders of Eastern Asia, and that in consonance with the principles of the Greater East Asia Joint Declaration, full support shall be accorded to their long-suppressed aspiration to achieve national independence.

No. 4. Treaty of Alliance between Japan and Thailand[4]

Signed in Bangkok, December 21, 1941.
Entered into effect, December 21, 1941.
Promulgated, December 27, 1941.

The Imperial Government of Japan and the Royal Government of Thailand, firmly convinced that the establishment of a new order in East Asia is the only method for realizing prosperity in that sphere and is the indispensable condition for the re-establishment and strengthening of world peace, and animated with the firm and unshakable desire to eliminate completely all evil influences hindering the achievement of that aim, have agreed to the following articles:

Article 1. An alliance is established between Japan and Thailand on the basis of mutual respect for independence and sovereignty.

Article 2. In the event that Japan or Thailand finds itself in armed conflict with another or several third Powers, Thailand or Japan will immediately range itself on the side of the other as its ally and will prepare itself to aid it with all political, economic and military means.

Article 3. The details relative to the execution of Article 2 will be determined by common agreement by the competent authorities of Japan and Thailand.

Article 4. Japan and Thailand, in the event of a war pursued in common, engage not to conclude either an armistice or a peace except by complete common agreement.

Article 5. The present Treaty goes into effect on its signature. It will remain in force for ten years. The two Parties will consult on the subject of the renewal of the present Treaty at a suitable time before the expiration of the above period.

No. 5. Treaty of Alliance between Japan and Burma[5]

Signed in Rangoon, August 1, 1943.
Entered into force, August 1, 1943.
Promulgated, August 2, 1943 *(Official Gazette,* dated August 3).

The Imperial Government of Japan and the Government of Burma, the Government of Japan having recognized Burma as an independent State,

Mutually respecting their sovereignty and independence, desiring to establish a joint construction in Greater East Asia based on justice and close cooperation, thereby contributing to world peace, conclude a treaty to the effect below with a firm and unshakeable will to eliminate all evil influences hindering its achievement.

Article 1. Japan and Burma will cooperate in all military, political and economic matters to pursue the Greater East Asia War to a successful conclusion.

Article 2. Japan and Burma will cooperate in a firm and mutual manner for the mutual construction of Greater East Asia and for the autonomous development and the prosperity of the countries of Greater East Asia.

Article 3. The details relative to the execution of this Treaty will be determined by common agreement by the competent authorities of the two countries.

Article 4. The present Treaty goes into effect from the day of signature.

No. 6. *Treaty of Alliance between Japan and the Republic of the Philippines*[6]

Signed at Manila, October 14, 1943.
Ratified by the Philippines, October 18, 1943.
Ratified by Japan, October 20, 1943.
Entered into force, October 20, 1943.
Promulgated, October 20, 1943.
Ratifications exchanged in Manila, October 28, 1943.

His Majesty, the Emperor of Japan, and the President of the Republic of the Philippines,

Japan having decided to recognize the Philippines as an independent State,

Desiring that the two countries, mutually respecting as good neighbors their autonomous independence, establish in firm collaboration a Greater East Asia based on justice in order to contribute thereby to the general world peace and desiring to eliminate completely with a strong and unshakable desire all evil influences hindering the achievement of that aim have resolved to conclude a Treaty to that effect . . .

Article 1. There will always be relations of good neighborhood and friendship between the high Contracting Parties on the basis of mutual respect for their sovereignty and territory.

Article 2. The High Contracting Parties assure each other of a firm collaboration in political, economic and military affairs in order to pursue the war of Greater East Asia to a complete victory.

Article 3. The High Contracting Parties will collaborate in a firm and mutual manner, for the construction of a Greater East Asia.

Article 4. The details necessary for the execution of the present Treaty will be determined by the competent authorities of the High Contracting Parties.

Article 5. The present Treaty will enter into force on the day of ratification by the High Contracting Parties.

Article 6. The present Treaty will be ratified as rapidly as possible. The exchange of the instruments of ratification will take place as soon as possible in Manila.

No. 7. Terms of Understanding Annexed to the Treaty of Alliance between Japan and the Philippines[7]

AD. Article 2.

It is understood that the principal means of firm cooperation in the military sphere in order to pursue the Greater East Asia War stipulated in this article will be as follows:

The Philippines will provide all facilities for military operations that will be undertaken by Japan; moreover, Japan and the Philippines will cooperate in a mutual and firm manner in order to safeguard the territorial integrity and independence of the Philippines.

No. 8. Statement of the Japanese Government on "Free India"[8]

October 23, 1943.

The Provisional Government of Free India having been established with Mr. Subhas Chandra Bose as its head, the Japanese Government, in their firm belief that it is a great forward step toward the realization of an independent India to which the Indian people have long aspired, have recognized it as the Provisional Government of Free India and hereby declare their intention to extend every possible cooperation and support in its effort to attain its object.

No. 9. Joint Declaration on Greater East Asia[9]

[Issued November 6, 1943, after the Greater East Asia Conference of November 5 and 6, 1943, in Tokyo, under the names of: Tojo Hideki, Prime Minister of Japan; Wang Chao-ming, President of the Executive Yuan of the Republic of China (Japanese-controlled);

Prince Wan Wai Thayanon, Thailand; Chang Ching-hui, Prime Minister of "Manchoukuo"; Jose P. Laurel, President of the Republic of the Philippines; and Ba Maw, Prime Minister of Burma.]

It is the basic principle for the establishment of world peace that the nations of the world have each its proper place, and enjoy prosperity in common through mutual aid and assistance.

The United States of America and the British Empire have in seeking their own prosperity oppressed other nations and peoples. Especially in East Asia, they indulged in insatiable aggression and exploitation, and sought to satisfy their inordinate ambition of enslaving the entire region, and finally they came to menace seriously the stability of East Asia. Herein lies the cause of the present war.

The countries of Greater East Asia, with a view to contributing to the cause of world peace, undertake to cooperate toward prosecuting the War of Greater East Asia to a successful conclusion, liberating their region from the yoke of British-American domination, and enduring their self-existence and self-defence, and in constructing a Greater East Asia in accordance with the following principles:

1. The countries of Greater East Asia through mutual cooperation will ensure the stability of their region and construct an order of common prosperity and well-being based upon justice.

2. The countries of Greater East Asia will ensure the fraternity of nations in their regions, by respecting one another's sovereignty and independence and practising mutual assistance and amity.

3. The countries of Greater East Asia by respecting one another's traditions and developing the creative faculties of each race, will enhance the culture and civilization of Greater East Asia.

4. The countries of Greater East Asia will endeavour to accelerate their economic development through close cooperation upon a basis of reciprocity and promote thereby the general prosperity of their region.

5. The countries of Greater East Asia will cultivate friendly relations with all the countries of the world, and work for the abolition of racial discrimination, the promotion of cultural intercourse, and the opening of resources throughout the world, and contribute thereby to the progress of mankind.

No. 10. Greater East Asia Declaration of 1945 [10]

(1) The foundation of an international order to be built will rest upon a concept of common prosperity and well-being through harmony and co-operation and through the abolition of all forms of

discrimination, racial and otherwise, under the principles of political equality, economic reciprocity, and respect for one another's national culture.

(2) Political status of equality will be secured to all nations, large and small, and they are to be afforded equal opportunity for the growth and development, while each nation is to choose its own form of government without interference from others.

(3) Peoples under colonial status are to be emancipated, and given each their proper place, and the way opened for them to contribute together with others toward advancement of civilization.

(4) Economic co-operation among nations is to be facilitated through the removal of monopolistic control of resources, commerce, and international communications; economic disequilibrium of the world to be rectified; and diffusion of economic prosperity through initiative and industry of individual nations to be encouraged
. . . [omission in original]

(5) The nations, while respecting the traditions of one another's culture, are to promote through cultural intercourse, international harmony and human progress.

(6) Under the principle of non-menace and nonaggression, such armaments as are likely to threaten other nations will be eliminated. Moreover, trade barriers will also be removed, while oppression or provocation through economic measures, as well as by armed force, is to be prevented.

(7) As for the security system, the establishment of all big powers and application of any uniform formula to enter the world . . . agency for each region, which is to operate co-jointly with such world-wide security machinery as may be required. Moreover, ways will be left open for the peaceful adjustment of an international order in accordance with various circumstances of the ever-growing world.

No. 11. Protocol on the Transfer of Japanese Oil and Coal Concessions in Northern Sakhalin, March 30, 1944[11]

The Government of Japan and the Government of the U.S.S.R. as a result of negotiations conducted with the view of putting into force the understanding regarding annulment of Japanese oil and coal concessions in northern Sakhalin which was reached between the two Governments in connection with the pact of neutrality of April 13, 1941, have agreed upon the following articles:

Article I. The Government of Japan shall transfer all rights concerning Japanese oil and coal concessions in northern Sakhalin in accordance with stipulations of the present protocol. . . .

Concession contracts concluded on Dec. 14, 1925, and additional contracts and agreements subsequently concluded between Japanese concessionaires on the one hand and the Government of the U.S.S.R. on the other hand shall be abrogated by virtue of the present protocol.

Article II. All property–installations, equipment, materials, spare stocks, provisions, etc. –possessed by the Japanese in northern Sakhalin shall be transferred in their actual state, unless otherwise provided for in the present protocol . . . to the possession of the Government of the U.S.S.R.

Article III. In connection with the preceding two articles, the Government of the U.S.S.R. agrees to pay to the Government of Japan the sum of 5,000,000 rubles in accordance with the stipulations of the terms for application of the protocol attached to the present protocol.

The Government of the U.S.S.R. will undertake to deliver each year to the Government of Japan 50,000 metric tons of oil produced in the Okha oil fields in northern Sakhalin on ordinary commercial terms for a period of five consecutive years after cessation of the present war.

Article IV. The Government of the U.S.S.R. guarantees removal from the concession territory, without hindrance and without taxation, of oil and coal stored and possessed by the Japanese concessionaires. . . .

Article V. The present protocol shall come into force on the date of its signature.

The present protocol is done in the Japanese and Russian languages both texts having equal force. In witness whereof the undersigned, duly authorized by their Governments, have signed the present protocol and have affixed their seals to it.

Done in duplicate in the city of Moscow on the 30th day of the third month of the 19th year of Showa, corresponding to March 30, 1944.

(Note: On the same day a protocol extending the term of a current fisheries convention for five years was also signed, but the Japanese had to accept higher rental rates for fishing areas and agree to both restriction of and exclusion from certain fishing areas. For the text of this protocol see Harriet L. Moore, *Soviet Far Eastern Policy: 1931-1945.* 1945: Princeton University Press. pp. 205-7.)

No. 12. *Soviet Denunciation of Neutrality Pact with Japan, April 6, 1945* [12]

The neutrality pact between the Soviet Union and Japan was signed

April 13, 1941, before Germany attacked the Soviet Union and before the war between Japan on the one side and Britain and the United States of America on the other broke out.

Since that time the situation is entirely altered, Germany attacked the Soviet Union, and Japan, an ally of Germany, helps the latter in her war against the Union of Soviet Socialist Republics. Besides, Japan is fighting against the United States and Britain, who are allies of the Soviet Union.

Under these circumstances the neutrality pact between the Soviet Union and Japan has lost its sense and a prolongation of this pact is impossible.

In accordance with the aforesaid and with Article III of the pact, which foresees a denunciation of the pact in the year before the expiration of the pact's five-year period of effectiveness, the Soviet Government declares to the Japanese Government its wish to denounce the pact of April 13, 1941.

No. 13. Soviet Declaration of War against Japan, August 8, 1945[13]

After the defeat and capitulation of Hitlerite Germany, Japan became the only great power that still stood for the continuation of the war.

The demand of the three powers, the United States, Great Britain and China on July 26 for the unconditional surrender of the Japanese forces was rejected by Japan and thus the proposal of the Japanese Government to the Soviet Union on mediation in the war in the Far East loses all basis.

Taking into consideration the refusal of Japan to capitulate, the Allies submitted to the Soviet government a proposal to join the war against Japanese aggression and thus shorten the duration of the war, reduce the number of victims, and facilitate the speedy restoration of universal peace.

Loyal to its Allied duty, the Soviet Government has accepted the proposal of the Allies and has joined in the declaration of the Allied powers of July 26.

The Soviet Government considers that this policy is the only means able to bring peace nearer, free the people from further sacrifice and suffering and give the Japanese people the possibility of avoiding the dangers and destruction suffered by Germany after her refusal to capitulate unconditionally.

In view of the above, the Soviet Government declares that from tomorrow, that is Aug. 9, the Soviet Government will consider itself to be at war with Japan.

6

JAPAN: THE LOST WAR AND THE PEACE

The crushing military defeat of Japan in 1945 resulted in a complete alteration of the pattern of Far Eastern international relations which had existed for half a century. Not only was Japan eliminated as the dominant power in Asia, but it was also forced to adapt itself to a completely new and different role both in its own immediate region and in world affairs.

Japan had successfully utilized war as an instrument of national policy as the preceding chapters have abundantly demonstrated, but it was a radical change in the nature of war that not only brought about Japan's defeat but made it virtually certain that it could not resort to war in the future, as it had in the past, to achieve its foreign policy goals. Creative military imagination, scientific and technological skill, and, above all, great industrial capacity enabled the United States to develop the new tactics and strategy necessary to defeat a Japan which in the early 1940's seemed secure behind the bulwarks provided by its own military machine and by great geographical distance as well. Viewed from the standpoint of a defeated Japan, the conclusion is simply that both the kind of war fought in 1944 and 1945 and a possible future major war lie beyond the economic capability of Japan.

As was stressed earlier, the economic base of Japan's war potential after 1895 was broad enough to sustain major and successful military offensives against neighbors without similar capabilities for war. It is now clear that only major continental powers have either the capability of creating the sophisticated weapons that are certain to be used in a major war in the future or the geographical area sufficient to absorb even temporarily the shattering blows of nuclear and thermonuclear attack. Japan's experience as the target of the only atomic bombs used in anger has demonstrated the vulnerability of all Japan to missile-delivered A- or H-bombs. Certainly, less than a dozen bombs with mass-destruction capability could eliminate any Japanese capacity to play an effective role in a future major war.

Thus, it is quite clear that Japan cannot in the future–barring an almost unthinkably drastic alteration in the world strategic situation–resort to war as an instrument of national policy as it once did. It cannot, for example, think in terms of attacks on the United States, continental China, or Russia as it did in the past.

If resort to major war seems barred to Japan, it seems equally unlikely that it can go to war against its small-power neighbors. In the first place, as limited as their armed strength may be, they are no longer the military vacuums that they were in the past. Of greater importance in the fact that the United Nations has demonstrated its ability to contain the outbreak of small-scale wars.

Finally, there is the extremely important consideration of the powerful anti-war sentiment inside Japan. The tragic and bitter experiences of the closing years of the Second World War produced a revulsion against war in all forms and under any circumstances that was one of the most important political and social facts after 1945.

The very necessity of defeating Japan projected the United States into Far Eastern international relations to an extent unprecedented in United States history. The seizure of power by the communists in China and their drive to consolidate their position, to create a new state with new power, and their determination to dominate Asia have completely altered the relationship, either present or potential, between Japan and the continent. The Soviet Union's development of massive military power and its relationship with Communist China have also significantly altered the position of Japan. Thus, the projection of new power and new policies into the Far East have created not only new problems but an entirely new position for Japan, the position of a secondary, not a dominant, power.

These were some of the strategic and international political considerations that were either explicit or implicit in those aspects of the new pattern of Far Eastern international relations that were expressed in the surrender terms, the surrender policy, and the peace settlement involving Japan and its former enemies.

The United States policy for Japan in the initial postsurrender period had a great, even revolutionary, impact on Japanese society. Scarcely any area of Japanese economic, political, or social activity was left untouched by the occupation, though in some areas the extent of change was perhaps illusory rather than real. Partly because of occupation policy, partly because of the enlightened administration of the occupation, and partly because of the option of the Japanese government and a substantial segment of Japanese society itself, Japan subsequently became a stable, democratic outpost for the free world in an Asia which was either communist-dominated, or unfriendly toward the Western democracies because of unhappy colonial memories, or neutralist, or preoccupied with the problems involved in the creation of stable, national societies.

The inconclusive, though useful, joint declaration between Japan and the Soviet Union, signed some five years after the general treaty of peace, reveals another aspect of Japan's new position in world affairs. The memories of the Treaty of Portsmouth, the rivalry that preceded the war and the Soviet attack on Japan in the closing stages of the Second World War are still fresh in the minds of both the Japanese and the Russian governments. The alignment of Japan on the side of the free world naturally affects Japan's relations with not only the Soviet Union but all the communist world.

It is one of the great ironies of the Japanese position that although it is firmly aligned with the free world both inside and outside the United Nations for political, diplomatic, economic, and psychological reasons, it lies thousands of miles away from the main centers of free world strength, but virtually in sight of Soviet territory and only a few hundred miles away from Communist China.

No. 1. Cairo Declaration: Statement on Conference of President Roosevelt, Generalissimo Chiang Kai-shek, and Prime Minister Churchill, Cairo, December 1, 1943[1]

The several military missions have agreed upon future military operations against Japan. The Three Great Allies expressed their resolve to bring unrelenting pressure against their brutal enemies by sea, land, and air. This pressure is already rising.

The Three Great Allies are fighting this war to restrain and punish the aggression of Japan. They covet no gain for themselves and have no thought of territorial expansion. It is their purpose that Japan shall be stripped of all the islands in the Pacific, which she has seized or occupied since the beginning of the first World War in 1914, and that all the territories Japan has stolen from the Chinese, such as Manchuria, Formosa, and the Pescadores, shall be restored to the Republic of China. Japan will also be expelled from all other territories which she has taken by violence and greed. The aforesaid three Great Powers, mindful of the enslavement of the people of Korea, are determined that in due course Korea shall become free and independent.

With these objects in view the three Allies, in harmony with those of the United Nations at war with Japan, will continue to persevere in the serious and prolonged operations necessary to procure the unconditional surrender of Japan.

No. 2. Statement by the President [Truman] of the United States on the Meaning of Unconditional Surrender for Japan, May 8, 1945[2]

Nazi Germany has been defeated.

The Japanese people have felt the weight of our land, air, and naval attacks. So long as their leaders and the armed forces continue the war, the striking power and intensity of our blows will steadily increase and will bring utter destruction to Japan's industrial production, to its shipping, and to everything that supports its military activity.

The longer the war lasts, the greater will be the suffering and hardships which the people of Japan will undergo—all in vain. Our blows will not cease until the Japanese military and naval forces lay down their arms in *unconditional surrender*.

Just what does the unconditional surrender of the armed forces mean for the Japanese people?

It means the end of the war.

It means the termination of the influences of the military leaders who have brought Japan to the present brink of disaster.

It means provision for the return of soldiers and sailors to their families, their farms, their jobs.

It means not prolonging the present agony and suffering of the Japanese in the vain hope of victory.

Unconditional surrender does not mean the extermination or enslavement of the Japanese people.

No. 3. The Yalta Agreement, February 11, 1945[3]

The leaders of the three Great Powers—the Soviet Union, the United States of America and Great Britain—have agreed that in two or three months after Germany has surrendered and the war in Europe has terminated the Soviet Union shall enter into the war against Japan on the side of the Allies on condition that:

1. The *status quo* in Outer Mongolia (The Mongolian People's Republic) shall be preserved;

2. The former rights of Russia violated by the treacherous attack of Japan in 1904 shall be restored, viz.:

(a) the southern part of Sakhalin as well as all the islands adjacent to it shall be returned to the Soviet Union,

(b) the commercial port of Dairen shall be internationalized, the pre-eminent interests of the Soviet Union in this port being safeguarded and the lease of Port Arthur as a naval base of the U.S.S.R. be restored;

(c) the Chinese Eastern Railroad and the South Manchurian Railroad which provides an outlet to Dairen shall be jointly operated by the establishment of a joint Soviet-Chinese Company, it being understood that the pre-eminent interests of the Soviet Union shall be safeguarded and that China shall retain full sovereignty in Manchuria;

3. The Kuril islands shall be handed over to the Soviet Union.

It is understood that the agreement concerning Outer Mongolia and the ports and railroads referred to above will require concurrence of Generalissimo Chiang Kai-shek. The President will take measures in order to obtain this concurrence on advice from Marshal Stalin.

The Heads of the three Great Powers have agreed that these claims of the Soviet Union shall be unquestionably fulfilled after Japan has been defeated.

For its part the Soviet Union expresses its readiness to conclude with the National Government of China a pact of friendship and alliance between the U.S.S.R. and China in order to render assistance to China with its armed forces for the purpose of liberating China from the Japanese yoke.

> [J. Stalin
> Franklin D. Roosevelt
> Winston S. Churchill]

No. 4. The Potsdam Declaration[4]

(1) We—the President of the United States, the President of the National Government of the Republic of China, and the Prime Minister of Great Britain, representing the hundreds of millions of our countrymen, have conferred and agree that Japan shall be given an opportunity to end this war.

(2) The prodigious land, sea and air forces of the United States, the British Empire and of China, many times reinforced by their armies and air fleets from the west, are poised to strike the final blows upon Japan. This military power is sustained and inspired

by the determination of all the Allied Nations to prosecute the war against Japan until she ceases to resist.

(3) The result of the futile and senseless German resistance to the might of the aroused free peoples of the world stands forth in awful clarity as an example to the people of Japan. The might that now converges on Japan is immeasurably greater than that which, when applied to the resisting Nazis, necessarily laid waste to the lands, the industry and the method of life of the whole German people. The full application of our military power, backed by our resolve, *will* mean the inevitable and complete destruction of the Japanese armed forces and just as inevitably the utter devastation of the Japanese homeland.

(4) The time has come for Japan to decide whether she will continue to be controlled by those self-willed militaristic advisers whose unintelligent calculations have brought the Empire of Japan to the threshold of annihilation, or whether she will follow the path of reason.

(5) Following are our terms. We will not deviate from them. There are no alternatives. We shall brook no delay.

(6) There must be eliminated for all time the authority and influence of those who have deceived and misled the people of Japan into embarking on world conquest, for we insist that a new order of peace, security and justice will be impossible until irresponsible militarism is driven from the world.

(7) Until such a new order is established *and* until there is convincing proof that Japan's war-making power is destroyed, points in Japanese territory to be designated by the Allies shall be occupied to secure the achievement of the basic objectives we are here setting forth.

(8) The terms of the Cairo Declaration shall be carried out and Japanese sovereignty shall be limited to the islands of Honshu, Hokkaido, Kyushu, Shikoku and such minor islands as we determine.

(9) The Japanese military forces, after being completely disarmed, shall be permitted to return to their homes with the opportunity to lead peaceful and productive lives.

(10) We do not intend that the Japanese shall be enslaved as a race or destroyed as a nation, but stern justice shall be meted out to all war criminals, including those who have visited cruelties upon our prisoners. The Japanese Government shall remove all obstacles to the revival and strengthening of democratic tendencies among the Japanese people. Freedom of speech, of religion, and of thought, as well as respect for the fundamental human rights shall be established.

(11) Japan shall be permitted to maintain such industries as will sustain her economy and permit the exaction of just reparations in kind, but not those which would enable her to re-arm for war. To this end, access to, as distinguished from control of, raw materials shall be permitted. Eventual Japanese participation in world trade relations shall be permitted.

(12) The occupying forces of the Allies shall be withdrawn from Japan as soon as these objectives have been accomplished and there has been established in accordance with the freely expressed will of the Japanese people a peacefully inclined and responsible government.

(13) We call upon the government of Japan to proclaim now the unconditional surrender of all Japanese armed forces, and to provide proper and adequate assurances of their good faith in such action. The alternative for Japan is prompt and utter destruction.

No. 5. Imperial Rescript on the End of the War, August 14, 1945[5]

To Our good and loyal subjects:

After pondering deeply the general trends of the world and the actual conditions obtaining in Our Empire today, We have decided to effect a settlement of the present situation by resorting to an extraordinary measure.

We have ordered Our Government to communicate to the Governments of the United States, Great Britain, China and the Soviet Union that Our Empire accepts the provisions of their Joint Declaration [Potsdam Declaration].

To strive for the common prosperity and happiness of all nations as well as the security and well-being of Our subjects is the solemn obligation which has been handed down by Our Imperial Ancestors, and which We lay close to heart. Indeed, We declared war on America and Britain out of Our sincere desire to ensure Japan's self-preservation and the stabilization of East Asia, it being far from Our thought either to infringe upon the sovereignty of other nations or to embark upon territorial aggrandizement. But now the war has lasted for nearly four years. Despite the best that has been done by everyone–the gallant fighting of military and naval forces, the diligence and assiduity of Our servants of the State and the devoted service of Our one hundred million people, the war situation has developed not necessarily to Japan's advantage, while the general trends of the world have all turned against her interest. Moreover, the enemy has begun to employ a new and most cruel bomb, the power of which to do damage is indeed incalculable, taking the toll of many innocent lives. Should We continue to fight, it would not only result in an ultimate collapse and obliteration of the Japanese nation, but also it would lead to the total extinction of human civilization. Such being the case, how are We to save the millions of Our subjects; or to atone Ourselves before the hallowed spirits of Our Imperial Ancestors? This is the reason why We have ordered the acceptance of the provisions of the Joint Declaration of the Powers.

We cannot but express the deepest sense of regret to our Allied nations of East Asia, who have consistently co-operated with the Empire towards the emancipation of East Asia. The thought of those officers and men as well as others who have fallen in the fields of battle, those who died at their posts of duty, or those who met with untimely death and all their bereaved families, pains Our heart night and day. The welfare of the wounded and the war-sufferers, and of those who have lost their home and livelihood, are the objects of Our profound solicitude. The hardships and sufferings to which Our nation is to be subjected hereafter will be certainly great. We are keenly aware of the inmost feelings of all ye, Our subjects. However, it is according to the dictate of time and fate that We have resolved to pave the way for a grand peace for all the generations to come by enduring the unendurable and suffering what is insufferable.

Having been able to safeguard and maintain the structure of the Imperial State, We are always with ye, Our good and loyal subjects, relying upon your sincerity and integrity. Beware most strictly of any outbursts of emotion which may engender needless complications, or any fraternal contention and strife which may create confusion, lead ye astray and cause ye to lose the confidence of the world. Let the entire nation continue as one family from generation to generation, ever firm in its faith of the imperishableness of its divine land, and mindful of its heavy burden of responsibilities, and the long road before it. Unite your total strength to be devoted to the construction for the future. Cultivate the ways of rectitude; foster nobility of spirit; and work with resolution so as ye may enhance the innate glory of the Imperial State and keep pace with the progress of the world.

No. 6. United States Initial Postsurrender Policy for Japan[6]

(The following statement of general initial policy relating to Japan after surrender was prepared jointly by the Department of State, the War Department, and the Navy Department and approved by the President on September 6. The document in substance was sent to

General MacArthur by radio on August 29 and, after approval by the President, by messenger on September 6.)

Purpose of This Document
 This document is a statement of general initial policy relating to Japan after surrender. It has been approved by the President and distributed to the Supreme Commander for the Allied Powers and to appropriate U.S. departments and agencies for their guidance. It does not deal with all matters relating to the occupation of Japan requiring policy determinations. Such matters as are not included or are not fully covered herein have been or will be dealt with separately.

Part I. Ultimate Objectives

 The ultimate objectives of the United States in regard to Japan, to which policies in the initial period must conform, are:
 (a) To insure that Japan will not again become a menace to the United States or to the peace and security of the world.
 (b) To bring about the eventual establishment of a peaceful and responsible government which will respect the rights of other states and will support the objectives of the United States as reflected in the ideals and principles of the Charter of the United Nations. The United States desires that this government should conform as closely as may be to principles of democratic self-government but it is not the responsibility of the Allied Powers to impose upon Japan any form of government not supported by the freely expressed will of the people.
 These objectives will be achieved by the following principal means:
 (a) Japan's sovereignty will be limited to the islands of Honshu, Hokkaido, Kyushu, Shikoku, and such minor outlying islands as may be determined, in accordance with the Cairo Declaration and other agreements to which the United States is or may be a party.
 (b) Japan will be completely disarmed and demilitarized. The authority of the militarists and the influence of militarism will be totally eliminated from her political, economic, and social life. Institutions expressive of the spirit of militarism and aggression will be vigorously suppressed.
 (c) The Japanese people shall be encouraged to develop a desire for individual liberties and respect for fundamental human rights, particularly the freedom of religion, assembly, speech, and the press. They shall also be encouraged to form democratic and representative organizations.

(d) The Japanese people shall be afforded opportunity to develop for themselves an economy which will permit the peacetime requirements of the population to be met.

Part II. Allied Authority

1. *Military Occupation*
    There will be a military occupation of the Japanese home islands to carry into effect the surrender terms and further the achievement of the ultimate objectives stated above. The occupation shall have the character of an operation in behalf of the principal allied powers acting in the interests of the United Nations at war with Japan. For that reason, participation of the forces of other nations that have taken a leading part in the war against Japan will be welcome and expected. The occupation forces will be under the command of a Supreme Commander designated by the United States.
    Although every effort will be made, by consultation and by constitution of appropriate advisory bodies, to establish policies for the conduct of the occupation and the control of Japan which will satisfy the principal Allied powers, in the event of any differences of opinion among them, the policies of the United States will govern.

2. *Relationship to Japanese Government*
    The authority of the Emperor and the Japanese Government will be subject to the Supreme Commander, who will possess all powers necessary to effectuate the surrender terms and to carry out the policies established for the conduct of the occupation and the control of Japan.
    In view of the present character of Japanese society and the desire of the United States to attain its objectives with a minimum commitment of its forces and resources, the Supreme Commander will exercise his authority through Japanese governmental machinery and agencies, including the Emperor, to the extent that this satisfactorily furthers United States objectives. The Japanese Government will be permitted, under his instructions, to exercise the normal powers of government in matters of domestic administration. This policy, however, will be subject to the right and duty of the Supreme Commander to require changes in governmental machinery or personnel or to act directly if the Emperor or other Japanese authority does not satisfactorily meet the requirements of the Supreme Commander in effectuating the surrender terms. This policy, moreover, does not commit the Supreme Commander to support the Emperor or any other Japanese governmental author-

ity in opposition to evolutionary changes looking toward the attainment of United States objectives. The policy is to use the existing form of Government in Japan, not to support it. Changes in the form of Government initiated by the Japanese people or government in the direction of modifying its feudal and authoritarian tendencies are to be permitted and favored. In the event that the effectuation of such changes involves the use of force by the Japanese people or government against persons opposed thereto, the Supreme Commander should intervene only where necessary to ensure the security of his forces and the attainment of all other objectives of the occupation.

3. *Publicity as to Policies*
The Japanese people, and the world at large, shall be kept fully informed of the objectives and policies of the occupation, and of progress made in their fulfilment.

Part III. Political

1. *Disarmament and Demilitarization*
Disarmament and demilitarization are the primary tasks of the military occupation and shall be carried out promptly and with determination. Every effort shall be made to bring home to the Japanese people the part played by the military and naval leaders, and those who collaborated with them, in bringing about the existing and future distress of the people.

Japan is not to have an army, navy, air force, secret police organization, or any civil aviation. Japan's ground, air and naval forces shall be disarmed and disbanded and the Japanese Imperial General Headquarters, the General Staff and all secret police organizations shall be dissolved. Military and naval materiel, military and naval vessels and military and naval installations, and military, naval and civilian aircraft shall be surrendered and shall be disposed of as required by the Supreme Commander.

High officials of the Japanese Imperial General Headquarters, and General Staff, other high military and naval officials of the Japanese Government, leaders of ultra-nationalist and militarist organizations and other important exponents of militarism and aggression will be taken into custody and held for future disposition. Persons who have been active exponents of militarism and militant nationalism will be removed and excluded from public office and from any other position of public or substantial private responsibility. Ultra-nationalistic or militaristic social, political, professional and commercial societies and institutions will be dissolved and prohibited. Militarism and ultra-nationalism, in doctrine and practice, including para-military training, shall be eliminated from the educational system. Former career military and naval officers, both commissioned and non-commissioned, and all other exponents of militarism and ultra-nationalism shall be excluded from supervisory and teaching positions.

2. *War Criminals*
Persons charged by the Supreme Commander or appropriate United Nations Agencies with being war criminals, including those charged with having visited cruelties upon United Nations prisoners or other nationals, shall be arrested, tried and, if convicted, punished. Those wanted by another of the United Nations for offenses against its nationals, shall, if not wanted for trial or as witnesses or otherwise by the Supreme Commander, be turned over to the custody of such other nation.

3. *Encouragement of Desire for Individual Liberties and Democratic Processes*
Freedom of religious worship shall be proclaimed promptly on occupation. At the same time it should be made plain to the Japanese that ultra-nationalistic and militaristic organizations and movements will not be permitted to hide behind the cloak of religion.

The Japanese people shall be afforded opportunity and encouraged to become familiar with the history, institutions, culture, and the accomplishments of the United States and the other democracies. Association of personnel of the occupation forces with the Japanese population should be controlled, only to the extent necessary, to further the policies and objectives of the occupation.

Democratic political parties, with rights of assembly and public discussion, shall be encouraged, subject to the necessity for maintaining the security of the occupying forces.

Laws, decrees and regulations which establish discriminations on ground of race, nationality, creed or political opinion shall be abrogated; those which conflict with the objectives and policies outlined in this document shall be repealed, suspended or amended as required; and agencies charged specifically with their enforcement shall be abolished or appropriately modified. Persons unjustly confined by Japanese authority on political grounds shall be released. The judicial, legal and police systems shall be reformed as soon as practicable to conform to the policies set forth in Articles 1 and

3 of this Part III and thereafter shall be progressively influenced, to protect individual liberties and civil rights.

Part IV. Economic

1. *Economic Demilitarization*
The existing economic basis of Japanese military strength must be destroyed and not be permitted to revive.

Therefore, a program will be enforced containing the following elements, among others; the immediate cessation and future prohibition of production of all goods designed for the equipment, maintenance, or use of any military force or establishment; the imposition of a ban upon any specialized facilities for the production or repair of implements of war, including naval vessels and all forms of aircraft; the institution of a system of inspection and control over selected elements in Japanese economic activity to prevent concealed or disguised military preparation; the elimination in Japan of those selected industries or branches of production whose chief value to Japan is in preparing for war; the prohibition of specialized research and instruction directed to the development of war-making power; and the limitation of the size and character of Japan's heavy industries to its future peaceful requirements, and restriction of Japanese merchant shipping to the extent required to accomplish the objectives of demilitarization.

The eventual disposition of those existing production facilities within Japan which are to be eliminated in accord with this program, as between conversion to other uses, transfer abroad, and scrapping will be determined after inventory. Pending decision, facilities readily convertible for civilian production should not be destroyed, except in emergency situations.

2. *Promotion of Democratic Forces*
Encouragement shall be given and favor shown to the development of organizations in labor, industry, and agriculture, organized on a democratic basis. Policies shall be favored which permit a wide distribution of income and of the ownership of the means of production and trade.

Those forms of economic activity, organization and leadership shall be favored that are deemed likely to strengthen the peaceful disposition of the Japanese people, and to make it difficult to command or direct economic activity in support of military ends.

To this end it shall be the policy of the Supreme Commander:

(a) To prohibit the retention in or selection for places of importance in the economic field of individuals who do not direct future Japanese economic effort solely towards peaceful ends; and

(b) To favor a program for the dissolution of the large industrial and banking combinations which have exercised control of a great part of Japan's trade and industry.

3. *Resumption of Peaceful Economic Activity*

The policies of Japan have brought down upon the people great economic destruction and confronted them with the prospect of economic difficulty and suffering. The plight of Japan is the direct outcome of its own behavior, and the Allies will not undertake the burden of repairing the damage. It can be repaired only if the Japanese people renounce all military aims and apply themselves diligently and with single purpose to the ways of peaceful living. It will be necessary for them to undertake physical reconstruction, deeply to reform the nature and direction of their economic activities and institutions, and to find useful employment for their people along lines adapted to and devoted to peace. The Allies have no intention of imposing conditions which would prevent the accomplishment of these tasks in due time.

Japan will be expected to provide goods and services to meet the needs of the occupying forces to the extent that this can be effected without causing starvation, widespread disease and acute physical distress.

The Japanese authorities will be expected, and if necessary directed, to maintain, develop, and enforce programs that serve the following purposes:

(a) To avoid acute economic distress.

(b) To assure just and impartial distribution of available supplies.

(c) To meet the requirements for reparations deliveries agreed upon by the Allied Governments.

(d) To facilitate the restoration of Japanese economy so that the reasonable peaceful requirements of the population can be satisfied.

In this connection, the Japanese authorities on their own responsibility shall be permitted to establish and administer controls over economic activities, including essential national public services, finance, banking, and production and distribution of essential commodities, subject to the approval and review of the Supreme Commander in order to assure their conformity with the objectives of the occupation.

4. *Reparations and Restitution*
Reparations
Reparations for Japanese agression shall be made:
(a) Through the transfer—as may be determined by the appropriate Allied authorities—of Japanese property located outside of the
territories to be retained by Japan.
(b) Through the transfer of such goods or existing capital equipment and facilities as are not necessary for a peaceful Japanese
economy or the supplying of the occupying forces. Exports other
than those directed to be shipped on reparation account or as restitution may be made only to those recipients who agree to provide
necessary imports in exchange or agree to pay for such exports in
foreign exchange. No form of reparation shall be exacted which will
interfere with or prejudice the program for Japan's demilitarization.
Restitution
Full and prompt restitution will be required of all identifiable
looted property.

5. *Fiscal, Monetary and Banking Policies*
The Japanese authorities will remain responsible for the management and direction of the domestic fiscal, monetary, and credit
policies subject to the approval and review of the Supreme Commander.

6. *International Trade and Financial Relations*
Japan shall be permitted eventually to resume normal trade relations with the rest of the world. During occupation and under
suitable controls, Japan will be permitted to purchase from foreign
countries raw materials and other goods that it may need for peaceful purposes, and to export goods to pay for approved imports.
Control is to be maintained over all imports and exports of goods,
and foreign exchange and financial transactions. Both the policies
followed in the exercise of these controls and their actual administration shall be subject to the approval and supervision of the Supreme Commander in order to make sure that they are not contrary
to the policies of the occupying authorities, and in particular that
all foreign purchasing power that Japan may acquire is used only
for essential needs.

7. *Japanese Property Located Abroad*
Existing Japanese external assets and existing Japanese assets

located in territories detached from Japan under the terms of surrender, including assets owned in whole or part by the Imperial Household and Government, shall be revealed to the occupying authorities and held for disposition according to the decision of the Allied authorities.

8. *Equality of Opportunity for Foreign Enterprise within Japan*
The Japanese authorities shall not give, or permit any Japanese business organization to give, exclusive or preferential opportunity or terms to the enterprise of any foreign country, or cede to such enterprise control of any important branch of economic activity.

9. *Imperial Household Property*
Imperial Household property shall not be exempted from any action necessary to carry out the objectives of the occupation.

No. 7. Treaty of Peace with Japan[7]

Whereas the Allied Powers and Japan are resolved that henceforth their relations shall be those of nations which, as sovereign equals, cooperate in friendly association to promote their common welfare and to maintain international peace and security, and are therefore desirous of concluding a Treaty of Peace which will settle questions still outstanding as a result of the existence of a state of war between them;

Whereas Japan for its part declares its intention to apply for membership in the United Nations and in all circumstances to conform to the principles of the Charter of the United Nations; to strive to realize the objectives of the Universal Declaration of Human Rights; to seek to create within Japan conditions of stability and well-being as defined in Articles 55 and 56 of the Charter of the United Nations and already initiated by post-surrender Japanese legislation; and in public and private trade and commerce to conform to internationally accepted fair practices;

Whereas the Allied Powers welcome the intentions of Japan set out in the foregoing paragraph;

The Allied Powers and Japan have therefore determined to conclude the present Treaty of Peace, and have accordingly appointed the undersigned Plenipotentiaries, who, after presentation of their full powers, found in good and due form, have agreed in the following provisions:

Chapter I. Peace

Article 1. (a) The state of war between Japan and each of the Allied Powers is terminated as from the date on which the present Treaty comes into force between Japan and the Allied Power concerned as provided for in Article 23.

(b) The Allied Powers recognize the full sovereignty of the Japanese people over Japan and its territorial waters.

Chapter II. Territory

Article 2. (a) Japan, recognizing the independence of Korea, renounces all right, title and claim to Korea, including the islands of Quelpart, Port Hamilton and Dagelet.

(b) Japan renounces all right, title and claim to Formosa and the Pescadores.

(c) Japan renounces all right, title and claim to the Kurile Islands, and to that portion of Sakhalin and the islands adjacent to it over which Japan acquired sovereignty as a consequence of the Treaty of Portsmouth of September 5, 1905.

(d) Japan renounces all right, title and claim in connection with the League of Nations Mandate System, and accepts the action of the United Nations Security Council of April 2, 1947, extending the trusteeship system to the Pacific Islands formerly under mandate to Japan.

(e) Japan renounces all claim to any right or title to or interest in connection with any part of the Antarctic area, whether deriving from the activities of Japanese nationals or otherwise.

(f) Japan renounces all right, title and claim to the Spratly Islands and to the Paracel Islands.

Article 3. Japan will concur in any proposal of the United States to the United Nations to place under its trusteeship system, with the United States as the sole administering authority, Nansei Shoto south of 29° north latitude (including the Ryukyu Islands and the Daito Islands), Nanpo Shoto south of Sofu Gan (including the Bonin Islands, Rosario Island and the Volcano Islands) and Parece Vela and Marcus Island. Pending the making of such a proposal and affirmative action thereon, the United States will have the right to exercise all and any powers of administration, legislation and jurisdiction over the territory and inhabitants of these islands, including their territorial waters.

Article 4. (a) Subject to the provisions of paragraph (b) of this

Article, the disposition of property of Japan and of its nationals in the areas referred to in Article 2, and their claims, including debts, against the authorities presently administering such areas and the residents (including juridical persons) thereof, and the disposition in Japan of property of such authorities and residents, and of claims, including debts, of such authorities and residents against Japan and its nationals, shall be the subject of special arrangements between Japan and such authorities. The property of any of the Allied Powers or its nationals in the areas referred to in Article 2 shall, insofar as this has not already been done, be returned by the administering authority in the condition in which it now exists. (The term nationals whenever used in the present Treaty includes juridical persons.)

(b) Japan recognizes the validity of dispositions of property of Japan and Japanese nationals made by or pursuant to directives of the United States Military Government in any of the areas referred to in Articles 2 and 3.

(c) Japanese owned submarine cables connecting Japan with territory removed from Japanese control pursuant to the present Treaty shall be equally divided, Japan retaining the Japanese terminal and adjoining half of the cable, and the detached territory the remainder of the cable and connecting terminal facilities.

Chapter III. Security

Article 5. (a) Japan accepts the obligations set forth in Article 2 of the Charter of the United Nations, and in particular the obligations

(i) to settle its international disputes by peaceful means in such a manner that international peace and security, and justice, are not endangered;

(ii) to refrain in its international relations from the threat or use of force against the territorial integrity or political independence of any State or in any other manner inconsistent with the Purposes of the United Nations;

(iii) to give the United Nations every assistance in any action it takes in accordance with the Charter and to refrain from giving assistance to any State against which the United Nations may take preventive or enforcement action.

(b) The Allied Powers confirm that they will be guided by the principles of Article 2 of the Charter of the United Nations in their relations with Japan.

(c) The Allied Powers for their part recognize that Japan as a sovereign nation possesses the inherent right of individual or collective self-defense referred to in Article 51 of the Charter of the United Nations and that Japan may voluntarily enter into collective security arrangements.

Article 6. (a) All occupation forces of the Allied Powers shall be withdrawn from Japan as soon as possible after the coming into force of the present Treaty, and in any case not later than 90 days thereafter. Nothing in this provision shall, however, prevent the stationing or retention of foreign armed forces in Japanese territory under or in consequence of any bilateral or multilateral agreements which have been or may be made between one or more of the Allied Powers, on the one hand, and Japan on the other.

(b) The provisions of Article 9 of the Potsdam Proclamation of July 26, 1945, dealing with the return of Japanese military forces to their homes, to the extent not already completed, will be carried out.

(c) All Japanese property for which compensation has not already been paid, which was supplied for the use of the occupation forces and which remains in the possession of those forces at the time of the coming into force of the present Treaty, shall be returned to the Japanese Government within the same 90 days unless other arrangements are made by mutual agreement.

Chapter IV. Political and Economic Clauses

Article 7. (a) Each of the Allied Powers, within one year after the present Treaty has come into force between it and Japan, will notify Japan which of its prewar bilateral treaties or conventions with Japan it wishes to continue in force or revive, and any treaties or conventions so notified shall continue in force or be revived subject only to such amendments as may be necessary to ensure conformity with the present Treaty. The treaties and conventions so notified shall be considered as having been continued in force or revived three months after the date of notification and shall be registered with the Secretariat of the United Nations. All such treaties and conventions as to which Japan is not so notified shall be regarded as abrogated.

(b) Any notification made under paragraph (a) of this Article may except from the operation or revival of a treaty or convention any territory for the international relations of which the notifying Power is responsible, until three months after the date on which notice is given to Japan that such exception shall cease to apply.

Article 8. (a) Japan will recognize the full force of all treaties now or hereafter concluded by the Allied Powers for terminating the state of war initiated on September 1, 1939, as well as any other arrangements by the Allied Powers for or in connection with the restoration of peace. Japan also accepts the arrangements made for terminating the former League of Nations and Permanent Court of International Justice.

(b) Japan renounces all such rights and interests as it may derive from being a signatory power of the Conventions of St. Germain-en-Laye of September 10, 1919, and the Straits Agreement of Montreux of July 20, 1936, and from Article 16 of the Treaty of Peace with Turkey signed at Lausanne on July 24, 1923.

(c) Japan renounces all rights, title and interests acquired under, and is discharged from all obligations resulting from, the Agreement between Germany and the Creditor Powers of January 20, 1930, and its Annexes, including the Trust Agreement, dated May 17, 1930; the Convention of January 20, 1930, respecting the Bank for International Settlements; and the Statutes of the Bank for International Settlements. Japan will notify to the Ministry of Foreign Affairs in Paris within six months of the first coming into force of the present Treaty its renunciation of the rights, title and interests referred to in this paragraph.

Article 9. Japan will enter promptly into negotiations with the Allied Powers so desiring for the conclusion of bilateral and multilateral agreements providing for the regulation or limitation of fishing and the conservation and development of fisheries on the high seas.

Article 10. Japan renounces all special rights and interests in China, including all benefits and privileges resulting from the provisions of the final Protocol signed at Peking September 7, 1901, and all annexes, notes and documents supplementary thereto, and agrees to the abrogation in respect to Japan of the said protocol, annexes, notes and documents.

Article 11. Japan accepts the judgments of the International Military Tribunal for the Far East and of other Allied War Crimes Courts both within and outside Japan, and will carry out the sentences imposed thereby upon Japanese nationals imprisoned in Japan. The power to grant clemency, to reduce sentences and to parole with respect to such prisoners may not be exercised except on the decision of the Government or Governments which imposed the sentence in each instance, and on the recommendation of Japan. In the case of persons sentenced by the International Military Tribunal for the Far East, such power may not be exercised except on the decision of a majority of the Governments represented on the Tribunal, and on the recommendation of Japan.

Article 12. (a) Japan declares its readiness promptly to enter into negotiations for the conclusion with each of the Allied Powers of treaties or agreements to place their trading, maritime and other commercial relations on a stable and friendly basis.

(b) Pending the conclusion of the relevant treaty or agreement, Japan will, during a period of four years from the first coming into force of the present Treaty

(1) accord to each of the Allied Powers, its nationals, products and vessels

(i) most-favored-nation treatment with respect to customs duties, charges, restrictions and other regulations on or in connection with the importation and exportation of goods;

(ii) national treatment with respect to shipping, navigation and imported goods, and with respect to national and juridical persons and their interests—such treatment to include all matters pertaining to the levying and collection of taxes, access to the courts, the making and performance of contracts, rights to property (tangible and intangible), participation in juridical entities constituted under Japanese law, and generally the conduct of all kinds of business and professional activities;

(2) ensure that external purchases and sales of Japanese state trading enterprises shall be based solely on commercial considerations.

(c) In respect to any matter, however, Japan shall be obliged to accord to an Allied Power national treatment, or most-favored-nation treatment, only to the extent that the Allied Power concerned accords Japan national treatment or most-favored-nation treatment, as the case may be, in respect of the same matter. The reciprocity envisaged in the foregoing sentence shall be determined, in the case of products, vessels and juridical entities of, and persons domiciled in, any non-metropolitan territory of an Allied Power, and in the case of juridical entities of, and persons domiciled in, any state or province of an Allied Power having a federal government, by reference to the treatment accorded to Japan in such territory, state or province.

(d) In the application of this Article, a discriminatory measure shall not be considered to derogate from the grant of national or most-favored-nation treatment, as the case may be, if such measure is based on an exception customarily provided for in the commercial treaties of the party applying it, or on the need to safeguard that party's external financial position or balance of payments (except in respect to shipping and navigation), or on the need to maintain its essential security interests, and provided such measure is proportionate to the circumstances and not applied in an arbitrary or unreasonable manner.

(e) Japan's obligations under this Article shall not be affected by the exercise of any Allied rights under Article 14 of the present Treaty; nor shall the provisions of this Article be understood as limiting the undertakings assumed by Japan by virtue of Article 15 of the Treaty.

Article 13. (a) Japan will enter into negotiations with any of the Allied Powers, promptly upon the request of such Power or Powers, for the conclusion of bilateral or multilateral agreements relating to international civil air transport.

(b) Pending the conclusion of such agreement or agreements, Japan will, during a period of four years from the first coming into force of the present Treaty, extend to such Power treatment not less favorable with respect to air-traffic rights and privileges than those exercised by any such Powers at the date of such coming into force, and will accord complete equality of opportunity in respect to the operation and development of air services.

(c) Pending its becoming a party to the Convention on International Civil Aviation in accordance with Article 93 thereof, Japan will give effect to the provisions of that Convention applicable to the international navigation of aircraft, and will give effect to the standards, practices and procedures adopted as annexes to the Convention in accordance with the terms of the Convention.

Chapter V. Claims and Properties

Article 14. (a) It is recognized that Japan should pay reparations to the Allied Powers for the damage and suffering caused by it during the war. Nevertheless it is also recognized that the resources of Japan are not presently sufficient, if it is to maintain a viable economy, to make complete reparation for all such damage and suffering and at the same time meet its other obligations.

Therefore,

1. Japan will promptly enter into negotiations with Allied Powers so desiring, whose present territories were occupied by Japanese forces and damaged by Japan, with a view to assisting to compensate those countries for the cost of repairing the damage done, by making available the services of the Japanese people in production, salvaging and other work for the Allied Powers in question. Such

arrangements shall avoid the imposition of additional liabilities on other Allied Powers, and, where the manufacturing of raw materials is called for, they shall be supplied by the Allied Powers in question, so as not to throw any foreign exchange burden upon Japan.

2. (I) Subject to the provisions of sub-paragraph (II) below, each of the Allied Powers shall have the right to seize, retain, liquidate, or otherwise dispose of all property, rights and interests of

(a) Japan and Japanese nationals,

(b) persons acting for or on behalf of Japan or Japanese nationals, and

(c) entities owned or controlled by Japan or Japanese nationals, which on the first coming into force of the present Treaty were subject to its jurisdiction. The property, rights, and interests specified in this sub-paragraph shall include those now blocked, vested or in the possession or under the control of enemy property authorities of Allied Powers, which belonged to, or were held or managed on behalf of, any of the persons or entities mentioned in (a), (b) or (c) above at the time such assets came under the controls of such authorities.

(II) The following shall be excepted from the right specified in sub-paragraph (I) above:

(i) property of Japanese natural persons who during the war resided with the permission of the Government concerned in the territory of one of the Allied Powers, other than territory occupied by Japan, except property subjected to restrictions during the war and not released from such restrictions as of the date of the first coming into force of the present Treaty;

(ii) all real property, furniture and fixtures owned by the Government of Japan and used for diplomatic or consular purposes, and all personal furniture and furnishings and other private property not of an investment nature which was normally necessary for the carrying out of diplomatic and consular functions, owned by Japanese diplomatic and consular personnel;

(iii) property belonging to religious bodies or private charitable institutions and used exclusively for religious or charitable purposes;

(iv) property, rights and interests which have come within its jurisdiction in consequence of the resumption of trade and financial relations subsequent to September 2, 1945, between the country concerned and Japan, except such as have resulted from transactions contrary to the laws of the Allied Power concerned;

(v) obligations of Japan or Japanese nationals, any right, title or interest in tangible property located in Japan, interests in enterprises organized under the laws of Japan, or any paper evidence thereof, provided that this exception shall only apply to obligations of Japan and its nationals expressed in Japanese currency.

(III) Property referred to in exceptions (i) through (v) above shall be returned subject to reasonable expenses for its preservation and administration. If any such property has been liquidated the proceeds shall be returned instead.

(IV) The right to seize, retain, liquidate or otherwise dispose of property as provided in sub-paragraph (I) above shall be exercised in accordance with the laws of the Allied Power concerned, and the owner shall have only such rights as may be given him by those laws.

(V) The Allied Powers agree to deal with Japanese trademarks and literary and artistic property rights on a basis as favorable to Japan as circumstances ruling in each country will permit.

(b) Except as otherwise provided in the present Treaty, the Allied Powers waive all reparations claims of the Allied Powers, other claims of the Allied Powers and their nationals arising out of any actions taken by Japan and its nationals in the course of the prosecution of the war, and claims of the Allied Powers for direct military costs of occupation.

Article 15. (a) Upon application made within nine months of the coming into force of the present Treaty between Japan and the Allied Power concerned, Japan will, within six months of the date of such application, return the property, tangible and intangible, and all rights or interests of any kind in Japan of each Allied Power and its nationals which was within Japan at any time between December 7, 1941, and September 2, 1945, unless the owner has freely disposed thereof without duress or fraud. Such property shall be returned free of all encumbrances and charges to which it may have become subject because of the war, and without any charges for its return. Property whose return is not applied for by or on behalf of the owner or by his Government within the prescribed period may be disposed of by the Japanese Government as it may determine. In cases where such property was within Japan on December 7, 1941, and cannot be returned or has suffered injury or damage as a result of the war, compensation will be made on terms not less favorable than the terms provided in the draft Allied Powers Property Compensation Law approved by the Japanese Cabinet on July 13, 1951.

(b) With respect to industrial property rights impaired during the war, Japan will continue to accord to the Allied Powers and their nationals benefits no less than those heretofore accorded by Cabinet Orders No. 309 effective September 1, 1949, No. 12 effective January 28, 1950, and No. 9 effective February 1, 1950. all as now amended, provided such nationals have applied for benefits within the time limits prescribed therein.

(c) (i) Japan acknowledges that the literary and artistic property rights which existed in Japan on December 6, 1941, in respect to the published and unpublished works of the Allied Powers and their nationals have continued in force since that date, and recognizes those rights which have arisen, or but for the war would have arisen, in Japan since that date, by the operation of any conventions and agreements to which Japan was a party on that date, irrespective of whether or not such conventions or agreements were abrogated or suspended upon or since the outbreak of the war by the domestic law of Japan or of the Allied Power concerned.

(ii) Without the need for application by the proprietor of the right and without the payment of any fee or compliance with any other formality, the period from December 7, 1941, until the coming into force of the present Treaty between Japan and the Allied Power concerned shall be excluded from the running of the normal term of such rights; and such period, with an additional period of six months, shall be excluded from the time within which a literary work must be translated into Japanese in order to obtain translating rights in Japan.

Article 16. As an expression of its desire to indemnify those members of the armed forces of the Allied Powers who suffered undue hardships while prisoners of war of Japan, Japan will transfer its assets and those of its nationals in countries which were neutral during the war, or which were at war with any of the Allied Powers, or, at its option, the equivalent of such assets, to the International Committee of the Red Cross which shall liquidate such assets and distribute the resultant fund to appropriate national agencies, for the benefit of former prisoners of war and their families on such basis as it may determine to be equitable. The categories of assets described in Article 14 (a) 2 (II) (ii) through (v) of the present Treaty shall be excepted from transfer, as well as assets of Japanese natural persons not residents of Japan on the first coming into force of the Treaty. It is equally understood that the transfer provision of this Article has no application to the 19,770 shares in the Bank for International Settlements presently owned by Japanese financial institutions.

Article 17. (a) Upon the request of any of the Allied Powers, the

Japanese Government shall review and revise in conformity with international law any decision or order of the Japanese Prize Courts in cases involving ownership rights of nationals of that Allied Power and shall supply copies of all documents comprising the records of these cases, including the decisions taken and orders issued. In any case in which such review or revision shows that restoration is due, the provisions of Article 15 shall apply to the property concerned.

(b) The Japanese Government shall take the necessary measures to enable nationals of any of the Allied Powers at any time within one year from the coming into force of the present Treaty between Japan and the Allied Power concerned to submit to the appropriate Japanese authorities for review any judgment given by a Japanese court between December 7, 1941, and such coming into force, in any proceedings in which any such national was unable to make adequate presentation of his case either as plaintiff or defendant. The Japanese Government shall provide that, where the national has suffered injury by reason of any such judgment, he shall be restored in the position in which he was before the judgment was given or shall be afforded such relief as may be just and equitable in the circumstances.

Article 18. (a) It is recognized that the intervention of the state of war has not affected the obligation to pay pecuniary debts arising out of obligations and contracts (including those in respect of bonds) which existed and rights which were acquired before the existence of a state of war, and which are due by the Government or nationals of Japan to the Government or nationals of one of the Allied Powers, or are due by the Government or nationals of one of the Allied Powers to the Government or nationals of Japan. The intervention of a state of war shall equally not be regarded as affecting the obligation to consider on their merits claims for loss or damage to property or for personal injury or death which arose before the existence of a state of war, and which may be presented or represented by the Government of one of the Allied Powers to the Government of Japan, or by the Government of Japan to any of the Governments of the Allied Powers. The provisions of this paragraph are without prejudice to the rights conferred by Article 14.

(b) Japan affirms its liability for the prewar external debt of the Japanese State and for debts of corporate bodies subsequently declared to be liabilities of the Japanese State, and expresses its intention to enter into negotiations at an early date with its creditors with respect to the resumption of payments on those debts;

to encourage negotiations in respect to other prewar claims and obligations; and to facilitate the transfer of sums accordingly.

Article 19. (a) Japan waives all claims of Japan and its nationals against the Allied Powers and their nationals arising out of the war or out of actions taken because of the existence of a state of war, and waives all claims arising from the presence, operations or actions of forces or authorities of any of the Allied Powers in Japanese territory prior to the coming into force of the present Treaty.

(b) The foregoing waiver includes any claims arising out of actions taken by any of the Allied Powers with respect to Japanese ships between September 1, 1939, and the coming into force of the present Treaty, as well as any claims and debts arising in respect to Japanese prisoners of war and civilian internees in the hands of the Allied Powers, but does not include Japanese claims specifically recognized in the laws of any Allied Power enacted since September 2, 1945.

(c) Subject to reciprocal renunciation, the Japanese Government also renounces all claims (including debts) against Germany and German nationals on behalf of the Japanese Government and Japanese nationals, including inter-governmental claims and claims for loss or damage sustained during the war, but excepting (a) claims in respect of contracts entered into and rights acquired before September 1, 1939, and (b) claims arising out of trade and financial relations between Japan and Germany after September 2, 1945. Such renunciation shall not prejudice actions taken in accordance with Articles 16 and 20 of the present Treaty.

(d) Japan recognizes the validity of all acts and omissions done during the period of occupation under or in consequence of directives of the occupation authorities or authorized by Japanese law at that time, and will take no action subjecting Allied nationals to civil or criminal liability arising out of such acts or omissions.

Article 20. Japan will take all necessary measures to ensure such disposition of German assets in Japan as has been or may be determined by those powers entitled under the Protocol of the proceedings of the Berlin Conference of 1945 to dispose of those assets, and pending the final disposition of such assets will be responsible for the conservation and administration thereof.

Article 21. Notwithstanding the provisions of Article 25 of the present Treaty, China shall be entitled to the benefits of Articles 10 and 14 (a) 2; and Korea to the benefits of Articles 2, 4, 9 and 12 of the present Treaty.

Chapter VI. Settlement of Disputes

Article 22. If in the opinion of any Party to the present Treaty there has arisen a dispute concerning the interpretation or execution of the Treaty, which is not settled by reference to a special claims tribunal or by other agreed means, the dispute shall, at the request of any party thereto, be referred for decision to the International Court of Justice. Japan and those Allied Powers which are not already parties to the Statute of the International Court of Justice will deposit with the Register of the Court, at the time of their respective ratifications of the present Treaty, and in conformity with the resolution of the United Nations Security Council, dated October 15, 1946, a general declaration accepting the jurisdiction, without special agreement, of the Court generally in respect to all disputes of the character referred to in this Article.

Chapter VII. Final Clauses

Article 23. (a) The present Treaty shall be ratified by the States which sign it, including Japan, and will come into force for all the States which have then ratified it, when instruments of ratification have been deposited by Japan and by a majority, including the United States of America as the principal occupying Power, of the following States, namely, Australia, Canada, Ceylon, France, Indonesia, the Kingdom of the Netherlands, New Zealand, Pakistan, the Republic of the Philippines, the United Kingdom of Great Britain and Northern Ireland, and the United States of America. The present Treaty shall come into force for each State which subsequently ratifies it, on the date of the deposit of its instrument of ratification.

(b) If the Treaty has not come into force within nine months after the date of the deposit of Japan's ratification, any State which has ratified it may bring the Treaty into force between itself and Japan by a notification to that effect given to the Governments of Japan and the United States of America not later than three years after the date of deposit of Japan's ratification.

Article 24. All instruments of ratification shall be deposited with the Government of the United States of America which will notify all the signatory States of each deposit, of the date of the coming into force of the Treaty under paragraph (a) of Article 23, and of any notifications made under paragraph (b) of Article 23.

Article 25. For the purposes of the present Treaty the Allied Powers shall be the States at war with Japan, or any State which previously formed a part of the territory of a State named in Article 23, provided that in each case the State concerned has signed and ratified the Treaty. Subject to the provisions of Article 21, the present Treaty shall not confer any rights, titles or benefits on any State which is not an Allied Power as herein defined; nor shall any right, title or interest of Japan be deemed to be diminished or prejudiced by any provision of the Treaty in favor of a State which is not an Allied Power as so defined.

Article 26. Japan will be prepared to conclude with any State which signed or adhered to the United Nations Declaration of January 1, 1942, and which is at war with Japan, or with any State which previously formed a part of the territory of a State named in Article 23, which is not a signatory of the present Treaty, a bilateral Treaty of Peace on the same or substantially the same terms as are provided for in the present Treaty, but this obligation on the part of Japan will expire three years after the first coming into force of the present Treaty. Should Japan make a peace settlement or war claims agreement with any State granting that State greater advantages than those provided by the present Treaty, those same advantages shall be extended to the parties to the present Treaty.

Article 27. The present Treaty shall be deposited in the archives of the Government of the United States of America which shall furnish each signatory State with a certified copy thereof.

In faith whereof the undersigned Plenipotentiaries have signed the present Treaty.

Done at the city of San Francisco this eighth day of September 1951, in the English, French and Spanish languages, all being equally authentic, and in the Japanese language.

[The above treaty was signed by plenipotentiaries of the following countries: Argentina, Australia, the Kingdom of Belgium, Bolivia, Brazil, Cambodia, Canada, Ceylon, Chile, Colombia, Costa Rica, Cuba, the Dominican Republic, Ecuador, Egypt, El Salvador, Ethiopia, France, Greece, Guatemala, Haiti, Honduras, Indonesia, Iran, Iraq, Laos, Lebanon, Liberia, the Grand Duchy of Luxembourg, Mexico, the Kingdom of the Netherlands, New Zealand, Nicaragua, the Kingdom of Norway, Pakistan, Panama, Paraguay, Peru, the Republic of the Philippines, Saudi Arabia, Syria, the Republic of Turkey, the Union of South Africa, the United Kingdom of Great Britain and Northern Ireland, the United States of America, Uruguay, Venezuela, Viet Nam, and Japan.]

No. 8. Treaty of Peace between the Republic of China and Japan (Signed at Taipei, on April 28, 1952)[8]

Article I. The state of war between the Republic of China and Japan is terminated as from the date on which the present Treaty enters into force.

Article II. It is recognized that under Article 2 of the Treaty of Peace with Japan signed at the city of San Francisco in the United States of America on September 8, 1951 (hereinafter referred to as the San Francisco Treaty), Japan has renounced all right, title and claim to Taiwan (Formosa) and Penghu (the Pescadores) as well as the Spratly Islands and the Paracel Islands.

Article III. The disposition of property of Japan and of its nationals in Taiwan (Formosa) and Penghu (the Pescadores), and their claims, including debts, against the authorities of the Republic of China in Taiwan (Formosa) and Penghu (the Pescadores) and the residents thereof, and the disposition in Japan of property of such authorities and residents and their claims, including debts, against Japan and its nationals, shall be the subject of special arrangements between the Government of the Republic of China and the Government of Japan. The terms nationals and residents whenever used in the present Treaty include juridical persons.

Article IV. It is recognized that all treaties, conventions and agreements concluded before December 9, 1941, between China and Japan have become null and void as a consequence of the war.

Article V. It is recognized that under the provisions of Article 10 of the San Francisco Treaty, Japan has renounced all special rights and interests in China, including all benefits and privileges resulting from the provisions of the final Protocol signed at Peking on September 7, 1901, and all annexes, notes and documents supplementary thereto, and has agreed to the abrogation in respect to Japan of the said protocol, annexes, notes and documents.

Article VI. (a) The Republic of China and Japan will be guided by the principles of Article 2 of the Charter of the United Nations in their mutual relations.

(b) The Republic of China and Japan will cooperate in accordance with the principles of the Charter of the United Nations and, in particular, will promote their common welfare through friendly cooperation in the economic field.

Article VII. The Republic of China and Japan will endeavor to conclude, as soon as possible, a treaty or agreement to place their trading, maritime and other commercial relations on a stable and friendly basis.

Article VIII. The Republic of China and Japan will endeavor to conclude, as soon as possible, an agreement relating to civil air transport.

Article IX. The Republic of China and Japan will endeavor to conclude, as soon as possible, an agreement providing for the regulation or limitation of fishing and the conservation and development of fisheries on the high seas.

Article X. For the purpose of the present Treaty, nationals of the Republic of China shall be deemed to include all the inhabitants and former inhabitants of Taiwan (Formosa) and Penghu (the Pescadores) and their descendants who are of the Chinese nationality in accordance with the laws and regulations which have been or may hereafter be enforced by the Republic of China in Taiwan (Formosa) and Penghu (the Pescadores); and juridical persons of the Republic of China shall be deemed to include all those registered under the laws and regulations which have been or may hereafter be enforced by the Republic of China in Taiwan (Formosa) and Penghu (the Pescadores).

Article XI. Unless otherwise provided for in the present Treaty and the documents supplementary thereto, any problem arising between the Republic of China and Japan as a result of the existence of a state of war shall be settled in accordance with the relevant provisions of the San Francisco Treaty.

Article XII. Any dispute that may arise out of the interpretation or application of the present Treaty shall be settled by negotiation or by other pacific means.

Article XIII. The present Treaty shall be ratified and the instruments of ratification shall be exchanged at Taipei as soon as possible. The present Treaty shall enter into force as from the date on which such instruments of ratification are exchanged.

Article XIV. The present Treaty shall be in the Chinese, Japanese and English languages. In case of any divergence of interpretation, the English text shall prevail.

No. 9. Protocol to the Treaty of Peace between the Republic of China and Japan[9]

1. (b) As a sign of magnanimity and good will towards the Japanese people, the Republic of China voluntarily waives the benefit of the services to be made available by Japan pursuant to Article 14 (a) of the San Francisco Treaty.

(c) Articles 11 and 18 of the San Francisco Treaty shall be excluded from the operation of Article XI of the present Treaty.

No. 10. Joint Declaration by the Union of Soviet Socialist Republics and Japan (Signed at Moscow, on October 19, 1956*)[10]

From 13 to 19 October 1956 negotiations were held at Moscow between the Delegations of the Union of Soviet Socialist Republics and Japan. . . .

In the course of the negotiations, which were held in an atmosphere of mutual understanding and co-operation, a full and frank exchange of views concerning relations between the Union of Soviet Socialist Republics and Japan took place. The Union of Soviet Socialist Republics and Japan were fully agreed that the restoration of diplomatic relations between them would contribute to the development of mutual understanding and co-operation between the two States in the interests of peace and security in the Far East.

As a result of these negotiations between the Delegations of the Union of Soviet Socialist Republics and Japan, agreement was reached on the following:

1. The state of war between the Union of Soviet Socialist Republics and Japan shall cease on the date on which this Declaration enters into force and peace, friendship and good-neighbourly relations between them shall be restored.

2. Diplomatic and consular relations shall be restored between the Union of Soviet Socialist Republics and Japan. For the purpose, it is intended that the two States shall proceed forthwith to exchange diplomatic representatives with the rank of Ambassador and that the question of the establishment of consulates in the territories of the USSR and Japan respectively shall be settled through the diplomatic channels.

3. The Union of Soviet Socialist Republics and Japan affirm that in their relations with each other they will be guided by the principles of the United Nations Charter, in particular the following principles set forth in Article 2 of the said Charter:

(a) To settle their international disputes by peaceful means in such a manner that international peace and security, and justice, are not endangered:

(b) To refrain in their international relations from the threat or use of force against the territorial integrity or political independ-

---

*Came into force on December 12, 1956, as from the date of the exchange of the instruments of ratification at Tokyo, in accordance with paragraph 10.

ence of any State or in any manner inconsistent with the Purposes of the United Nations.

The USSR and Japan affirm that, in accordance with Article 51 of the United Nations Charter, each of the two States has the inherent right of individual or collective self-defence.

The USSR and Japan reciprocally undertake not to intervene directly or indirectly in each other's domestic affairs for any economic, political or ideological reasons.

4. The Union of Soviet Socialist Republics will support Japan's application for membership in the United Nations.

5. On the entry into force of this Joint Declaration, all Japanese citizens convicted in the Union of Soviet Socialist Republics shall be released and repatriated to Japan.

With regard to those Japanese whose fate is unknown, the USSR, at the request of Japan, will continue its efforts to discover what has happened to them.

6. The Union of Soviet Socialist Republics renounces all reparations claims against Japan.

The USSR and Japan agree to renounce all claims by either State, its institutions or citizens, against the other State, its institutions or citizens, which have arisen as a result of the war since 9 August 1945.

7. The Union of Soviet Socialist Republics and Japan agree that they will enter into negotiations as soon as may be possible for the conclusion of treaties or agreements with a view to putting their trade, navigation and other commercial relations on a firm and friendly basis.

8. The Convention on deep-sea fishing in the north-western sector of the Pacific Ocean between the Union of Soviet Socialist Republics and Japan and the Agreement between the Union of Soviet Socialist Republics and Japan on co-operation in the rescue of persons in distress at sea, both signed at Moscow on 14 May 1956, shall come into effect simultaneously with this Joint Declaration.

Having regard to the interest of both the USSR and Japan in the conservation and rational use of the natural fishery resources and other biological resources of the sea, the USSR and Japan shall, in a spirit of co-operation, take measures to conserve and develop fishery resources, and to regulate and restrict deep-sea fishing.

9. The Union of Soviet Socialist Republics and Japan agree to continue, after the restoration of normal diplomatic relations between the Union of Soviet Socialist Republics and Japan, negotiations for the conclusion of a Peace Treaty.

In this connexion, the Union of Soviet Socialist Republics, desiring to meet the wishes of Japan and taking into consideration the interests of the Japanese State, agrees to transfer to Japan the Habomai Islands and the island of Shikoton [sic], the actual transfer of these islands to Japan to take place after the conclusion of a Peace Treaty between the Union of Soviet Socialist Republics and Japan.

10. This Joint Declaration is subject to ratification. It shall enter into force on the date of the exchange of instruments of ratification. The exchange of the instruments of ratification shall take place at Tokyo as soon as may be possible.

IN WITNESS WHEREOF the undersigned plenipotentiaries have signed this Joint Declaration.

DONE in two copies, each in the Russian and Japanese languages, both texts being equally authentic.

Moscow, 19 October 1956.

By authorization of
the Presidium of the Supreme
Soviet of the Union of Soviet
Socialist Republics:
N. Bulganin
D. Shepilov

By authorization of
the Government of
Japan:
I. Hatoyama
I. Kono
S. Matsumoto

No. 11. Reparations Agreement between the Republic of the Philippines and Japan* (Signed at Manila, May 9, 1956)[11]

Article 1. Japan, by way of reparations, shall supply the Republic of the Philippines with the services of the Japanese people and the products of Japan in the form of capital goods, the total value of which will be so much in yen as shall be equivalent to five hundred fifty million United States dollars ($550,000,000) at present computed at one hundred ninety-eight billion yen (¥198,000,000,000), within the period and in the manner hereinafter prescribed.

Article 2. The supply of the services and products referred to in the preceding Article shall be made on an annual average of so much in yen as shall be equivalent to twenty-five million United States dollars ($25,000,000) at present computed at nine billion yen (¥9,000,000,000), during the ten-year period from the date of coming into force of the present Agreement; and on an annual average of so much in yen as shall be equivalent to thirty million United States dollars ($30,000,000) at present computed at ten billion eight hundred million yen (¥10,800,000,000), during the succeeding ten-year

---

*Came into force on 23 July, 1956. . . .

period. However, by agreement between the two Governments, this latter period may be reduced to a period shorter than ten years, provided the outstanding balance is settled in full within the remainder of the reduced period.

Article 3. 1. The services and products to be supplied by way of reparations shall be those requested by the Government of the Republic of the Philippines and agreed upon between the two Governments. These services and products shall consist of such items as may be needed for projects to be chosen from among those enumerated in the Annex to the present Agreement, provided that such items as may be requested by the Government of the Republic of the Philippines for projects other than those listed in the aforesaid Annex may, by agreement between the two Governments, be included in the services and products to be supplied by way of reparations.

2. The products to be supplied by way of reparations shall be capital goods. However, products other than capital goods may, by agreement between the two Governments, be supplied by Japan at the request of the Government of the Republic of the Philippines.

Article 4. 1. The two Governments shall fix through consultation an annual schedule (hereinafter referred to as the "Schedule") specifying the services and products to be supplied by Japan each year.

2. The Schedule for the first year shall be fixed within sixty days from the date of the coming into force of the present Agreement. The Schedule for each succeeding year shall, until the reparations obligation specified in Article I above shall have been fulfilled, be fixed prior to the beginning of that year.

Article 5. 1. Japan agrees that the Mission mentioned in Article 7, paragraph 1 of the present Agreement shall have the authority to conclude, in behalf of the Government of the Republic of the Philippines, contracts directly with any Japanese national or any Japanese juridical person controlled by Japanese nationals, in order to have the services and products supplied in accordance with the Schedule for each year.

2. Every such contract (including modifications thereof) shall conform with

(a) the provisions of the present Agreement, (b) the provisions of such arrangements as may be made by the two Governments for the implementation of the present Agreement and (c) the Schedule then applicable. Every proposed contract shall, before it is entered into, be verified by the Government of Japan as to the conformity of the same with the above-mentioned criteria. The Government of Japan shall receive a copy of each contract from the Mission on the day following the date such contract is entered into. In case any proposed contract cannot be entered into due to non-verification, such proposed contract shall be referred to the Joint Committee mentioned in Article 10 of the present Agreement and acted upon in accordance with the recommendation of the Joint Committee. Such recommendation shall be made within a period of thirty days following the receipt of the proposed contract by the Joint Committee. A contract which has been concluded in the manner hereinabove provided, shall hereinafter be referred to as a "Reparations Contract."

3. Every Reparations Contract shall contain a provision to the effect that disputes arising out of or in connection with such Contract shall, at the request of either party thereto, be referred for settlement to an arbitration board of commerce in accordance with such arrangement as may be made between the two Governments.

4. Notwithstanding the provisions of paragraph 1 above, the supply of services and products as reparations may be made without Reparations Contracts, but only by agreement in each case between the two Governments.

Article 6. 1. In the discharge of the reparations obligation under Article 1 of the present Agreement, the Government of Japan shall, through procedures to be determined under Article 11, make payments to cover the obligations incurred by the Mission under Reparations Contracts and the expenses for the supply of services and products referred to in Article 5, paragraph 4 of the present Agreement. These payments shall be made in Japanese yen.

2. By and upon making a payment in yen under the preceding paragraph, Japan shall be deemed to have supplied the Republic of the Philippines with the services and products thus paid for and shall be released from its reparations obligations to the extent of the equivalent value in United States dollars of such yen payment in accordance with Articles 1 and 2 of the present Agreement.

Article 7. 1. Japan agrees to the establishment in Japan of a Mission of the Government of the Republic of the Philippines (hereinafter referred to as "the Mission") as its sole and exclusive agent to be charged with the implementation of the present Agreement, including the conclusion and performance of Reparations Contracts.

2. Such office or offices of the Mission in Japan as are necessary for the effective performance of its functions and used exclusively for that purpose may be established at Tokyo and/or other places to be agreed upon between the two Governments.

3. The premises of the office or offices, including the archives, of the Mission in Japan shall be inviolable. The Mission shall be

entitled to use cipher. The real estate which is owned by the Mission and used directly for the purpose of its functions shall be exempt from the Tax on Acquisition of Real Property and the Property Tax. The income of the Mission which may be derived from the performance of its functions shall be exempt from taxation in Japan. The property imported for the official use of the Mission shall be exempt from customs duties and any other charges imposed on or in connection with importation.

4. The Mission shall be accorded such administrative assistance by the Government of Japan as other foreign missions usually enjoy and as may be required for the effective performance of its functions.

5. The Chief and two senior officials of the Mission as well as the chiefs of such offices as may be established in pursuance of paragraph 2 above, who are nationals of the Republic of the Philippines, shall be accorded diplomatic privileges and immunities generally recognized under international law and usage. If it is deemed necessary for the effective performance of the functions of the Mission, the number of such senior officials may be increased by agreement between the two Governments.

6. Other members of the staff of the Mission who are nationals of the Republic of the Philippines and who are not ordinarily resident in Japan shall be exempt from taxation in Japan upon emoluments which they may receive in the discharge of their duties, and, in accordance with Japanese laws and regulations, from customs duties and any other charges imposed on or in connection with importation of property for their personal use.

7. In the event any dispute arising out of or in connection with a Reparations Contract has not been settled by arbitration or the arbitration award rendered has not been complied with, the matter may be taken, as a last resort, to the appropriate Japanese court. In such a case and solely for the purpose of whatever judicial proceedings may be necessary, the person holding the position of Chief of the Legal Section of the Mission may sue or be sued, and accordingly he may be served with process and other pleadings at his office in the Mission. However, he shall be exempt from the obligation to give security for the costs of legal proceedings. While the Mission enjoys inviolability and immunity as provided for in paragraphs 3 and 5 above, the final decision rendered by the appropriate judicial body in such a case will be accepted by the Mission as binding upon it.

8. In the enforcement of any final court decision, the land and buildings, as well as the movable property therein, owned by the

Mission and used for the performance of its functions shall in no case be subject to execution.

Article 8. 1. The services which have already been supplied or may hereafter be supplied in accordance with the exchange of notes effected at Manila on January 24, 1953, in connection with the survey of sunken vessels in Philippine territorial waters or in accordance with the Interim Agreement on Reparations Concerning Salvage of Sunken Vessels between the Republic of the Philippines and Japan signed at Manila on March 12, 1953, shall constitute part of the reparations under Article 1 of the present Agreement.

Article 9. 1. The two Governments shall take measures necessary for the smooth and effective implementation of the present Agreement.

2. Those materials, supplies, and equipment which are necessary for the projects mentioned in Article 3 but are not included in the Schedule will be provided by the Government of the Republic of the Philippines. No Japanese labor will be utilized in such projects as may be undertaken in the Philippines except the services of Japanese technicians. The incidental expenses in local currency for such Japanese technicians as well as the expenses for local labor shall be borne by the Government of the Republic of the Philippines.

3. Japanese nationals who may be needed in the Philippines in connection with the supply of services or products under the present Agreement shall, during the required period of their stay in the Philippines, be accorded such facilities as may be necessary for the performance of their work.

4. With respect to the income derived from the supply of services or products under the present Agreement, Japanese nationals and juridical persons shall be exempt from taxation in the Philippines.

5. The products of Japan supplied under the present Agreement shall not be re-exported from the territories of the Republic of the Philippines.

Article 10. There shall be established a Joint Committee to be composed of representatives of the two Governments as an organ of consultation between them, with powers to recommend on matters concerning the implementation of the present Agreement.

Article 11. Details including procedures for the implementation of the present Agreement shall be agreed upon through consultation between the two Governments.

Article 12. 1. The two Governments shall endeavor, through constant consultation, to preclude the likelihood of disputes arising out of or in connection with the implementation of the present Agreement.

Article 12. 1. The two Governments shall endeavor, through constant consultation, to preclude the likelihood of disputes arising out of or in connection with the implementation of the present Agreement.

2. Any dispute between the two Governments concerning the interpretation and implementation of the present Agreement shall be settled primarily through diplomatic channels. If the two Governments fail to reach a settlement, the dispute shall be referred for decision to a tribunal of three arbitrators, one to be appointed by each Government and third to be agreed upon by the two arbitrators so chosen, provided that such third arbitrator shall not be a national of either country. Each Government shall appoint an arbitrator within a period of thirty days from the date of receipt by either Government from the other Government of a note requesting arbitration of the dispute and the third arbitrator shall be agreed upon within a further period of thirty days. If, within the periods respectively referred to, either Government fails to appoint an arbitrator or the third arbitrator is not agreed upon, the President of the International Court of Justice may be requested by either Government to appoint such arbitrator or the third arbitrator, as the case may be. The two Governments agree to abide by any award given under this paragraph.

Article 13. The present Agreement shall be ratified. The Agreement shall enter into force either on the date of exchange of the instruments of ratification or on the date the Republic of the Philippines deposits its instrument of ratification of the Treaty of Peace with Japan signed at the city of San Francisco on September 8, 1951, in accordance with Article 24 of the said Treaty, whichever date is the later.

Article 14. The present Agreement is written in the English and Japanese languages, both being equally authentic.

In witness whereof the undersigned Plenipotentiaries have signed the present Agreement and have affixed thereunto their seals.

Done in duplicate at the city of Manila, this ninth day of May of the year one thousand nine hundred and fifty-six, Anno Domini, and of the Independence of the Republic of the Philippines, the tenth; corresponding to the ninth day of the fifth month of the thirty-first year of Showa.

7

CHINA: THE UNITED STATES AND THE SOVIET UNION, 1945-50

In a Far East that witnessed far-reaching and dramatic shifts in its international relations after 1945, the most significant development was the emergence of communist power in China under a regime that was determined to make China dominant not only in Asia but in world affairs as well. Much of the story lies in the 1945-49 civil war, the treatment of which is outside the scope of this study. Though the present chapter deals with only a narrow segment of the role of China in Far Eastern international relations since 1945, almost all the material in the final three chapters deals directly or indirectly with the problems created by the existence of the two Chinas and the national and international tensions caused thereby.

The documents in this chapter reveal in outline how the two great powers, the United States and the Soviet Union, became involved in China after the defeat of Japan, to the detriment of the former and the benefit of the latter. The United States was drawn into the internal affairs of China when, for purely military reasons, it seemed of overwhelming importance to strengthen the Nationalist Government's internal position in order better to enable it to wage effective war, even though it be only defensive, against the common Japanese enemy. For reasons of friendship to a recent fighting ally, of a traditional sympathetic interest in the problems of China (as revealed in earlier documents), and of a desire to avert a civil war which might develop into a threat to general peace, the United States attempted to effect a peaceful settlement of the conflict between the Nationalists and the Communists. This policy failed, possibly because of its own inherent weaknesses, but certainly because neither party to the civil strife was willing to accommodate itself to the requisite conditions for a negotiated and peaceful settlement. At any rate United States policy between 1945 and 1949, whatever its merits and demerits, also determined to a large extent the pattern of United States relations with the Nationalists on Taiwan and the Communists on the mainland in subsequent years. No later than the outbreak of the conflict in Korea less than a year after the Nationalist Government was forced to flee to Taiwan, the United States became firmly committed to the support and defense of the government that its policy had failed to keep in power on the mainland.

Likewise, United States policy both before and after 1949 made it the target of bitter attack by the communist government. This attack was obviously generated by its alliance with the Soviet Union, its theoretical view of world affairs, the communist confrontation of the free world, and by relatively narrow considerations of national policy. (For a good example of the Chinese Communist attitude toward the United States, see in Chapter 8 the attack on the United States before the United Nations Security Council in late 1950.)

It is clear from the 1945 treaty between the Soviet Union and the Nationalist Government and the related agreements that the Soviet aim was to reconstruct in the Far East, and especially in the vitally important area of Manchuria, the position that the Imperial Russian government had lost in 1905. It also turned out that the Soviet position in Manchuria played a decisive role in the outcome of the civil war, not only because the Soviet Union was in a position to aid the communists directly, but also because it denied to the Nationalists effective access to the area, vital to the postwar economic reconstruction of China.

The Soviet-Chinese Communist alliance of 1950, entered into at almost exactly the midpoint in time between the end of the civil war and the outbreak of the Korean conflict, established the basis of the relationship between a great and an emergent communist power. This alliance, directed against "Japan or any other state, which should unite in any form with Japan in acts of aggression, " was a key element in the communist alignment against the free world. It is significant that the Soviet Union was willing even at that early date to surrender, at least formally, its position in Manchuria to a government that it could reasonably expect to favor its interests in that area.

(Note: See also the Yalta Agreement, page 120.)

No. 1. Statement by President Truman on United States Policy toward China, December 15, 1945[1]

The Government of the United States holds that peace and prosperity in this new and unexplored era ahead depend upon the ability of the sovereign nations to combine for collective security in the United Nations Organization.

It is the firm belief of this Government that a strong, united, and democratic China is of the utmost importance to the success of this United Nations Organization and for world peace. A China disorganized and divided either by foreign aggression, such as that undertaken by the Japanese, or by violent internal strife is an undermining influence to world stability and peace, now and in the future. The United States Government has long subscribed to the principle that the management of internal affairs is the responsibility of the peoples of the sovereign nations. Events of this century, however, would indicate that a breach of peace anywhere in the world threatens the peace of the entire world. It is thus in the most vital interest of the United States and all the United Nations that the people of China overlook no opportunity to adjust their internal differences promptly by methods of peaceful negotiation.

The Government of the United States believes it essential:

1. That a cessation of hostilities be arranged between the armies of the National Government and the Chinese Communists and other dissident Chinese armed forces for the purpose of completing the return of all China to effective Chinese control, including the immediate evacuation of the Japanese forces.

2. That a national conference of representatives of major political elements be arranged to develop an early solution to the present internal strife—a solution which will bring about the unification of China.

The United States and the other United Nations have recognized the present National Government of the Republic of China as the only legal government in China. It is the proper instrument to achieve the objective of a unified China.

The United States and the United Kingdom by the Cairo Declaration of 1943 and the Union of Soviet Socialist Republics by adhering to the Potsdam Declaration of last July and by the Sino-Soviet treaty and agreements of August 1945 are all committed to the liberation of China, including the return of Manchuria to Chinese control. These agreements were made with the National Government of the Republic of China.

In continuation of the constant and close collaboration with the National Government of the Republic of China in the prosecution of this war, in consonance with the Potsdam Declaration, and to remove possibility of Japanese influence remaining in China, the United States has assumed a definite obligation in the disarmament and evacuation of the Japanese troops. Accordingly the United States has been assisting and will continue to assist the National Government of the Republic of China in effecting the disarmament and evacuation of Japanese troops in the liberated areas. The United States Marines are in North China for that purpose.

The United States recognizes and will continue to recognize the National Government of China and cooperate with it in international affairs and specifically in eliminating Japanese influences from China. The United States is convinced that a prompt arrangement for a cessation of hostilities is essential to the effective achievement of this end. The United States support will not extend to United States military intervention to influence the course of any Chinese internal strife.

The United States has already been compelled to pay a great price to restore the peace which was first broken by Japanese aggression in Manchuria. The maintenance of peace in the Pacific may be jeopardized, if not frustrated, unless Japanese influence in China is wholly removed and unless China takes her place as a unified, democratic, and peaceful nation. This is the purpose of the maintenance for the time being of United States military and naval forces in China.

The United States is cognizant that the present National Government of China is a "one-party government" and believes that peace, unity, and democratic reform in China will be furthered if the basis of this Government is broadened to include other political elements in the country. Hence, the United States strongly advocates that the national conference of representatives of major political elements in the country agree upon arrangements which would give those elements a fair and effective representation in the Chinese National Government. It is recognized that this would require modification of the one-party "political tutelage" established as an interim arrangement in the progress of the nation toward democracy by the father of the Chinese Republic, Dr. Sun Yat-sen.

The existence of autonomous armies such as that of the Communist Army is inconsistent with, and actually makes impossible, political unity in China. With the institution of a broadly representative government, autonomous armies should be eliminated as such and all armed forces in China integrated effectively into the Chinese National Army.

In line with its often expressed views regarding self-determination, the United States Government considers that the detailed steps necessary to the achievement of political unity in China must be worked out by the Chinese themselves and that intervention by any foreign government in these matters would be inappropriate. The

United States Government feels, however, that China has a clear responsibility to the other United Nations to eliminate armed conflict within its territory as constituting a threat to world stability and peace—a responsibility which is shared by the National Government and all Chinese political and military groups.

As China moves toward peace and unity along the lines described above, the United States would be prepared to assist the National Government in every reasonable way to rehabilitate the country, improve the agrarian and industrial economy, and establish a military organization capable of discharging China's national and international responsibilities for the maintenance of peace and order. In furtherance of such assistance, it would be prepared to give favorable consideration to Chinese requests for credits and loans under reasonable conditions for projects which would contribute toward the development of a healthy economy throughout China and healthy trade relations between China and the United States.

No. 2. Statement by President Truman on United States Policy toward China, December 18, 1946[2]

. . . Thus during the past year we have successfully assisted in the repatriation of the Japanese and have subsequently been able to bring most of our own troops home. We have afforded appropriate assistance in the reoccupation of the country from the Japanese. We have undertaken some emergency measures of economic assistance to prevent the collapse of China's economy and have liquidated our own wartime financial account with China.

It is a matter of deep regret that China has not yet been able to achieve unity by peaceful methods. Because he knows how serious the problem is, and how important it is to reach a solution, General Marshall has remained at his post even though active negotiations have been broken off by the Communist Party. We are ready to help China as she moves toward peace and genuine democratic government.

The views expressed a year ago by this Government are valid today. The plan for political unification agreed to last February is sound. The plan for military unification of last February has been made difficult of implementation by the progress of the fighting since last April, but the general principles involved are fundamentally sound.

China is a sovereign nation. We recognize that fact and we recognize the National Government of China. We continue to hope that the Government will find a peaceful solution. We are pledged not to interfere in the internal affairs of China. Our position is clear.

While avoiding involvement in their civil strife, we will persevere with our policy of helping the Chinese people to bring about peace and economic recovery in their country.

As ways and means are presented for constructive aid to China, we will give them careful and sympathetic consideration. . . . When conditions in China improve, we are prepared to consider aid in carrying out other projects, unrelated to civil strife, which would encourage economic reconstruction and reform in China and which, in so doing, would promote a general revival of commercial relations between American and Chinese businessmen.

We believe that our hopes for China are identical with what the Chinese people themselves most earnestly desire. We shall therefore continue our positive and realistic policy toward China which is based on full respect for her national sovereignty and our traditional friendship for the Chinese people and is designed to promote international peace.

No. 3. Personal Statement by the Special Representative [Marshall] of the President, January 7, 1947[3]

The President has recently given a summary of the developments in China during the past year and the position of the American Government toward China. Circumstances now dictate that I should supplement this with impressions gained at firsthand.

In this intricate and confused situation, I shall merely endeavor here to touch on some of the more important considerations—as they appeared to me—during my connection with the negotiations to bring about peace in China and a stable democratic form of government.

In the first place, the greatest obstacle to peace has been the complete, almost overwhelming suspicion with which the Chinese Communist Party and the Kuomintang regard each other.

On the one hand, the leaders of the Government are strongly opposed to a Communist form of government. On the other, the Communists frankly state that they are Marxists and intend to work toward establishing a Communistic form of government in China, though first advancing through the medium of a democratic form of government of the American or British type.

The leaders of the Government are convinced in their minds that the Communist-expressed desire to participate in a government of the type endorsed by the Political Consultative Conference last January had for its purpose only a destructive intention. The Communists felt, I believe, that the Government was insincere in its apparent acceptance of the P.C.C. resolutions for the formation of the new Government and intended by coercion of military force

and the action of secret police to obliterate the Communist Party.
Combined with this mutual deep distrust was the conspicuous error
by both parties of ignoring the effect of the fears and suspicions of
the other party in estimating the reason for proposals or opposition
regarding the settlement of various matters under negotiation. They
each sought only to take counsel of their own fears. They both,
therefore, to that extent took a rather lopsided view of each situation and were susceptible to every evil suggestion or possibility.
This complication was exaggerated to an explosive degree by the
confused reports of fighting on the distant and tremendous fronts of
hostile military contact. Patrol clashes were deliberately magnified
into large offensive actions. The distortion of the facts was utilized
by both sides to heap condemnation on the other. It was only through
the reports of American officers in the field teams from Executive
Headquarters that I could get even a partial idea of what was actually
happening and the incidents were too numerous and the distances too
great for the American personnel to cover all of the ground. I must
comment here on the superb courage of the officers of our Army
and Marines in struggling against almost insurmountable and mad-
dening obstacles to bring some measure of peace to China.

I think the most important factors involved in the recent break-
down of negotiations are these:

On the side of the National Government, which is in effect the
Kuomintang there is a dominant group of reactionaries who have
been opposed, in my opinion, to almost every effort I have made to
influence the formation of a genuine coalition Government. This has
usually been under the cover of political or party action, but since
the Party was the Government, this action, though subtle or indirect, has been devastating in its effect. They were quite frank
in publicly stating their belief that co-operation by the Chinese
Communist Party in the Government was inconceivable and that only
a policy of force could definitely settle the issue. This group includes military as well as political leaders.

On the side of the Chinese Communist Party, there are, I believe,
liberals as well as radicals, though this view is vigorously opposed
by many who believe that the Chinese Communist Party discipline
is too rigidly enforced to admit of such differences of viewpoint.
Nevertheless, it has appeared to me that there is a definite liberal
group among the Communists, especially of young men who have
turned to the Communists in disgust at the corruption evident in the
local governments–men who would put the interest of the Chinese
people above ruthless measures to establish a Communist ideology
in the immediate future. The dyed-in-the-wool Communists do not

hesitate at the most drastic measures to gain their end as, for instance, the destruction of communications in order to wreck the economy of China and produce a situation that would facilitate the overthrow or collapse of the Government, without any regard to the immediate suffering of the people involved. They completely distrust the leaders of the Kuomintang and appear convinced that every Government proposal is designed to crush the Chinese Communist Party. I must say that the quite evidently inspired mob actions of last February and March, some within a few blocks of where I was then engaged in completing negotiations, give the Communists good excuse for such suspicions.

However, a very harmful and immensely provocative phase of the Chinese Communist Party procedure has been in the character of its propaganda. I wish to state to the American people that in the deliberate misrepresentation and abuse of the action, policies and purposes of our Government this propaganda has been without regard for the truth, without any regard whatsoever for the facts, and has given plain evidence of a determined purpose to mislead the Chinese people and the world and to arouse a bitter hatred of Americans. It has been difficult to remain silent in the midst of such public abuse and wholesale disregard of facts, but a denial would merely lead to the necessity of daily denials; an intolerable course of action for an American official. In the interest of fairness, I must state that the Nationalist Government publicity agency has made numerous misrepresentations, though not of the vicious nature of the Communist propaganda. Incidentally, the Communist statements regarding the Anping incident which resulted in the death of three Marines and the wounding of twelve others were almost pure fabrication, deliberately representing a carefully arranged ambuscade of a Marine convoy with supplies for the maintenance of Executive Headquarters and some UNRRA supplies, as a defense against a Marine assault. The investigation of this incident was a tortuous procedure of delays and maneuvers to disguise the true and privately admitted facts of the case.

Sincere efforts to achieve settlement have been frustrated time and again by extremist elements of both sides. The agreements reached by the Political Consultative Conference a year ago were a liberal and forward-looking charter which then offered China a basis for peace and reconstruction. However, irreconcilable groups within the Kuomintang Party, interested in the preservation of their own feudal control of China, evidently had no real intention of implementing them. Though I speak as a soldier, I must here also deplore the dominating influence of the military. Their dominance accentuates the weakness of civil government in China. At the same time, in pondering the situation in China, one must have clearly in mind not the workings of small Communist groups or committees to which we are accustomed in America, but rather of millions of people and an army of more than a million men.

I have never been in a position to be certain of the development of attitudes in the innermost Chinese Communist circles. Most certainly, the course which the Chinese Communist Party has pursued in recent months indicated an unwillingness to make a fair compromise. It has been impossible even to get them to sit down at a conference table with Government representatives to discuss given issues. Now the Communists have broken off negotiations by their last offer, which demanded the dissolution of the National Assembly and a return to the military positions of January 13th which the Government could not be expected to accept.

Between this dominant reactionary group in the Government and the irreconcilable Communists, who, I must state, did not so appear last February, lies the problem of how peace and well-being are to be brought to the long-suffering and presently inarticulate mass of people of China. The reactionaries in the Government have evidently counted on substantial American support regardless of their actions. The Communists by their unwillingness to compromise in the national interest are evidently counting on an economic collapse to bring about the fall of the Government, accelerated by extensive guerrilla action against the long lines of rail communications—regardless of the cost in suffering to the Chinese people.

The salvation of the situation, as I see it, would be the assumption of leadership by the liberals in the Government and in the minority parties, a splendid group of men, but who as yet lack the political power to exercise a controlling influence. Successful action on their part under the leadership of Generalissimo Chiang Kai-shek would, I believe, lead to unity through good government.

In fact, the National Assembly has adopted a democratic constitution which in all major respects is in accordance with the principles laid down by the all-party Political Consultative Conference of last January. It is unfortunate that the Communists did not see fit to participate in the Assembly, since the constitution that has been adopted seems to include every major point that they wanted.

Soon the Government in China will undergo major reorganization pending the coming into force of the constitution following elections to be completed before Christmas Day, 1947. Now that the form for a democratic China has been laid down by the newly adopted constitution, practical measures will be the test. It remains to be seen to what extent the Government will give substance to the form by a genuine welcome of all groups actively to share in the responsibility of Government.

The first step will be the reorganization of the State Council and the executive branch of Government to carry on administration pending the enforcement of the constitution. The manner in which this is done and the amount of representation accorded to liberals and to non-Kuomintang members will be significant. It is also to be hoped that during this interim period, the door will remain open for Communists or other groups to participate if they see fit to assume their share of responsibility for the future of China.

It has been stated officially and categorically that the period of political tutelage under the Kuomintang is at an end. If the termination of one-party rule is to be a reality, the Kuomintang should cease to receive financial support from the Government.

I have spoken very frankly because in no other way can I hope to bring the people of the United States to even a partial understanding of this complex problem. I have expressed all these views privately in the course of negotiations: they are well known, I think, to most of the individuals concerned. I express them now publicly, as it is my duty to present my estimate of the situation and its possibilities to the American people who have a deep interest in the development of conditions in the Far East promising an enduring peace in the Pacific.

No. 4. Treaty of Friendship and Alliance between the Republic of China and the Union of Soviet Socialist Republics, August 14, 1945[4]

The President of the National Government of the Republic of China and the Praesidium of the Supreme Soviet of the Union of Soviet Socialist Republics, being desirous of strengthening the friendly relations which have always prevailed between the Republic of China and the Soviet Union, by means of an alliance and good neighbourly postwar collaboration;

Determined to assist each other in the struggle against aggression on the part of the enemies of the United Nations in this World War and to collaborate in the common war against Japan until that country's unconditional surrender;

Expressing their unswerving resolve to collaborate in maintaining peace and security for the benefit of the peoples of both countries and of all peace-loving nations;

Acting in accordance with the principles proclaimed in the joint Declaration of the United Nations of 1 January, 1942, in the Declaration of the Four Powers signed in Moscow on 30 October, 1943, and in the Charter of the "United Nations" International Organization;

Have decided to conclude the present Treaty . . .

Article I. The High Contracting Parties undertake jointly with the other United Nations to wage war against Japan until final victory is achieved. The High Contracting Parties mutually undertake to afford one another all necessary military and other assistance and support in this war.

Article II. The High Contracting Parties undertake not to enter into separate negotiations with Japan or conclude, except by mutual consent, any armistice or peace treaty either with the present Japanese Government or any other Government or authority set up in Japan that does not clearly renounce all aggressive intentions.

Article III. On the conclusion of the war against Japan, the High Contracting Parties undertake to carry out jointly all measures in their power to render impossible a repetition of aggression and violation of the peace by Japan.

Should either of the High Contracting Parties become involved in hostilities with Japan in consequence of an attack by the latter against that Party, the other High Contracting Party will at once render to the High Contracting Party so involved in hostility all the military and other support and assistance in its power.

This Article shall remain in force until such time as, at the request of both High Contracting Parties, responsibility for the prevention of further aggression by Japan is placed upon the "United Nations" Organization.

Article IV. Each High Contracting Party undertakes not to conclude any alliance and not to take any part in any coalition directed against the other Contracting Party.

Article V. The High Contracting Parties, having regard to the interests of the security and economic development of each of them, agree to work together in close and friendly collaboration after the re-establishment of peace and to act in accordance with the principles of mutual respect for each other's sovereignty and territorial integrity and non-intervention in each other's internal affairs.

Article VI. The High Contracting Parties agree to afford one another all possible economic assistance in the post-war period in order to facilitate and expedite the rehabilitation of both countries and to make their contribution to the prosperity of the world.

Article VII. Nothing in this Treaty should be interpreted in such a way as to prejudice the rights and duties of the High Contracting

Parties as Members of the Organization of the "United Nations."
Article VIII. The present Treaty is subject to ratification in the
shortest possible time. The instruments of ratification shall be exchanged in Chungking as soon as possible.

The Treaty comes into force immediately upon ratification, and
shall remain in force for thirty years. Should neither of the High
Contracting Parties make, one year before the date of the Treaty's
expiry, a statement of its desire to denounce it, the Treaty will
remain in force for an unlimited period, provided that each High
Contracting Party may invalidate it by announcing its intention to
do so to the other Contracting Party one year in advance.

In witness whereof the respective Plenipotentiaries have signed
this Treaty and affixed thereto their seals.

Done in Moscow, the 14 August 1945 and the 14th day of August
in the year 34 of the Chinese Republic in two copies, each copy in
both Chinese and Russian, both texts being of equal validity.

No. 5. Note from the People's Commissar for Foreign
Affairs of the Union of Soviet Socialist Republics to
Mr. Wang, Minister of Foreign Affairs of the
National Government of the Chinese Republic[5]

Moscow, 14 August 1945

. . . I have the honour to place on record that the following provisions are understood by both Contracting Parties as follows:

(1) In accordance with the spirit of the . . . Treaty and to implement its general idea and its purposes, the Soviet Government
agrees to render China moral support and assist her with military
supplies and other material resources, it being understood that this
support and assistance will go exclusively to the National Government as the Central Government of China.

(2) During the negotiations on the ports of Dairen and Port Arthur
and on the joint operation of the Chinese Changchun Railway, the
Soviet Government regarded the Three Eastern Provinces as part
of China and again affirmed its respect for the complete sovereignty
of China over the Three Eastern Provinces and recognition of their
territorial and administrative integrity.

(3) With regard to recent events in Sinkiang, the Soviet Government confirms that, as stated in Article 5 of the Treaty of Friendship and Alliance, it has no intention of interfering in the internal
affairs of China.

Should you confirm your agreement with this understanding of the above-mentioned points, the present Note and your answer to it will form part of the above-mentioned Treaty of Friendship and Alliance. . . .

(signed) V. Molotov

No. 6. Note from Mr. Wang Shih-chieh, Minister of Foreign Affairs of the National Government of the Republic of China, to Mr. Molotov[6]

. . . 14 August 1945

In view of the frequently manifested desire for independence of the people of Outer Mongolia, the Chinese Government states that, after the defeat of Japan, if this desire is confirmed by a plebiscite of the people of Outer Mongolia, the Chinese Government will recognize the independence of Outer Mongolia within her existing frontiers.

The above statement will have binding force after the ratification of the Treaty of Friendship and Alliance. . . .

No. 7. Agreement between the Chinese Republic and the Union of Soviet Socialist Republics on the Chinese Changchun Railway (Signed at Moscow, on August 14, 1945)[7]

Article 1. After the expulsion of the Japanese armed forces from the Three Eastern Provinces of China, the main trunk lines of the Chinese Eastern Railway and the South Manchurian Railway . . . shall be combined to form a single railway system to be known as "Chinese Changchun Railway, " and shall become the joint property of the USSR and the Chinese Republic and be jointly exploited by them. Only such lands and branch lines shall become joint property and be jointly exploited as were constructed by the Chinese Eastern Railway while it was under Russian and joint Soviet-Chinese management and by the South Manchurian Railway while under Russian management, and which are intended to serve the direct needs of those railways. Ancillary undertakings directly serving the needs of those railways and constructed during the above-mentioned periods shall also be included. All other railway branch lines, ancillary undertakings and lands will be the exclusive property of the Chinese Government. The joint exploitation of the above-mentioned railways shall be effected by a single administration under Chinese sovereignty as a purely commercial transport undertaking.

Article 2. The Contracting Parties agree that ownership of the above-mentioned railway shall be vested equally in both Parties, and shall not be transferable either in part or in whole.

Article 3. For the purpose of jointly exploiting the above-mentioned railway, the Contracting Parties agree to establish a Sino-Soviet Chinese Changchun Railway Company. The company shall have a Board of Directors consisting of ten members, five of whom will be appointed by the Chinese Government and five by the Soviet Government. The Head Office shall be at Changchun.

Article 4. The Chinese Government shall appoint from among the Chinese Directors a President and a Vice-President of the Board of Directors. The Soviet Government shall appoint from among the Soviet Directors a Deputy President and a Deputy Vice-President of the Board of Directors. . . .

Article 5. The Company shall establish a Supervisory Committee consisting of six members, three of whom shall be appointed by the Chinese Government and three by the Soviet Government. The Chairman of the Supervisory Committee shall be chosen from among the members of Soviet nationality and the Vice-Chairman from among the members of Chinese nationality. In deciding upon matters in the Supervisory Committee, the Chairman's vote shall count as two votes. Five members of the Committee shall form a legal quorum.

Article 6. For conducting the routine business, the Board of Directors shall appoint one of its Soviet members as Manager and one of its Chinese members as Deputy Manager of the Chinese Changchun Railway.

Article 9. The Chinese Government shall be responsible for the security of the railway. For the purpose of protecting the railway premises, equipment and other property, and to prevent goods in transit being destroyed, lost or stolen, the Chinese Government shall create and control a railway police force. . . .

Article 10. The railway shall be employed for the transport of Soviet troops only during hostilities against Japan.

The Soviet Government shall have the right to employ the railway for transporting without Customs inspection and in sealed wagons, military property in transit, such property to be protected by the railway police, and the Soviet Government shall not provide it with any armed escort of its own.

Article 11. Goods in transit from one Soviet station to another and goods passing in either direction between Soviet territory and the ports of Dairen and Port Arthur shall be exempt from any duties or any other kind of taxes or levies imposed by the Chinese Government. Upon arrival in Chinese territory such goods shall be liable to Customs inspection. . . .

Article 17. The present Agreement shall remain in force for a period of thirty years. Thereafter the full ownership of the Chinese Changchun Railway and all its assets shall revert without charge to the Chinese Republic. . . .

No. 8. Agreement on the Port of Dairen (Signed at Moscow, on August 14, 1945)[8]

. . . the Chinese Republic, in order to protect the interests of the Union of Soviet Socialist Republics in Dairen as a port for the import and export of goods, hereby agrees:

1. To proclaim Dairen a free port, open to the trade and shipping of all countries.

2. The Chinese Government agrees to allocate docks and warehouse accommodation in the said free port to be leased to the USSR under a separate agreement.

3. The administration in Dairen will be Chinese.

The Harbour Master shall be a Soviet citizen to be appointed by the Manager of the Chinese Changchun Railway by agreement with the Mayor of the town of Dairen. The Assistant Harbour Master shall be a Chinese citizen appointed by the same procedure. . . .

5. Goods entering the said free port from abroad and proceeding via the Chinese Changchun Railway directly into the territory of the USSR, goods leaving the USSR via the same railway and entering the free port for export, and materials and equipment sent from the USSR for the construction of harbour installations shall be exempt from customs duties. The said goods must be conveyed in sealed wagons. . . .

6. The present Agreement shall remain in force for a period of 30 years. . . .

No. 9. Agreement on Port Arthur (Signed at Moscow, on August 14, 1945)[9]

1. In order to strengthen the security of China and the USSR and prevent a repetition of aggression on the part of Japan, the Government of the Chinese Republic agrees to the joint use by both Contracting Parties of Port Arthur as a naval base. . . .

3. The Contracting Parties have agreed to make Port Arthur a

naval base only, to be used and be made available to the warships and commercial vessels of China and the USSR only.

A Sino-Soviet Military Commission, consisting of two Chinese and three Soviet representatives will be established to deal with questions arising in connexion with the joint use of the aforementioned naval base. The chairman of the Commission shall be appointed by the Soviet authorities and the vice-chairman by the Chinese authorities.

4. The defence of the aforementioned naval base shall be entrusted by the Government of China to the Government of the USSR. For purposes of such defence of the naval base, the Government of the USSR shall erect there the necessary installations, the expense of which shall be borne by the Government of the USSR.

5. The civil administration in the area concerned will be Chinese, but the interests of the USSR will be taken into account when appointments to responsible positions in the said area are made by the Chinese Government. The civil administration in the town of Port Arthur shall be appointed and dismissed by the Chinese Government in agreement with the Soviet Military Command. . . .

6. The Government of the USSR has the right to maintain its own military, naval and air forces in the area . . . and to determine their disposition. . . .

9. The present Agreement shall remain in force for a period of thirty years.

No. 10. Agreement on Relations between the Soviet Commander-in-Chief and the Chinese Administration Following the Entry of Soviet Forces into the Territory of the Three Eastern Provinces of China in Connection with the Present Joint War against Japan (Signed at Moscow, on August 14, 1945) [10]

1. After the entry, as a result of military operations, of Soviet troops into the territory of the Three Eastern Provinces of China, the supreme authority and responsibility in the zone of military activity in all matters relating to the conduct of the war shall during the period necessary for conducting such operations, be vested in the Commander-in-Chief of the Soviet Armed Forces. . . .

5. As soon as any part of a recaptured territory ceases to be a

zone of direct military operations, the National Government of the Chinese Republic shall assume complete power in respect of civil affairs and shall render the Soviet Commander-in-Chief all assistance and support through its civil and military organs. . . .

No. 11. Treaty of Friendship, Alliance, and Mutual Assistance between the Union of Soviet Socialist Republics and the People's Republic of China (Signed in Moscow, February 14, 1950)[11]

The Presidium of the Supreme Soviet of the Union of Soviet Socialist Republics and the Central People's Government of the People's Republic of China;

Filled with determination jointly to prevent, by the consolidation of friendship and co-operation between the Union of Soviet Socialist Republics and the People's Republic of China, the rebirth of Japanese imperialism and a repetition of aggression on the part of Japan or any other state, which should unite in any form with Japan in acts of aggression;

Imbued with the desire to consolidate lasting peace and universal security in the Far East and throughout the world in conformity with the aims and principles of the United Nations Organization;

Profoundly convinced that the consolidation of good neighborly relations and friendship between the Union of Soviet Socialist Republics and the People's Republic of China meets the fundamental interests of the peoples of the Soviet Union and China;

Resolved for this purpose to conclude the present Treaty and appointed as their plenipotentiary representatives;

The Presidium of the Supreme Soviet of the Union of Soviet Socialist Republics—Andrei Yanuaryevich Vyshinsky, Minister of Foreign Affairs of the Union of Soviet Socialist Republics;

The Central People's Government of the People's Republic of China—Chou En-lai, Prime Minister of the State Administrative Council and Minister of Foreign Affairs of China;

Who, after exchange of their credentials, found in due form and good order, agreed upon the following:

Article I. Both High Contracting Parties undertake jointly to take all the necessary measures at their disposal for the purpose of preventing a repetition of aggression and violation of peace on the part of Japan or any other state which should unite with Japan, directly or indirectly, in acts of aggression. In the event of one of the High Contracting Parties being attacked by Japan or states allied by it, and thus being involved in a state of war, the other High Contracting

Party will immediately render military and other assistance with all the means at its disposal.

The High Contracting Parties also declare their readiness in the spirit of sincere co-operation to participate in all international actions aimed at ensuring peace and security throughout the world, and will do all in their power to achieve the speediest implementation of these tasks.

Article II. Both the High Contracting Parties undertake by means of mutual agreement to strive for the earliest conclusion of a peace treaty with Japan, jointly with the other Powers which were allies during the Second World War.

Article III. Both High Contracting Parties undertake not to conclude any alliance directed against the other High Contracting Party, and not to take part in any coalition or in actions or measures directed against the other High Contracting Party.

Article IV. Both Contracting Parties will consult each other in regard to all important international problems affecting the common interests of the Soviet Union and China, being guided by the interests of the consolidation of peace and universal security.

Article V. Both the High Contracting Parties undertake, in the spirit of friendship and co-operation and in conformity with the principles of equality, mutual interests, and also mutual respect for the state sovereignty and territorial integrity and non-interference in internal affairs of the other High Contracting Party— to develop and consolidate economic and cultural ties between the Soviet Union and China, to render each other every possible economic assistance, and to carry out the necessary economic co-operation.

Article VI. The present Treaty comes into force immediately upon its ratification; the exchange of instruments of ratification will take place in Peking.

The present Treaty will be valid for 30 years. If neither of the High Contracting Parties gives notice one year before the expiration of this term of its desire to denounce the Treaty, it shall remain in force for another five years and will be extended in compliance with this rule.

Done in Moscow on February 14, 1950, in two copies, each in the Russian and Chinese languages, both texts having equal force.

[Signatures]

No. 12. Agreement between the Union of Soviet Socialist Republics and the People's Republic of China on the Chinese Changchun Railway, Port Arthur and Dalny (Signed in Moscow, February 14, 1950)[12]

The Presidium of the Supreme Soviet of the Union of Soviet Socialist Republics and the Central People's Government of the People's Republic of China state that since 1945 radical changes have occurred in the situation in the Far East, namely: Imperial Japan suffered defeat; the reactionary Kuomintang Government was overthrown; China has become a People's Democratic Republic, and in China a new People's Government was formed which has united the whole of China, carried out a policy of friendship and co-operation with the Soviet Union, and proved its ability to defend the state independence and territorial integrity of China, the national honor and dignity of the Chinese people.

The Presidium of the Supreme Soviet of the Union of Soviet Socialist Republics and the Central People's Government of the People's Republic of China maintain that this new situation permits a new approach to the question of the Chinese Changchun Railway, Port Arthur and Dalny [Dairen].

In conformity with these new circumstances, the Presidium of the Supreme Soviet of the Union of Soviet Socialist Republics and the Central People's Government of the People's Republic of China have decided to conclude the present agreement on the Chinese Changchun Railway, Port Arthur and Dalny.

Article I. Both High Contracting Parties have agreed that the Soviet Government transfer gratis to the Government of the People's Republic of China all its rights in the joint administration of the Chinese Changchun Railway, with all the property belonging to the Railway. The transfer will be effected immediately upon the conclusion of a peace treaty with Japan, but not later than the end of 1952.

Pending the transfer, the now existing position of the Soviet-Chinese joint administration of the Chinese Changchun Railway remains unchanged; however, the order of filling posts by representatives of the Soviet and Chinese sides, upon the coming into force of the present Agreement, will be changed, and there will be established an alternating filling of posts for a definite period of time (Director of the Railway, Chairman of the Central Board, and others).

As regards concrete methods of effecting the transfer, they will be agreed upon and determined by the Governments of both High Contracting Parties.

Article II. Both High Contracting Parties have agreed that Soviet troops will be withdrawn from the jointly utilized naval base of Port Arthur and that the installations in this area will be handed over to the Government of the People's Republic of China immediately upon the conclusion of a peace treaty with Japan, but not later than the end of 1952, with the Government of the People's Republic of China compensating the Soviet Union for expenses incurred in the restoration and construction of installations effected by the Soviet Union since 1945.

For the period pending the withdrawal of Soviet troops and the transfer of the above installations, the Governments of the Soviet Union and China will appoint an equal number of military representatives for organizing a joint Chinese-Soviet Military Commission which will be alternately presided over by both sides and which will be in charge of military affairs in the area of Port Arthur; concrete measures in this sphere will be determined by the joint Chinese-Soviet Military Commission within three months upon the coming into force of the present Agreement and shall be implemented upon the approval of these measures by the Governments of both countries.

The civil administration in the aforementioned area shall be in the direct charge of the Government of the People's Republic of China. Pending the withdrawal of Soviet troops, the zone of billeting of Soviet troops in the area of Port Arthur will remain unaltered in conformity with the now existing frontiers.

In the event of either of the High Contracting Parties being subjected to aggression on the part of Japan or any state which should unite with Japan and as a result of this being involved in military operations, China and the Soviet Union may, on the proposal of the Government of the People's Republic of China and with the agreement of the Soviet Government, jointly use the naval base of Port Arthur in the interests of conducting joint military operations against the aggressor.

Article III. Both High Contracting Parties have agreed that the question of Port Dalny must be further considered upon the conclusion of a peace treaty with Japan.

As regards the administration in Dalny, it fully belongs to the Government of the People's Republic of China.

All property now existing in Dalny provisionally in charge of or under lease to the Soviet side, is to be taken over by the Government of the People's Republic of China. For carrying out work involved in the receipt of the aforementioned property, the Governments of the Soviet Union and China appoint three representatives from each side for organizing a joint commission which in the course of three months after the coming into force of the present agreement shall determine the concrete methods of transfer of property, and after approval of the proposals of the Joint Commission by the Governments of both countries will complete their implementation in the course of 1950.

Article IV. The present agreement comes into force on the day of its ratification. The exchange of instruments of ratification will take place in Peking.

Done in Moscow on February 14, in two copies, each in the Russian and Chinese language, both texts having equal force.

[Signatures of Vyshinsky and Chou]

No.13. Agreement between the Government of the Union of Soviet Socialist Republics and the Central People's Government of the People's Republic of China on Granting Credits to the People's Republic of China[13]

In connection with the consent of the Government of the Union of Soviet Socialist Republics to grant the request of the Central People's Government of the People's Republic of China on giving China credits for paying for equipment and other materials which the Soviet Union has agreed to deliver to China, both Governments have agreed upon the following:

Article I. The Government of the Union of Soviet Socialist Republics grants the Central People's Government of the People's Republic of China credits, calculated in dollars, amounting to 300,000,000 American dollars, taking 35 American dollars to one ounce of fine gold.

In view of the extreme devastation of China as a result of prolonged hostilities on its territory, the Soviet Government has agreed to grant credits on favorable terms of one per cent annual interest.

Article II. The credits mentioned in Article I will be granted in the course of five years, as from January 1, 1950, in equal portions of one-fifth of the credits in the course of each year, for payments for delivery from the USSR of equipment and materials, including equipment for electric power stations, metallurgical and engineering plants, equipment for mines for the production of coal and ores, railway and other transport equipment, rails and other material for the restoration and development of the national economy of China.

The assortment, quantities, prices and dates of deliveries of equipment and materials will be determined under a special agreement of the parties; prices will be determined on the basis of prices obtaining on the world markets.

Any credits which remain unused in the course of one annual period may be used in subsequent annual periods.

Article III. The Central People's Government of the People's Republic of China repays the credits mentioned in Article I as well as interest on them with deliveries of raw materials, tea, gold, American dollars. Prices for raw materials and tea, quantities and dates of deliveries will be determined on the basis of prices obtaining on the world markets.

Repayment of credits is effected in the course of 10 years in equal annual parts—one-tenth yearly of the sum total of received credits no later than December 31 of every year. The first payment is effected not later than December 31, 1954, and the last on December 31, 1963.

Payment of interest on credits, calculated from the day of drawing the respective fraction of the credits, is effected every six months.

Article IV. For clearance with regard to the credits envisaged by the present agreement the State Bank of the USSR and National Bank of the People's Republic of China shall open special accounts and jointly establish the order of clearance and accounting under the present agreement.

Article V. The present agreement comes into force on the day of its signing and is subject to ratification. The exchange of instruments of ratification will take place in Peking.

Done in Moscow on February 14, 1950, in two copies, each in the Russian and Chinese languages, both texts having equal force.

[Signatures of Vyshinsky and Chou]

8

THE PROBLEM OF KOREA: 1945-

The tragedy of modern Korea has been that it has had no control over and even little influence on its own destiny. We have already seen how in the last decade of the nineteenth century it was the object of international rivalry among Imperial China, Imperial Russia, and Imperial Japan; nothing that the Koreans could do could prevent Japanese victory in that struggle and the consequent annexation. Then for more than a third of a century Korea was a Japanese colony with all the consequences: loss of independence, political oppression, and economic exploitation.

The ending of Japanese colonial rule in 1945 seemed to mean not only political independence, but also the opportunity for the construction of a new and modern Korean society. But it was the unhappy fate of the country not only to be split into two halves but to become the scene of an even greater and potentially more dangerous rivalry than it had seen a half-century earlier.

The peculiar and temporary circumstances of the surrender of the Japanese military forces in Korea led to an informal agreement between the United States and Soviet governments to share in the acceptance of the surrender, with the United States acting south of the thirty-eighth parallel and the Soviet Union north of it. The Soviet Union immediately chose to treat the thirty-eighth parallel as a political boundary, not as a line of demarkation set up as a military convenience. This not only divided Korea unnaturally but also made it into a key area of United States-Soviet confrontation, which served initially to exacerbate relations between the two governments and later became the scene of a military conflict between forces representing the free and the communist worlds. It was the entry of Chinese Communist "volunteers," armed with Soviet weapons, in the winter of 1950-51 which threatened to convert the conflict into a major war.

That the conflict remained localized in Korea and was not carried into Chinese Communist territory in Manchuria or elsewhere is explainable at least in part by the reluctance of the United Nations and its member states to risk a general war over the issue of Korea. What lay behind this reluctance was, of course, a keen awareness of the consequences of atomic warfare which would have been virtually certain had the conflict become general as a result of the extension of United Nations military action beyond Korea. Many Americans, including some in positions of great responsibility, remained convinced that a direct attack on Communist China would not have precipitated a general war, but the issue was never put to the test. Had the Korean conflict occurred before nuclear weapons changed the nature of war and consequently altered the attitudes of governments toward it as a means of resolving international disputes, it seems reasonable to assume that there would have been considerably less reluctance to extend military operations. Thus, the conflict was fought with only conventional weapons which virtually guaranteed that it would end in a military stalemate without a solution by arms of either the local issue of Korean unification or the broader issue of free world-communist tension in the area.

Because the United Nations has not solved, by either political or military means, the basic problem, the establishment of a "unified, independent, and democratic" government in Korea, it is widely held that it has failed in its task. Yet the nonachievement of a solution should not be equated with failure. To evaluate the accomplishment of the United Nations in Korea it is necessary to glance backward at earlier acts of aggression or breaches of the peace in the Far East. In the first decade of the twentieth century no government and no international organization stood in the way of Japan's nonmilitary aggression against Korea; the loss of Korean independence was regarded as a natural consequence of weakness on the Korean side and strength on the Japanese. Two decades later the League of Nations was unable to stop Japan's military aggression in Manchuria, thus opening the way for a general collapse of international peace and security. Thus, although the United Nations certainly failed to achieve its stated objective of the peaceful unification of Korea under an independent and democratic government, it definitely prevented the loss of freedom by half the country and the successful exercise of aggression by a regime aided and abetted by two strong communist powers.

The propaganda attack, delivered before the United Nations Security Council by a representative of the Chinese Communist government, did not achieve its objective of an indictment of United States "aggression" in both Taiwan and Korea and did not prevent the United Nations from branding Communist China as an aggressor in Korea. It is, however, a statement of the Chinese Communist attitude toward the United States that remained virtually unchanged in subsequent years. This attitude and the policy based on it made it impossible for the two governments to arrive at a modus vivendi, maintained tensions across the Straits of Taiwan, and was one of the principal reasons for the construction of the free world security network in the Western Pacific.

No. 1. Excerpt from the Cairo Declaration Dealing with Korea[1]

The aforesaid three great powers, mindful of the enslavement of the people of Korea, are determined that in due course Korea shall become free and independent.

(Note: In the Potsdam Declaration [which see] it was provided that the terms of the Cairo Declaration would be carried out.)

No. 2. Report of the Meeting of the Ministers of Foreign Affairs of the Union of Soviet Socialist Republics, the United States of America, and the United Kingdom, Moscow, December 27, 1945 (The Moscow Agreement)[2]

Korea

1. With a view to the re-establishment of Korea as an independent state, the creation of conditions for developing the country on democratic principles and the earliest possible liquidation of the disastrous results of the protracted Japanese domination in Korea, there shall be set up a provisional Korean democratic government which shall take all the necessary steps for developing the industry, transport and agriculture of Korea and the national culture of the Korean people.

2. In order to assist the formation of a provisional Korean government and with a view to the preliminary elaboration of the appropriate measures, there shall be established a Joint Commission consisting of representatives of the United States command in southern Korea and the Soviet command in northern Korea. In preparing their proposals the Commission shall consult with the Ko-

ean democratic parties and social organizations. The recommendations worked out by the Commission shall be presented for the consideration of the Governments of the Union of Soviet Socialist Republics, China, the United Kingdom and the United States prior to final decision by the two Governments represented on the Joint Commission.

3. It shall be the task of the Joint Commission, with the participation of the provisional Korean democratic government and of the Korean democratic organizations to work out measures also for helping and assisting (trusteeship) the political, economic, and social progress of the Korean people, the development of democratic self-government and the establishment of the national independence of Korea.

The proposals of the Joint Commission shall be submitted, following consultation with the provisional Korean Government for the joint consideration of the Governments of the United States, Union of Soviet Socialist Republics, United Kingdom and China for the working out of an agreement concerning a four-power trusteeship of Korea for a period of up to five years.

4. For the consideration of urgent problems affecting both southern and northern Korea and for the elaboration of measures establishing permanent co-ordination in administrative-economic matters between the United States command in southern Korea and the Soviet command in northern Korea, a conference of the representatives of the United States and Soviet commands in Korea shall be convened within a period of two weeks.

No. 3. Presentation of the Problem of Korea to the General Assembly of the United Nations by Secretary of State Marshall, September 17, 1947[3]

I turn now to the question of the independence of Korea. At Cairo in December, 1943, the United States, the United Kingdom, and China joined in declaring that in due course Korea should become free and independent. This multilateral pledge was reaffirmed in the Potsdam Declaration of July 1945, and subscribed to by the Union of Soviet Socialist Republics when it entered the war against Japan.

In Moscow, in December of 1945, the Foreign Ministers of the USSR, the United Kingdom and the United States concluded an agreement designed to bring about the independence of Korea. This agreement was later adhered to by the Government of China. It provided for the establishment of a Joint United States and Union of Soviet Socialist Republics Commission to meet in Korea and, through consultations with Korean democratic parties and social organizations, to decide on methods for establishing a provisional Korean Government. The Joint Commission was then to consult with that provisional Government on methods of giving aid and assistance to Korea, any agreement reached being submitted for approval to the four Powers adhering to the Moscow Agreement.

For about two years, the United States Government has been trying to reach agreement with the Soviet Government, through the Joint Commission and otherwise, on methods of implementing the Moscow Agreement, and thus bringing about the independence of Korea. The United States representatives have insisted that any settlement of the Korean problem must in no way infringe the fundamental democratic right of freedom of opinion. That is still the position of my Government.

Today the independence of Korea is no further advanced than it was two years ago. Korea remains divided at the 38th parallel with Soviet forces in the industrial north and United States forces in the agricultural south. There is little or no exchange of goods or services between the two zones. Korea's economy is thus crippled.

The Korean people—not former enemies but a people liberated from forty years of Japanese oppression—are still not free. This situation must not be allowed to continue indefinitely. In an effort to make progress the United States Government recently made certain proposals designed to achieve the purposes of the Moscow Agreement and requested the Powers adhering to that agreement to join in discussion of these proposals. China and the United Kingdom agreed to this procedure. The Soviet Government did not. Furthermore, the United States and Soviet delegations to the Joint Commission have not even been able to agree on a joint report on the status of their deliberations. It appears evident that further attempts to solve the Korean problem by means of bilateral negotiations will only serve to delay the establishment of an independent, united Korea.

It is therefore the intention of the United States Government to present the problem of Korean independence to this session of the General Assembly. Although we shall be prepared to submit suggestions as to how the early attainment of Korean independence might be effected, we believe that this is a matter which now requires the impartial judgment of the other Members. We do not want the inability of two Powers to reach agreement to delay any further the urgent and rightful claims of the Korean people to independence.

No. 4. Resolution of the General Assembly of the United Nations on Korea, Adopted November 14, 1947[1]

A. *Inasmuch* as the Korean question which is before the General Assembly is primarily a matter for the Korean people itself and concerns its freedom and independence, and

Recognizing that this question cannot be correctly and fairly resolved without the participation of representatives of the indigenous populations,

The General Assembly,

1. *Resolves* that elected representatives of the Korean people be invited to take part in the consideration of the question;

2. *Further resolves* that in order to facilitate and expedite such participation and to observe that the Korean representatives are in fact duly elected by the Korean people and not mere appointees by military authorities in Korea, there be forthwith established a United Nations Temporary Commission on Korea, to be present in Korea, with right to travel, observe and consult throughout Korea.

B. *The General Assembly,*

Recognizing the urgent and rightful claims to independence of the people of Korea;

Believing that the national independence of Korea should be reestablished and all occupying forces then withdrawn at the earliest practicable date;

Recalling its previous conclusion that the freedom and independence of the Korean people cannot be correctly or fairly resolved without the participation of representatives of the Korean people, and its decision to establish a United Nations Temporary Commission on Korea (hereinafter called the "Commission") for the purpose of facilitating and expediting such participation by elected representatives of the Korean people,

1. *Decides* that the Commission shall consist of representatives of Australia, Canada, China, El Salvador, France, India, Philippines, Syria, Ukrainian Soviet Socialist Republic;

2. *Recommends* that the elections be held not later than 31 March 1948 on the basis of adult suffrage and by secret ballot to choose representatives with whom the Commission may consult regarding the prompt attainment of the freedom and independence of the Korean people and which representatives, constituting a National Assembly, may establish a National Government of Korea. The number of representatives from each voting area or zone should be proportionate to the population, and the elections should be under the observation of the Commission;

3. *Further recommends* that as soon as possible after the elections, the National Assembly should convene and form a National Government and notify the Commission of its formation

4. *Further recommends* that immediately upon the establishment of a National Government, that Government should, in consultation with the Commission: (a) constitute its own national security forces and dissolve all military or semi-military formations not included therein: (b) take over the functions of government from the military commands and civilian authorities of north and south Korea, and (c) arrange with the occupying Powers for the complete withdrawal from Korea of their armed forces as early as practicable and if possible within ninety days;

5. *Resolves* that the Commission shall facilitate and expedite the fulfillment of the foregoing programme for the attainment of the national independence of Korea and withdrawal of occupying forces, taking into account its observations and consultations in Korea. The Commission shall report, with its conclusions, to the General Assembly and may consult with the Interim Committee (if one be established) with respect to the application of this resolution in the light of developments;

6. *Calls upon* the Member States concerned to afford every assistance and facility to the Commission in the fulfillment of its responsibilities;

7. *Calls upon* all Members of the United Nations to refrain from interfering in the affairs of the Korean people during the interim period preparatory to the establishment of Korean independence, except in pursuance of the decisions of the General Assembly; and thereafter, to refrain completely from any and all acts derogatory to the independence and sovereignty of Korea.

No. 5. Statement of the Policy of the United States Government toward the New Korean Government[5]

August 12, 1948

In the Joint Declaration issued at Cairo on December 1, 1943, the three subscribing Powers—the United States, China, and Great Britain—expressed their determination "that in due course Korea shall become free and independent." This determination was reaffirmed in the Potsdam Declaration of July 26, 1945, with which the Soviet Union associated itself upon its declaration of war against Japan on August 8 of that year. On December 27, 1945, in Moscow the Foreign Ministers of the Soviet Union, the United States, and

Great Britain concluded an agreement, later adhered to by the Government of China, designed to re-establish Korea as an independent state.

Although the annexation of Korea by Japan was effectively terminated with the occupation of that country by the armed forces of the Soviet Union and the United States in August and September 1945, the freedom and independence of Korea so solemnly pledged by the Four Powers have proved slow of realization. After nearly two years of painstaking but unavailing effort to give effect to those pledges through negotiations with the other occupying power, the United States Government, on September 17, 1947, laid the problem of Korean independence before the General Assembly of the United Nations. The will of an overwhelming majority of that body was expressed in two resolutions adopted by it on November 14, 1947, the purpose of which was to make it possible for the Korean people to attain their long-sought freedom and independence through the holding of free and democratic elections and the establishment, on the basis thereof, of a national government.

In pursuance of those resolutions, elections were held in Korea on May 10 of this year, under the observation of the United Nations Temporary Commission on Korea, for the purpose of electing representatives to a National Assembly which might in turn form a national government. The National Assembly so elected convened on May 31 and has proceeded to form a government—a government in which it is hoped that the people of North Korea, who were prevented from participating in the May 10 elections by the refusal of the Soviet Union to permit the implementation of the General Assembly resolutions in its zone of occupation, will be free in due course to assume their rightful role. Notification of the formation of the new Government was communicated to the United Nations Temporary Commission on Korea on August 6, 1948.

It is the view of the United States Government that the Korean Government so established is entitled to be regarded as the Government of Korea envisaged by the General Assembly resolution of November 14, 1947. Pending consideration by the General Assembly at its forthcoming Third Session of the report of the United Nations Temporary Commission on Korea, the United States, pursuant to its responsibility as occupying power, is sending to Seoul a special representative who will be authorized to carry on negotiations with that Government, in consultation with the United Nations Temporary Commission on Korea, concerning the implementation of the further provisions set forth in paragraph 4 of the second of the General Assembly resolutions of November 14, 1947. As such special representative the President has named John J. Muccio of Rhode Island, who will have the personal rank of ambassador.

No. 6. The Problem of the Independence of Korea⁶

The General Assembly,

Having regard to its resolution 112 (II) of 14 November 1947 concerning the problem of the independence of Korea,

Having considered the report of the United Nations Temporary Commission on Korea (hereinafter referred to as the "Temporary Commission"), and the report of the Interim Committee of the General Assembly regarding its consultation with the Temporary Commission,

Mindful of the fact that, due to difficulties referred to in the report of the Temporary Commission, the objectives set forth in the resolution of 14 November 1947 have not been fully accomplished, and in particular that unification of Korea has not yet been achieved,

1. *Approves* the conclusions of the reports of the Temporary Commission;

2. *Declares* that there has been established a lawful government (the Government of the Republic of Korea) having effective control and jurisdiction over that part of Korea where the Temporary Commission was able to observe and consult and in which the great majority of the people of all Korea reside; that this Government is based on elections which were a valid expression of the free will of the electorate of that part of Korea and which were observed by the Temporary Commission; and that this is the only such Government in Korea;

3. *Recommends* that the occupying Powers should withdraw their occupation forces from Korea as early as practicable;

4. *Resolves* that, as a means to the full accomplishment of the objectives set forth in the resolution of 14 November 1947, a Commission on Korea consisting of Australia, China, El Salvador, France, India, the Philippines and Syria, shall be established to continue the work of the Temporary Commission and carry out the provisions of the present resolution, having in mind the status of the Government of Korea as herein defined, and in particular to:

(a) Lend its good offices to bring about the unification of Korea and the integration of all Korean security forces in accordance with the principles laid down by the General Assembly in the resolution of 14 November 1947;

(b) Seek to facilitate the removal of barriers to economic, social and other friendly intercourse caused by the division of Korea;

(c) Be available for observation and consultation in the further development of representative government based on the freely-expressed will of the people;

(d) Observe the actual withdrawal of the occupying forces and verify the fact of withdrawal when such has occurred; and for this purpose, if it so desires, request the assistance of military experts of the two occupying Powers;

5. *Decides* that the Commission:

(a) Shall, within thirty days of the adoption of the present resolution, proceed to Korea, where it shall maintain its seat;

(b) Shall be regarded as having superseded the Temporary Commission established by the resolution of 14 November 1947;

(c) Is authorized to travel, consult and observe throughout Korea;

(d) Shall determine its own procedures;

(e) May consult with the Interim Committee with respect to the discharge of its duties in the light of developments, and within the terms of the present resolution;

(f) Shall render a report to the next regular session of the General Assembly and to any prior special session which might be called to consider the subject matter of the present resolution, and shall render such interim reports as it may deem appropriate to the Secretary-General for distribution to Members;

6. *Requests* that the Secretary-General shall provide the Commission with adequate staff and facilities, including technical advisers as required; and authorizes the Secretary-General to pay the expenses and *per diem* of a representative and an alternate from each of the States members of the Commission;

7. *Calls upon* the Member States concerned, the Government of the Republic of Korea, and all Koreans to afford every assistance and facility to the Commission in the fulfillment of its responsibilities;

8. *Calls upon* Member States to refrain from any acts derogatory to the results achieved and to be achieved by the United Nations in bringing about the complete independence and unity of Korea;

9. *Recommends* that Member states and other nations, in establishing their relations with the Government of the Republic of Korea, take into consideration the facts set out in paragraph 2 of the present resolution.

Hundred and eighty-seventh plenary meeting,
12 December 1948

No. 7. The United Nations Commission on Korea to the Secretary-General[7]

[Seoul, June 25, 1950.]

Government of Republic of Korea states that about 04:00 hrs. 25 June attacks were launched in strength by North Korean forces all along the 38th parallel. Major points of attack have included Ongjin Peninsula, Kaesong area and Chunchon and east coast where seaborne landings have been reported north and south of Kangnung. Another seaborne landing reported imminent under air cover in Pohang area on southeast coast. The latest attacks have occurred along the parallel directly north of Seoul along shortest avenue of approach. Pyongyang radio allegation at 13:35 hrs. of South Korean invasion across parallel during night declared entirely false by President and Foreign Minister in course of conference with Commission members and Principal Secretary. Allegations also stated People's Army instructed repulse invading forces by decisive counter attack and placed responsibility for consequences on South Korea. Briefing on situation by President included statement thirty-six tanks and armoured cars used in northern attacks at four points. Following emergency Cabinet meeting Foreign Minister issuing broadcast to people of South Korea encouraging resistance against dastardly attack. President expressed complete willingness for Commission broadcast urging cease-fire and for communication to United Nations to inform of gravity of situation. Although North Korean declaration of war rumoured at 11:00 hrs. over Pyongyang radio, no confirmation available from any source. President not treating broadcast as official notice. United States Ambassador, appearing before Commission, stated his expectation Republican Army would give good account of itself.

[Omitted here is brief paragraph telling of additional local military actions.]

Commission wishes to draw attention of Secretary-General to serious situation developing which is assuming character of full-scale war and may endanger the maintenance of international peace and security. It suggests that he consider possibility of bringing matter to notice of Security Council. Commission will communicate more fully considered recommendation later.

No. 8. Resolution Adopted by the Security Council, June 25, 1950[8]

The Security Council

Recalling the finding of the General Assembly in its resolution of 21 October 1949 that the Government of the Republic of Korea is a lawfully established government "having effective control and jurisdiction over that part of Korea where the United Nations Temporary Commission on Korea was able to observe and consult and in which the great majority of the people of Korea reside; and that this Government is based on elections which were a valid expression of the free will of the electorate of that part of Korea and which were observed by the Temporary Commission; and that this is the only such Government in Korea";

Mindful of the concern expressed by the General Assembly in its resolutions of 12 December 1948 and 21 October 1949 of the consequences which might follow unless Member States refrained from acts derogatory to the results sought to be achieved by the United Nations in bringing about the complete independence and unity of Korea; and the concern expressed that the situation described by the United Nations Commission on Korea in its report menaces the safety and well-being of the Republic of Korea and of the people of Korea and might lead to open military conflict there;

Noting with grave concern the armed attack upon the Republic of Korea by forces from North Korea,

Determines that this action constitutes a breach of the peace,

I. *Calls for* the immediate cessation of hostilities, and calls upon the authorities of North Korea to withdraw forthwith their armed forces to the 38th parallel;

II. *Requests* the United Nations Commission on Korea

(a) To communicate its fully considered recommendations on the situation with the least possible delay;

(b) To observe the withdrawal of the North Korean forces to the 38th parallel; and

(c) To keep the Security Council informed on the execution of this resolution;

III. *Calls upon* all Members to render every assistance to the United Nations in execution of this resolution and to refrain from giving assistance to the North Korean authorities.

No. 9. *Resolution Adopted by the Security Council, June 27, 1950*⁹

The Security Council,

Having determined that the armed attack upon the Republic of Korea by forces from North Korea constitutes a breach of the peace,

Having called for an immediate cessation of hostilities, and

Having called upon the authorities of North Korea to withdraw forthwith their armed forces to the 38th parallel, and

Having noted from the report of the United Nations Commission for Korea that the authorities in North Korea have neither ceased hostilities nor withdrawn their armed forces to the 38th parallel and that urgent military measures are required to restore international peace and security, and

Having noted the appeal from the Republic of Korea to the United Nations for immediate and effective steps to secure peace and security,

Recommends that the Members of the United Nations furnish such assistance to the Republic of Korea as may be necessary to repel the armed attack and to restore international peace and security in the area.

No. 10. Statement by the President [Harry S. Truman], June 27, 1950[10]

In Korea, the Government forces, which were armed to prevent border raids and to preserve internal security, were attacked by invading forces from North Korea. The Security Council of the United Nations called upon the invading troops to cease hostilities and to withdraw to the 38th parallel. This they have not done but, on the contrary, have pressed the attack. The Security Council called upon all members of the United Nations to render every assistance to the United Nations in execution of this resolution. In these circumstances, I have ordered United States air and sea forces to give the Korean Government troops cover and support.

The attack upon Korea makes it plain beyond all doubt that communism has passed beyond the use of subversion to conquer independent nations and will now use armed invasion and war. It has defied the orders of the Security Council of the United Nations issued to preserve international peace and security. In these circumstances, the occupation of Formosa by Communist forces would be a direct threat to the security of the Pacific area and to United States forces performing their lawful and necessary functions in that area.

Accordingly, I have ordered the Seventh Fleet to prevent any attack on Formosa. As a corollary of this action, I am calling upon the Chinese Government on Formosa to cease all air and sea operations against the mainland. The Seventh Fleet will see that this is done. The determination of the future status of Formosa must await the restoration of security in the Pacific, a peace settlement with Japan, or consideration by the United Nations.

I have also directed that United States Forces in the Philippines be strengthened and that military assistance to the Philippine Government be accelerated.

I have similarly directed acceleration in the furnishing of military assistance to the forces of France and the Associated States in Indochina and the dispatch of a military mission to provide close working relations with those forces.

I know that all members of the United Nations will consider carefully the consequences of this latest aggression in Korea in defiance of the Charter of the United Nations. A return to the rule of force in international affairs would have far-reaching effects. The United States will continue to uphold the rule of law.

I have instructed Ambassador Austin, as the Representative of the United States to the Security Council, to report these steps to the Council.

No. 11. Resolution Adopted by the Security Council, July 7, 1950 [11]

The Security Council,

Having determined that the armed attack upon the Republic of Korea by forces from North Korea constitutes a breach of the peace,

Having recommended that Members of the United Nations furnish such assistance to the Republic of Korea as may be necessary to repel the armed attack and to restore international peace and security in the area,

1. *Welcomes* the prompt and vigorous support which governments and peoples of the United Nations have given to its resolutions of 25 and 27 June 1950 to assist the Republic of Korea in defending itself against armed attack and thus to restore international peace and security in the area,

2. *Notes* that Members of the United Nations have transmitted to the United Nations offers of assistance for the Republic of Korea;

3. *Recommends* that all Members providing military forces and other assistance pursuant to the aforesaid Security Council resolutions make such forces and other assistance available to a unified command under the United States;

4. *Requests* the United States to designate the commander of such forces;

5. *Authorizes* the unified command at its discretion to use the United Nations flag in the course of operations against North Korean forces concurrently with the flags of the various nations participating;

6. *Requests* the United States to provide the Security Council with reports as appropriate on the course of action taken under the unified command.

No.12. The Deputy Minister of Foreign Affairs of the Union of Soviet Socialist Republics to the Secretary-General[12]

[July 11, 1950]

The Soviet Government has received your telegram citing the text of the Security Council Resolution of 7 July, which calls for the provision of military forces and other assistance to the so-called "unified command under the United States," requests the United States to designate the commander of such forces, and authorizes the use of the United Nations flag in the course of operations in Korea.

The Soviet Government finds that the adoption of this resolution constitutes the same flagrant violations of the United Nations Charter as the Security Council resolution of 27 June on the Korean question. The resolution was adopted in the absence of two permanent members of the Security Council—the Union of Soviet Socialist Republics and China—and received only six votes, the seventh vote being that of the Kuomintang representative, who has no legal right to represent China.

In these circumstances this Security Council resolution also can clearly have no legal force. Moreover, the Soviet Government considers it necessary to draw attention to the following. The above-mentioned decision of the Security Council is directed towards the illegal use of the United Nations flag as a cloak for United States military operations in Korea, which are a direct aggression by the United States against the Korean people.

All this gives the Soviet Government grounds for declaring that the Security Council resolution of 7 July, first, is illegal, and, secondly, constitutes a direct act of assistance to armed aggression against the Korean people.

A. Gromyko

No.13. The Problem of the Independence of Korea[General Assembly Resolution] Approved October 7, 1950 (294th Meeting)[13]

The General Assembly,

Having regard to its resolutions of 14 November 1947 . . . of 12 December 1948 . . . and of 21 October 1949 . . .

Having received and considered the report of the United Nations Commission on Korea,

Mindful of the fact that the objectives set forth in the resolutions referred to above have not been fully accomplished and, in particular, that the unification of Korea has not yet been achieved, and that an attempt has been made by an armed attack from North Korea to extinguish by force the Government of the Republic of Korea,

Recalling the General Assembly declaration of 12 December 1948 that there has been established a lawful government (the Government of the Republic of Korea) having effective control and jurisdiction over that part of Korea where the United Nations Temporary Commission on Korea was able to observe and consult and in which the great majority of the people of Korea resides; that this Government is based on elections which were a valid expression of the free will of the electorate of that part of Korea and which were observed by the Temporary Commission; and that this is the only such Government in Korea,

Having in mind that United Nations armed forces are at present operating in Korea in accordance with the recommendations of the Security Council of 27 June 1950, subsequent to its resolution of 25 June 1950, that Members of the United Nations furnish such assistance to the Republic of Korea as may be necessary to repel the armed attack and to restore international peace and security in the area,

Recalling that the essential objective of the resolutions of the General Assembly referred to above was the establishment of a unified, independent and democratic Government of Korea,

1. *Recommends that*

(a) All appropriate steps be taken to ensure conditions of stability throughout Korea;

(b) All constituent acts be taken, including the holding of elections, under the auspices of the United Nations, for the establishment of a unified, independent and democratic government in the sovereign State of Korea;

(c) All sections and representative bodies of the population of Korea, South and North, be invited to co-operate with the organs of the United Nations in the restoration of peace, in the holding of elections and in the establishment of a unified government;

(d) United Nations forces should not remain in any part of Korea otherwise than so far as necessary for achieving the objectives specified in sub-paragraphs (a) and (b) above;

(e) All necessary measures be taken to accomplish the economic rehabilitation of Korea;

2. *Resolves that*

(a) A commission consisting of Australia, Chile, Netherlands, Pakistan, Philippines, Thailand and Turkey, to be known as the

United Nations Commission for the Unification and Rehabilitation of Korea, be established to (i) assume the functions hitherto exercised by the present United Nations Commission on Korea; (ii) represent the United Nations in bringing about the establishment of a unified, independent and democratic government of all Korea; (iii) exercise such responsibilities in connection with relief and rehabilitation in Korea as may be determined by the General Assembly after receiving the recommendations of the Economic and Social Council. The United Nations Commission for the Unification and Rehabilitation of Korea should proceed to Korea and begin to carry out its functions as soon as possible;

(b) Pending the arrival in Korea of the United Nations Commission for the Unification and Rehabilitation of Korea, the Governments of the States represented on the Commission should form an Interim Committee composed of representatives meeting at the seat of the United Nations to consult with and advise the United Nations Unified Command in the light of the above recommendation; the Interim Committee should begin to function immediately upon the approval of the present resolution by the General Assembly;

(c) The Commission shall render a report to the next regular session of the General Assembly and to any prior special session which might be called to consider the subject matter of the present resolution; and shall render such interim reports as it may deem appropriate to the Secretary-General for transmission to Members;

The General Assembly furthermore,

Mindful of the fact that at the end of the present hostilities the task of rehabilitating the Korean economy will be of great magnitude,

3. *Requests* the Economic and Social Council, in consultation with the specialized agencies, to develop plans for relief and rehabilitation on the termination of hostilities and to report to the General Assembly within three weeks of the adoption of the present resolution by the General Assembly;

4. *Also recommends* the Economic and Social Council to expedite the study of long-term measures to promote the economic development and social progress of Korea, and meanwhile to draw the attention of the authorities which decide requests for technical assistance to the urgent and special necessity of affording such assistance to Korea;

5. *Expresses* its appreciation of the services rendered by the members of the United Nations Commission on Korea in the performance of their important and difficult task;

6. *Requests* the Secretary-General to provide the United Nations Commission for the Unification and Rehabilitation of Korea with

adequate staff and facilities, including technical advisers as required; and authorizes the Secretary-General to pay the expenses and per diem of a representative and alternate from each of the States members of the Commission.

No. 14. Address of Ambassador Wu Hsiu-chuan of the Central People's Government of the People's Republic of China, before the Security Council of the United Nations, November 28, 1950[14]

Mr. President, members of the Security Council: on the instructions of the Central People's Government of the People's Republic of China, I am here in the name of the 475 million people of China to accuse the United States Government of the unlawful and criminal act of armed aggression against the territory of China, Taiwan—including the Penghu Islands. . . .

After instigating the puppet Government of Syngman Rhee in South Korea to start the civil war in Korea, President Truman stated on 27 June 1950 that the United States Government had decided to prevent by force the liberation of Taiwan by the Central People's Government of the People's Republic of China. At the same time the United States armed forces, on the order of President Truman, began the full-scale, open invasion of Taiwan to carry out the policy of the United States Government of preventing by force the liberation of Taiwan by the Chinese People's Liberation Army.

The Central People's Government of the People's Republic of China in a statement issued on 28 June 1950, pointed out that the statement by President Truman on 27 June together with the actions of the United States armed forces constituted armed aggression against Chinese territory and a gross, total violation of the United Nations Charter. The Chinese people cannot tolerate such barbaric, illegal and criminal acts of aggression by the United States Government. . . .

Whatever decision the United Nations General Assembly may take on the so-called question of the status of Taiwan, whether it be to hand over the island to the United States so that it might administer it openly under the disguise of "trusteeship," or "neutralization," or whether it be to procrastinate by way of "investigation," thereby maintaining the present state of actual United States occupation, it will, in substance, be stealing China's legitimate territory and supporting United States aggression against Taiwan in opposition to the Chinese people. Any such decision would be unjustifiable and unlawful. Any such decision would in no way shake the resolve of the Chinese people to liberate Taiwan, nor would it prevent action by the Chinese people to liberate Taiwan. . . .

The civil war in Korea was created by the United States—but in no sense whatsoever can the civil war in Korea be used as a justification or pretext for United States aggression against Taiwan. . . .

. . . The creation of civil war in Korea by the United States government was designed to furnish a pretext for launching armed aggression against Korea and against our territory, Taiwan, for tightening its control in Viet-Nam and in the Philippines. . . .

. . . The armed invasion and occupation of Taiwan by the United States Government is an act of aggression in that it constitutes flagrant intervention in China's domestic affairs, and armed occupation of Chinese territory. It is an open and wanton act of provocation against all the 475 million Chinese people. . . .

. . . the armed aggression of the United States Government against the Chinese territory, Taiwan, is not an isolated affair. It is an integral part of the over-all plan of the United States Government to intensify its aggression, control and enslavement of the Asian countries and the peoples of Korea, Viet-Nam, the Philippines, Japan, etc. . . .

. . . Korea is about 5,000 miles away from the boundaries of the United States. To say that the civil war in Korea would affect the security of the United States is a flagrant, deceitful absurdity. But there is only a narrow river between Korea and China. The United States armed aggression in Korea inevitably threatens China's security. . . .

Now the United States forces of aggression in Korea are approaching our north-eastern frontiers. The flames of the war of aggression waged by the United States against Korea are swiftly sweeping toward China.

Under such circumstances, the United States armed aggression against Korea cannot be regarded as a matter which concerns the Korean people alone. No, decidedly not. The United States aggression against Korea gravely endangers the security of the People's Republic of China.

The Korean People's Democratic Republic is a country bound by close ties of friendship to the People's Republic of China. Only a river separates the two countries geographically. The Chinese people cannot afford to stand idly by in the face of this serious situation brought about by the United States Government's aggression against Korea and the dangerous tendency towards the extension of the war. . . .

The Chinese people have witnessed with their own eyes Taiwan fall prey to aggression and the flames of the United States war of aggression against Korea leap towards them. Thus stirred into righteous anger, they are volunteering in great numbers to go to the aid of the Korean people. Resistance to United States aggression is based on self-evident principles of justice and reason. The Chinese People's Government sees no reason whatever to prevent voluntary departure for Korea to participate under the command of the Government of the Korean People's Democratic Republic, in the great liberation struggle of the Korean people against United States aggression.

In making Japan its main war base in the East, launching armed aggression against Korea and Taiwan, carrying out active intervention against Viet-Nam and tightening its control over other countries in Asia, the United States Government is systematically building up a military encirclement of the People's Republic of China, in preparation for further attack on the People's Republic of China, and to stir up a Third World War.

In the name of the Central People's Government of the People's Republic of China, I therefore propose to the United Nations Security Council:

First, that the United Nations Security Council should openly condemn, and take concrete steps to apply severe sanctions against the United States Government for its criminal acts of armed aggression against the territory of China, Taiwan, and armed intervention in Korea.

Second, that the United Nations Security Council should immediately adopt effective measures to bring about the complete withdrawal by the United States Government of its forces of armed aggression from Taiwan, in order that peace and security in the Pacific and in Asia may be ensured;

Third, that the United Nations Security Council should immediately adopt effective measures to bring about the withdrawal from Korea of the armed forces of the United States and all other countries and to leave it to the people of North and South Korea to settle the domestic affairs of Korea themselves, so that a peaceful solution of the Korean question may be achieved.

No.15. Resolution of the General Assembly on the Intervention of the Central People's Government of the People's Republic of China in Korea, Adopted February 1, 1951 [15]

The General Assembly,

Noting that the Security Council, because of lack of unanimity of the permanent members, has failed to exercise its primary responsibility for the maintenance of international peace and security in regard to Chinese Communist intervention in Korea,

Noting that the Central People's Government of the People's Republic of China has not accepted United Nations proposals to bring about a cessation of hostilities in Korea with a view to peaceful settlement, and that its armed forces continue their invasion of Korea and their large-scale attacks upon United Nations forces there,

1. *Finds* that the Central People's Government of the People's Republic of China by giving direct aid and assistance to those who were already committing aggression in Korea and by engaging in hostilities against United Nations forces there has itself engaged in aggression in Korea;

2. *Calls upon* the Central People's Government of the People's Republic of China to cause its forces and nationals in Korea to cease hostilities against the United Nations forces and to withdraw from Korea;

3. *Affirms* the determination of the United Nations to continue its action in Korea to meet the aggression;

4. *Calls upon* all States and authorities to continue to lend every assistance to the United Nations action in Korea;

5. *Calls upon* all States and authorities to refrain from giving any assistance to the aggressors in Korea;

6. *Requests* a Committee composed of the members of the Collective Measures Committee as a matter of urgency to consider additional measures to be employed to meet this aggression and to report thereon to the General Assembly, it being understood that the Committee is authorized to defer its report if the Good Offices Committee referred to in the following paragraph reports satisfactory progress in its efforts;

7. *Affirms* that it continues to be the policy of the United Nations to bring about a cessation of hostilities in Korea and the achievement of United Nations objectives in Korea by peaceful means, and requests the President of the General Assembly to designate forthwith two persons who would meet with him at any suitable opportunity to use their good offices to this end.

No. 16. Agreement between the Commander-in-Chief, United Nations Command, on the One Hand, and the Supreme Commander of the Korean People's Army and the Commander of the Chinese People's Volunteers, on the Other Hand, concerning a Military Armistice in Korea[16]

Preamble

The undersigned, the Commander-in-Chief, United Nations Command, on the one hand, and the Supreme Commander of the Korean

People's Army and the Commander of the Chinese People's Volunteers, on the other hand, in the interest of stopping the Korean conflict, with its great toll of suffering and bloodshed on both sides, and with the objective of establishing an armistice which will insure a complete cessation of hostilities and of all acts of armed force in Korea until a final peaceful settlement is achieved, do individually, collectively, and mutually agree to accept and to be bound and governed by the conditions and terms of armistice set forth in the following articles and paragraphs, which said conditions and terms are intended to be purely military in character and to pertain solely to the belligerents in Korea.

Article I. Military Demarcation Line and Demilitarized Zone.

1. A military demarcation line shall be fixed and both sides shall withdraw two (2) kilometers from this line so as to establish a demilitarized zone between the opposing forces. A demilitarized zone shall be established as a buffer zone to prevent the occurrence of incidents which might lead to a resumption of hostilities. . . .

Article II. Concrete Arrangements for Cease-Fire and Armistice.

A. *General.* 13. In order to insure the stability of the military armistice so as to facilitate the attainment of a peaceful settlement through the holding by both sides of a political conference of a higher level, the Commanders of the opposing sides shall:

(a) Within seventy-two (72) hours after this armistice agreement becomes effective, withdraw all of their military forces, supplies, and equipment from the demilitarized zone except as otherwise provided herein. . . .

(c) Cease the introduction into Korea of reinforcing military personnel; provided, however, that the rotation of units and personnel, the arrival in Korea of personnel on a temporary duty basis, and the return to Korea of personnel after short periods of leave or temporary duty outside of Korea shall be permitted within the scope prescribed below: [There follow a careful definition of "rotation" and a description of the manner in which it is to be carried out and supervised.]

(d) Cease the introduction into Korea of reinforcing combat aircraft, armored vehicles, weapons, and ammunition; provided, however, that combat aircraft, armored vehicles, weapons, and ammunition which are destroyed, damaged, worn out, or used up during the period of the armistice may be replaced on the basis of piece-for-piece of the same effectiveness and the same type. [There follow detailed provisions as to how replacement is to be carried out.]

B. *Military Armistice Commission.*

19. A Military Armistice Commission is hereby established.

24. The general mission of the Military Armistice Commission shall be to supervise the implementation of this armistice agreement and to settle through negotiations any violations of this armistice agreement.

28. The Military Armistice Commission, or the senior member of either side thereof, is authorized to request the Neutral Nations Supervisory Commission to conduct special observations and inspections at places outside the demilitarized zone where violations of this armistice agreement have been reported to have occurred.

C. *Neutral Nations Supervisory Commission*.

36. A Neutral Nations Supervisory Commission is hereby established.

37. The Neutral Nations Supervisory Commission shall be composed of four (4) senior officers, two (2) of whom shall be appointed by neutral nations nominated by the Commander-in-Chief, United Nations Command, namely, Sweden and Switzerland, and two (2) of whom shall be appointed by neutral nations nominated jointly by the Supreme Commander of the Korean People's Army and the Commander of the Chinese People's Volunteers, namely, Poland and Czechoslovakia.

41. The mission of the Neutral Nations Supervisory Commission shall be to carry out the functions of supervision, observation, inspection, and investigation, as stipulated in sub-paragraphs 13 (2) and 13 (d) and paragraph 28 hereof, and to report the results of such supervision, observation, inspection, and investigation to the Military Armistice Commission.

Article III. Arrangements Relating to Prisoners of War. [The major provisions of this article are covered in the excerpts from the "Text of Agreement on Prisoners of War," given immediately below.]

Article IV. Recommendations to the Governments Concerned On Both Sides.

60. In order to insure the peaceful settlement of the Korean question, the military commanders of both sides hereby recommend to the governments of the countries concerned on both sides that, within three (3) months after the armistice agreement is signed and becomes effective, a political conference of a higher level of both sides be held by representatives appointed respectively to settle through negotiation the questions of the withdrawal of all foreign forces from Korea, the peaceful settlement of the Korean question, etc.

Done at Panmunjom, Korea, at 1000 hours on the 27th day of July 1953, in English, Korean, and Chinese, all texts being equally authentic.

No. 17. *Agreement on Prisoners of War*[17]

Within two months after the armistice agreement becomes effective both sides shall, without offering any hindrance, directly repatriate and hand over in groups all those prisoners of war in its custody who insist on repatriation to the side to which they belonged at the time of capture. . . .

I, *General*. 1. In order to ensure that all prisoners of war have the opportunity to exercise their right to be repatriated following an armistice, Sweden, Switzerland, Poland, Czechoslovakia and India shall each be requested by both sides to appoint a member to a neutral nations repatriation commission which shall be established to take custody in Korea of those prisoners of war who, while in the custody of the detaining powers, have not exercised their right to be repatriated. . . .

II, *Custody of Prisoners of War*. 4. All prisoners of war who have not exercised their right of repatriation following the effective date of the armistice arrangement shall be released from the military control and from the custody of the detaining side as soon as practicable and, in all cases, within sixty (60) days subsequent to the effective date of the armistice agreement to the neutral nations repatriation commission at locations in Korea to be designated by the detaining side.

III, *Explanation*. 8. The neutral nations repatriation commission, after having received and taken into custody all those prisoners of war who have not exercised their right to be repatriated, shall immediately make arrangements so that within ninety (90) days after the neutral nations repatriation commission takes over the custody, the nations to which the prisoners of war belong shall have freedom and facilities to send representatives to the locations where such prisoners of war are in custody to explain to all the prisoners of war depending upon these nations their rights and to inform them of any matters relating to their return to their homelands, particularly of their full freedom to return home to lead a peaceful life. . . .

9

TRUCE IN INDOCHINA: 1954

In the decade of the 1950's the three principal areas of tension in the Far East were China, Korea, and Viet Nam, each made so because of the existence in each country of two governments claiming legitimacy, one aligned on the side of the free world and the other with the communist world. Alone of the three, Viet Nam was a former possession of a Western colonial power.

The dissolution of Western colonialism in Southeastern Asia, the Philippines, and Indonesia was a great fact of post-1945 Far Eastern international relations, second in significance only to the emergence of communist power on the Chinese mainland. However, it was only in Viet Nam that the dissolution of colonial rule finally involved an international conference. That no less than nine governments attended the Geneva Conference of 1954 which witnessed the arrangement of a settlement in Indochina revealed how the dissolution of French colonial rule in the area, a process that had been initiated by the ejection of the French by the Japanese occupation in the spring of 1945 (see p. 109 above), had become an issue extending far beyond both the area and the relationship between the metropolitan government and the colonial area.

The Indochinese crisis originated at least in part from the reluctance of the French government to grant independence on any terms save its own. Under almost any circumstances this might have been a tactical error of some moment, but its consequences were compounded by the fact that one Vietnamese independence group was communist, that it had consistently been supported by the Soviet government, and that by 1950 it was receiving direct, but concealed, military aid from the Chinese Communist government. The military defeat suffered by the French at Dien Bien Phu in April, 1954, was the direct reason for the calling of the Geneva Conference.

Lying behind the conference and the settlement was the Chinese Communist policy not only of direct involvement in the Vietnamese situation but also of general probing into all of Southeastern Asia. What made the situation even more critical for the free world was that all the governments in the area either in existence or about to be born—Laos, Cambodia, Thailand, Burma, Malaya and Indonesia—were confronted with serious political and economic problems which resulted in varying degrees of internal instability, an open invitation to further communist penetration.

Although provision was made in the Geneva settlement for the unification of Viet Nam by peaceful means, it remained impossible because of the hostility between the two local governments and because of the involvement of the interests of the free and communist worlds. As in the case of China and Korea, no settlement in Viet Nam seemed possible without a resolution of the fundamental issues splitting the United States and the Soviet Union and the two worlds which they led.

(Note: For extensive documentation of the Indochinese situation see *Conflict in Indo-China & International Repercussions: A Documentary History, 1945-1955*, edited by Allen B. Cole. Cornell University Press, 1956.)

No. 1. Final Declaration of the Geneva Conference on the Problem of Restoring Peace in Indo-China, in Which the Representatives of Cambodia, the Democratic Republic of Viet Nam, France, Laos, the People's Republic of China, State of Viet Nam, the Union of Soviet Socialist Republics, the United Kingdom, the United States of America Took Part, July 21, 1954[1]

1. The Conference takes note of the agreements ending hostilities in Cambodia, Laos and Viet Nam and organizing international control and the supervision of the execution of the provisions of these agreements.

2. The Conference expresses satisfaction at the ending of hostilities in Cambodia, Laos and Viet Nam; the Conference expresses its conviction that the execution of the provisions set out in the present declaration and in the agreements on the cessation of hostilities will permit Cambodia, Laos and Viet Nam henceforth to play their part, in full independence and sovereignty, in the peaceful community of nations.

3. The Conference takes note of the declarations made by the Governments of Cambodia and of Laos of their intention to adopt meas-

ures permitting all citizens to take their place in the national community, in particular by participating in the next general elections, which, in conformity with the constitution of each of these countries, shall take place in the course of the year 1955, by secret ballot and in conditions of respect for fundamental freedoms.

4. The Conference takes note of the clauses in the agreement on the cessation of hostilities in Viet Nam prohibiting the introduction into Viet Nam of foreign troops and military personnel as well as of all kinds of arms and munitions. The Conference also takes note of the declarations made by the Governments of Cambodia and Laos of their resolution not to request foreign aid, whether in war material, in personnel or in instructors except for the purpose of the effective defence of their territory and, in the case of Laos, to the extent defined by the agreements on the cessation of hostilities in Laos.

5. The Conference takes note of the clauses in the agreement on the cessation of hostilities in Viet Nam to the effect that no military base under the control of a foreign State may be established in the regrouping zones of the two parties, the latter having the obligation to see that the zones allotted to them shall not constitute part of any military alliance and shall not be utilized for the resumption of hostilities or in the service of an aggressive policy. The Conference also takes note of the declarations of the Governments of Cambodia and Laos to the effect that they will not join in any agreement with other States if this agreement includes the obligation to participate in a military alliance not in conformity with the principles of the Charter of the United Nations or, in the case of Laos, with the principles of the agreement on the cessation of hostilities in Laos or, so long as their security is not threatened, the obligation to establish bases on Cambodian or Laotian territory for the military forces of foreign Powers.

6. The Conference recognizes that the essential purpose of the agreement relating to Viet Nam is to settle military questions with a view to ending hostilities and that the military demarcation line is provisional and should not in any way be interpreted as constituting a political or territorial boundary. The Conference expresses its conviction that the execution of the provisions set out in the present declaration and in the agreement on the cessation of hostilities creates the necessary basis for the achievement in the near future of a political settlement in Viet Nam.

7. The Conference declares that, so far as Viet Nam is concerned, the settlement of political problems, effected on the basis of respect for the principles of independence, unity and territorial integrity, shall permit the Vietnamese people to enjoy the fundamental free-

doms, guaranteed by democratic institutions established as a result of free general elections by secret ballot. In order to ensure that sufficient progress in the restoration of peace has been made, and that all the necessary conditions obtain for free expression of the national will, general elections shall be held in July 1956, under the supervision of an international commission composed of representatives of the Member States of the International Supervisory Commission, referred to in the agreement on the cessation of hostilities. Consultations will be held on this subject between the competent representative authorities of the two zones from July 20, 1955, onwards.

8. The provisions of the agreements on the cessation of hostilities intended to ensure the protection of individuals and of property must be most strictly applied and must, in particular, allow everyone in Viet Nam to decide freely in which zone he wishes to live.

9. The competent representative authorities of the Northern and Southern zones of Viet Nam, as well as the authorities of Laos and Cambodia, must not permit any individual or collective reprisals against persons who have collaborated in any way with one of the parties during the war, or against members of such persons' families.

10. The Conference takes note of the declaration of the Government of the French Republic to the effect that it is ready to withdraw its troops from the territory of Cambodia, Laos and Viet Nam, at the request of the Governments concerned and within periods which shall be fixed by agreement between the parties except in the cases where, by agreement between the two parties, a certain number of French troops shall remain at specified points and for a specified time.

11. The Conference takes note of the declaration of the French Government to the effect that for the settlement of all the problems connected with the re-establishment and consolidation of peace in Cambodia, Laos and Viet Nam, the French Government will proceed from the principle of respect for the independence and sovereignty, unity and territorial integrity of Cambodia, Laos and Viet Nam.

12. In their relations with Cambodia, Laos and Viet Nam, each member of the Geneva Conference undertakes to respect the sovereignty, the independence, the unity and the territorial integrity of the above-mentioned States, and to refrain from any interference in their internal affairs.

13. The members of the Conference agree to consult one another on any question which may be referred to them by the International

Supervisory Commission, in order to study such measures as may prove necessary to ensure that the agreements on the cessation of hostilities in Cambodia, Laos and Viet Nam are respected.

No. 2. Agreement on the Cessation of Hostilities in Viet Nam, July 20, 1954[2]

Article 1. A provisional military demarcation line shall be fixed, on either side of which the forces of the two parties shall be re-grouped after their withdrawal, the forces of the People's Army of Viet Nam to the north of the line and the forces of the French Union to the south. [Note: In an Annex to this Agreement the following statement appears: "The provisional military demarcation line is fixed as follows, reading from east to west:−The mouth of the Song Ben Hat (Cua Tung River) and the course of that river (known as the Rao Thanh in the mountains) to the village of Bo Ho Su, then the parallel of Bo Ho Su to the Laos-Viet Nam frontier."]

It is also agreed that a demilitarized zone shall be established on either side of the demarcation line, to a width of not more than 5 kms. from it, to act as a buffer zone and to avoid any incidents which might result in the resumption of hostilities.

Article 16. With effect from the date of entry into force of the present Agreement, the introduction into Viet Nam of any troop reinforcements and additional military personnel is prohibited. [The exception of meticulously defined "rotation of personnel" is then made.]

Article 17. With effect from the date of entry into force of the present Agreement, the introduction into Viet Nam in the form of all types of arms, munitions and other war material, such as combat aircraft, naval craft, pieces of ordnance, jet engines and jet weapons and armoured vehicles is prohibited. [The exception of carefully limited "replacement" is then made.]

Article 28. Responsibility for the execution of the agreement on the cessation of hostilities shall rest with the parties.

Article 29. An International Commission shall ensure control and supervision of this agreement.

Article 34. An International Commission shall be set up for the control and supervision over the application of the provisions of the agreement on the cessation of hostilities in Viet Nam. It shall be composed of representatives of the following States: Canada, India and Poland.

It shall be presided over by the Representative of India.

No. 3. United States Declaration on Indochina[3]

Following is the text of a statement made by Under Secretary

Walter B. Smith at the concluding Indochina plenary session at Geneva on July 2, 1954:
"As I stated on July 18, my Government is not prepared to join in a declaration by the Conference such as is submitted. However, the United States makes this unilateral declaration of its position in these matters:

DECLARATION

"The Government of the United States, being resolved to devote its efforts to the strengthening of peace in accordance with the principles and purposes of the United Nations, takes note of the agreements concluded at Geneva on July 20 and 21, 1954, between the (a) Franco-Laotian Command and the Command of the Peoples Army of Viet-Nam, (b) the Royal Khmer Army Command and the Command of the Peoples Army of Viet-Nam, (c) Franco-Vietnamese Command and the Command of the Peoples Army of Viet-Nam and of paragraphs 1 to 12 inclusive of the declaration presented to the Geneva Conference on July 21, 1954, declares with regard to the aforesaid agreements and paragraphs that (i) it will refrain from the threat or the use of force to disturb them, in accordance with Article 2 (4) of the Charter of the United Nations dealing with the obligation of members to refrain in their international relations from the threat or use of force, and (ii) it would view any renewal of the aggression in violation of the aforesaid agreements with grave concern and as seriously threatening international peace and security.
"In connection with the statement in the declaration concerning free elections in Viet-Nam, my Government wishes to make clear its position which it has expressed in a declaration made in Washington on June 29, 1954, as follows:

In the case of nations now divided against their will, we shall continue to seek to achieve unity through free elections supervised by the United Nations to insure that they are conducted fairly.

"With respect to the statement made by the representative of the State of Viet-Nam, the United States reiterates its traditional position that peoples are entitled to determine their own future and that it will not join in an arrangement which would hinder this. Nothing in its declaration just made is intended to or does indicate any departure from this traditional position.
"We share the hope that the agreements will permit Cambodia, Laos and Viet-Nam to play their part in full independence and sovereignty, in the peaceful community of nations, and will enable the peoples of that area to determine their own future."

No. 4. Joint Sino-Vietnamese Communique, July 7, 1955[4]

During the visit in China of the delegation of the Government of the Democratic Republic of Vietnam headed by President Ho Chi Minh, talks were held in Peking from June 27 to July 7 between a delegation of the Government of the People's Republic of China and the Government of the Democratic Republic of Vietnam on the basis of principles laid down through consultation by Chairman Mao Tsetung of the People's Republic of China and President Ho Chi Minh of the Democratic Republic of Vietnam. [Omitted is the list of delegates from both sides.]

In the course of the talks, the two parties discussed matters of common interest to the People's Republic of China and the Democratic Republic of Vietnam and questions of major significance in the present international situation.

The two parties note with satisfaction that the regrouping and transfer of military forces as provided in the Geneva agreements have been completed, and that the International Commissions for supervision and control in the three Indochinese States, composed of representatives of India, Poland, and Canada, and with the Indian representatives as Chairmen, have made important contributions in supervising and controlling the implementation of the Geneva agreements. The two parties express the hope that the International Commissions for supervision and control will continue to play an active role in ensuring the thorough implementation of the Geneva agreements.

However, the two parties are aware that the implementation of the Geneva agreements has been obstructed and sabotaged and is threatened with new sabotage. Shortly after the Geneva Conference, the United States Government violated the Geneva agreements by including South Vietnam, Cambodia, and Laos in the so-called area "protected" by the Manila Treaty and by stepping up the equipping and training of troops in South Vietnam in order to convert the southern part of Vietnam into a colony and war base of the United States. At present, the United States is actively obstructing the holding of consultations for the general elections in Vietnam in an attempt to sabotage the cause of consolidating the peace and achieving the unification of Vietnam. The United States, again in violation of the Geneva agreements, signed a military assistance agreement with Cambodia and is further attempting to conclude a similar agreement with Laos so as to destroy the neutrality of Cambodia and Laos and jeopardize peace in Indo-China. The two parties to the talks are in agreement that these and similar violations of the Geneva agreements must be stopped and the Geneva agreements must be carried through.

In accordance with the agreement reached in Geneva on the peaceful unification of Vietnam through general elections, consultations shall be held on the subject of general elections between the competent authorities of the two zones in Vietnam from July 20, 1955, so that free general elections may be held in July 1956 under the supervision of the International Commission composed of the representatives of India, Poland, and Canada to bring about the unification of Vietnam. The Government of the Democratic Republic of Vietnam is determined to continue to carry out the Geneva agreements faithfully and has already declared its readiness to hold consultations with the competent authorities of South Vietnam on matters concerning the general elections. The two parties to the talks are of the common opinion that the countries which participated in the Geneva Conference have the responsibility to guarantee the implementation of the Geneva agreements. The two parties fully endorse the appeal and exhortation made by the Chairman of the Council of Ministers of the Soviet Union and the Prime Minister of India in their joint declaration of June 22, 1955, namely that all governments concerned with the carrying out of the Geneva agreements should do their utmost to discharge their obligations so that the purposes of the agreements may be completely achieved; and that where elections are to be held as a preliminary to a political settlement, the efforts of the governments concerned should be directed to the full implementation of the provisions of the agreements. The two parties are deeply convinced that the efforts of the Vietnamese people to achieve the unification of their country through consultations between the northern and the southern zones and through free general elections will certainly enjoy full support of all countries and peoples who love peace and uphold the Geneva agreements.

The historic Asian-African Conference has set an example of working in harmony by countries with different social systems. The two parties to the talks are pleased to note that the influence of the Asian-African Conference is increasing. They warmly support the series of important steps taken recently by the Soviet Union, India and other peaceloving countries, which help to advance the cause of peace. As a result of the efforts of the peaceloving countries and peoples, there have appeared signs of the easing of international tension. But the threat of a new war has not been eliminated, the international situation has not yet been fundamentally improved, and the rulers of certain important countries are still flaunting their so-called "policy of strength."

[Note: In *Conflict in Indochina & International Repercussions* (cited above) the following paragraph appears at this point: "The two parties consider that the 'policy of strength' based on the organization of military blocs, establishment of military bases, expanding of armaments, and conduct of war propaganda goes entirely against the common desire of the people of the world to maintain international peace and collective security. " This was not given in the copy of the communique, also released by the New China News Agency, available to the present editor.]

The two parties to the talks are pleased to note that the 5 principles of peaceful co-existence are being recognized and accepted by more and more countries. They consider that the establishment of mutual confidence between nations, the elimination of international tensions and the development of friendly co-operation between various countries depend on the universal and extensive acceptance of these principles by all countries of the world as the principles guiding their relations with one another. The two parties reiterate that the People's Republic of China and the Democratic Republic of Vietnam are ready, on the basis of the 5 principles of peaceful co-existence, to establish normal and cordial relations with all countries, particularly to establish friendly and good neighborly relations with the countries around them.

The Chinese and the Vietnamese peoples have always given each other deep sympathy and support in their respective national liberation movements. At present, the Chinese people are engaged in a struggle to safeguard the sovereignty and territorial integrity of their fatherland and to liberate their territory, Taiwan. The Vietnamese people are engaged in a struggle to unify their country through consultations between the northern and the southern zones and through the holding of free general elections so as to build a peaceful, united, independent, democratic, prosperous and strong new Vietnam. The two parties to the talks express full sympathy and support for the just struggles of the Chinese and Vietnamese peoples and are deeply convinced that their struggles will certainly triumph.

The two parties to the talks are of the opinion that the economic and technical co-operation between the People's Republic of China and the Democratic Republic of Vietnam will be helpful to the efforts of the two peoples in peaceful construction. In order to assist the Vietnamese people to heal the wounds left by a protracted war and rehabilitate and develop their national economy, the Government of the People's Republic of China decided to present without compensation to the Government of the Democratic Republic of Vietnam 800 million Chinese yuan. The Government of the People's Republic of China will use the above sum to help Vietnam rebuild railways, river docks, highways and bridges, restore and construct textile mills, tanneries, medical equipment factories, electrical equipment factories, agriculture implement factories, paper mills, etc. The two parties also agree to co-operate fully with each other on the technical side. China will help to design and construct the factories, railways, highways, bridges, etc. which Vietnam considers necessary to repair or build, and will also dispatch technical personnel to Vietnam. At the same time, Vietnam will dispatch workers as apprentices to certain enterprises in China.

In order to promote the economic development of the two countries and to improve the livelihood of their peoples, the two parties further agree to expand step by step their mutual trade on the basis of equality and mutual benefit.

The Chinese and the Vietnamese peoples have long and traditional cultural ties in history. In order further to extend their co-operation, exchange experiences and study from each other in the fields of culture, education and health, the two parties agree to exchange cultural visits, and exchange students, and books and literature. The People's Republic of China will dispatch technical personnel to Vietnam and present it as gifts material, and apparatus for cultural, educational and health work so as to assist the work of the Vietnamese people in these fields. The two parties are of the common view that the strengthening of the cultural interflow between the two peoples will further consolidate and develop their close friendship.

The two parties are deeply convinced that their talks held in an atmosphere of sincerity and harmony are not only in the interest of strengthening the unity and friendship of the two peoples and of their just struggle, but are certainly also in the interest of the common cause of safeguarding peace of the peoples of the world.

No. 5. Joint Communique of Soviet Government and Government of Democratic Republic of Viet Nam, July 18, 1955[5]

Both governments have noted with satisfaction that the relations of friendship and growing economic and cultural cooperation that have developed between the People's Republic of China and the Democratic Republic of Viet Nam accord with the interests of the peoples of China and Viet Nam and constitute a major factor in the cause of preserving and strengthening peace in the Far East.

The governments of the USSR and the Democratic Republic of Viet Nam have noted with profound satisfaction that at the foundation of the relations that have developed between the USSR and the Democratic Republic of Viet Nam lie reciprocal feelings of friendship and solidarity binding the Soviet and Vietnamese peoples.

Both governments are unanimous in their aspiration to promote and strengthen political, economic and cultural cooperation between the Soviet Union and the Democratic Republic of Viet Nam.

The question of economic cooperation between the USSR and the Democratic Republic of Viet Nam, on whose national economy heavy material damage was inflicted as a result of protracted war, were [sic] discussed in the course of the negotiations.

In this connection the Soviet Government has allocated 400,000,000 rubles as a free gift to assist in raising the living standards of the population and restoring the economy of the Democratic Republic of Viet Nam, including the restoration and construction of 25 industrial enterprises and public utilities.

The Government of the USSR will render assistance to the Democratic Republic of Viet Nam in the training of Vietnamese specialists at establishments of higher learning and secondary technical schools in the USSR, as well as assistance in the organization of the training of specialists at educational establishments in Viet Nam; technical assistance will be provided in geological prospecting and also in the undertaking of health and prophylactic measures to fight contagious diseases, etc.

Both governments have reached unanimity on the necessity of extending reciprocal trade between their two countries and have concluded a trade agreement to this end.

Both governments express the firm conviction that the interchange of views that has taken place will undoubtedly facilitate the further development of friendly relations between the USSR and the Democratic Republic of Viet Nam to the benefit of the peoples of both countries and will serve the interests of strengthening peace and security the world over.

10

FREE WORLD SECURITY
IN THE FAR EAST

The security system established by the treaties set forth in this chapter constituted the free world's response to the serious political and strategic situation created by the emergence in 1945 of the Soviet Union as a dominant force in Northeast Asia and the Chinese Communist victory in the civil war in 1949.

Although the ANZUS Pact and the United States-Philippines security treaty were a part of the general peace settlement with Japan, constituting assurances to these three wartime allies of the United States in the war against Japan that there would not in the future be a threat to them from a possibly resurgent Japanese military power, they have stood mainly as a part of the security system containing the communist threat.

The 1951 treaty with Japan was obviously designed to guarantee the security of Japan against a possible extension of communist military power. However, the treaty was a vital necessity to the United Nations and United States military forces operating in the Korean theater. The treaty of peace contained a provision for the return of full sovereignty to Japan and thus in turn made necessary the conclusion of treaty arrangements which would permit the continued use of bases in Japan by United Nations forces which were operating against the communist aggressor in Korea and were to continue to do so for almost two more years. The conclusion of a new security treaty in 1960, the immediate cause of a political crisis inside Japan, reflected not only an understandable Japanese desire for a treaty based on equality of partnership of the signatories, but also the altered strategic situation in the Far East in which communist aggression in the vicinity of Japan was a possibility, not an actuality.

The United States security treaty with the Republic of Korea was a necessary element of the Korean truce arrangements. It is highly doubtful that Mr. Syngman Rhee, then president of the Republic, would have accepted the truce without the assurance of United States assistance in the event of a recurrence of North Korean aggression. The United States treaty with Nationalist China also grew out of the Korean conflict in part because of the initial United States guarantee of Taiwan against invasion from the mainland, given when the communist attack on Korea began in 1950.

The Southeast Asia Collective Defense Treaty was, of course, a broad response of the free world to the situation created in Viet Nam by the withdrawal of the French as a result of the Geneva agreement of 1954. Of great political significance was the Pacific Charter which, although it was only a statement of position, nevertheless was also a renunciation of colonialism by three governments which were formerly the leading Western colonial powers in Asia, Great Britain, France, and the United States.

From its very nature the security system established by the treaties here presented had to be defensive. By no stretch of the imagination could any of the signatories, except the United States, be regarded as military powers capable of carrying out sustained and effective military operations in a possible major Far Eastern military theater. Australia, New Zealand and the European partners are prevented from doing so by distance, limited manpower, and restricted industrial bases—restricted in terms of modern, large-scale warfare, if not in terms of the satisfaction of their peacetime economic requirements. Similar limitations but of a greater order prevent the resort to offensive military operations by the Asian partners of the security system. There is the additional military factor that without exception the Asian partners are directly dependent on the United States for their military hardware.

Furthermore, if the United States were to put itself in the inconceivable position of initiating a "brush-fire" war anywhere in Asia it would still be confronted with the massive geographical fact of its separation from a possible theater of war by the vast distances of the Pacific, rendered less formidable than in 1940, for example, by technical advances in military aircraft, but constituting a complex and expensive logistical problem.

If the parties to the security arrangements were ever to embark on offensive war against the communist powers in Asia, they would have to contend with the handicaps just mentioned, and would also be confronted with the hard strategic fact that they would be attempting to carry war to an enemy with the great advantage of interior lines of communication fighting close to its centers of strength.

In the six years between 1954–when it was completed in all essentials–and 1960, the security system did function effectively. Between 1950 and 1954 the communist world twice attempted to solve political problems by aggressive means, but did not do so thereafter. Clearly, there were other factors operating, but at a minimum the free world security system was a problem requiring serious consideration by any potential communist aggressor.

No. 1. Security Treaty between Australia, New Zealand, and the United States (ANZUS Pact)[1]

The Parties to this Treaty,

Reaffirming their faith in the purposes and principles of the Charter of the United Nations and their desire to live in peace with all peoples and all Governments, and desiring to strengthen the fabric of peace in the Pacific Area,

Noting that the United States already has arrangements pursuant to which its armed forces are stationed in the Philippines, and has armed forces and administrative responsibilities in the Ryukyus, and upon the coming into force of the Japanese Peace Treaty may also station armed forces in and about Japan to assist in the preservation of peace and security in the Japan Area,

Recognizing that Australia and New Zealand as members of the British Commonwealth of Nations have military obligations outside as well as within the Pacific Area,

Desiring to declare publicly and formally their sense of unity, so that no potential aggressor could be under the illusion that any of them stand alone in the Pacific Area, and

Desiring further to coordinate their efforts for collective defense for the preservation of peace and security pending the development of a more comprehensive system of regional security in the Pacific Area,

Therefore declare and agree as follows:

Article I. The Parties undertake, as set forth in the Charter of the United Nations, to settle any international disputes in which they may be involved by peaceful means in such a manner that international peace and security and justice are not endangered and to refrain in their international relations from the threat or use of force in any manner inconsistent with the purposes of the United Nations.

Article II. In order more effectively to achieve the objective of this Treaty the Parties separately and jointly by means of continuous and effective self-help and mutual aid will maintain and develop their individual and collective capacity to resist armed attack.

Article III. The Parties will consult together whenever in the opinion of any of them the territorial integrity, political independence or security of any of the Parties is threatened in the Pacific.

Article IV. Each Party recognizes that an armed attack in the Pacific Area on any of the Parties would be dangerous to its own peace and safety and declares that it would act to meet the common danger in accordance with its constitutional processes.

Any such armed attack and all measures taken as a result thereof shall be immediately reported to the Security Council of the United Nations. Such measures shall be terminated when the Security Council has taken the measures necessary to restore and maintain international peace and security.

Article V. For the purpose of Article IV, an armed attack on any of the Parties is deemed to include an armed attack on the metropolitan territory of any of the Parties, or on the island territories under its jurisdiction in the Pacific or on its armed forces, public vessels or aircraft in the Pacific.

Article VI. This Treaty does not affect and shall not be interpreted as affecting in any way the rights and obligations of the parties under the Charter of the United Nations or the responsibility of the United Nations for the maintenance of international peace and security.

Article VII. The Parties hereby establish a Council, consisting of their Foreign Ministers or their Deputies, to consider matters concerning the implementation of this Treaty. The Council should be so organized as to be able to meet at any time.

Article VIII. Pending the development of a more comprehensive system of regional security in the Pacific Area and the development by the United Nations of more effective means to maintain international peace and security, the Council established by Article VII is authorized to maintain a consultative relationship with States, Regional Organizations, Associations of States, or other authorities in the Pacific area in a position to further the purposes of this Treaty and to contribute to the security of that Area.

Article IX. This Treaty shall be ratified by the Parties in accordance with their respective constitutional processes. The instruments of ratification shall be deposited as soon as possible with the Government of Australia, which will notify each of the other signatories of such deposit. The Treaty shall enter into force as soon as the ratifications of the signatories have been deposited.

Article X. This Treaty shall remain in force indefinitely. Any Party may cease to be a member of the Council established by Article VII one year after notice has been given to the Government of

Australia, which will inform the Governments of the other Parties of the deposit of such notice.

Article XI. This Treaty in the English language shall be deposited in the archives of the Government of Australia. Duly certified copies thereof will be transmitted by that Government to the Governments of each of the other signatories.

In witness whereof the undersigned plenipotentiaries have signed this treaty.

Done at San Francisco this first day of September, 1951.

No. 2. Mutual Defense Treaty between the United States and the Republic of the Philippines[2]

The Parties to this Treaty,

Reaffirming their faith in the purposes and principles of the Charter of the United Nations and their desire to live in peace with all peoples and all Governments, and desiring to strengthen the fabric of peace in the Pacific Area,

Recalling with mutual pride the historic relationship which brought their two peoples together in a common bond of sympathy and mutual ideals to fight side-by-side against imperialist aggression during the last war,

Desiring to declare publicly and formally their sense of unity and their common determination to defend themselves against external armed attack, so that no potential aggressor could be under the illusion that either of them stands alone in the Pacific Area,

Desiring further to strengthen their present efforts for collective defense for the preservation of peace and security pending the development of a more comprehensive system of regional security in the Pacific Area,

Agreeing that nothing in this present instrument shall be considered or interpreted as in any way or sense altering or diminishing any existing agreements or understandings between the United States of America and the Republic of the Philippines,

Have agreed as follows:

Article I. The Parties undertake, as set forth in the Charter of the United Nations, to settle any international disputes in which they may be involved by peaceful means in such a manner that international peace and security and justice are not endangered and to refrain in their international relations from the threat or use of force in any manner inconsistent with the purposes of the United Nations.

Article II. In order more effectively to achieve the objective of this Treaty the Parties separately and jointly by self-help and mutual aid will maintain and develop their individual and collective capacity to resist armed attack.

Article III. The Parties through their Foreign Ministers or their deputies, will consult together from time to time regarding the implementation of the Treaty and whenever in the opinion of either of them the territorial integrity, political independence or security of either of the Parties is threatened by external armed attack in the Pacific.

Article IV. Each Party recognizes that an armed attack in the Pacific Area on either of the Parties would be dangerous to its own peace and safety and declares that it would act to meet the common dangers in accordance with its constitutional processes.

Any such armed attack and all measures taken as a result thereof shall be immediately reported to the Security Council of the United Nations. Such measures shall be terminated when the Security Council has taken the measures necessary to restore and maintain international peace and security.

Article V. For the purpose of Article **IV,** an armed attack on either of the Parties is deemed to include an armed attack on the metropolitan territory of the Parties, or on the island territories under its jurisdiction in the Pacific or on its armed forces, public vessels or aircraft in the Pacific.

Article VI. This Treaty does not affect and shall not be interpreted as affecting in any way the rights and obligations of the Parties under the Charter of the United Nations or the responsibility of the United Nations for the maintenance of international peace and security.

Article VII. This Treaty shall be ratified by the United States of America and the Republic of the Philippines in accordance with their respective constitutional processes and will come into force when instruments of ratification thereof have been exchanged by them at Manila.

Article VIII. This Treaty shall remain in force indefinitely. Either Party may terminate it one year after notice has been given to the other Party.

Article IX. This Treaty in the English language shall be deposited in the archives of the Government of the Philippines. Duly certified copies thereof will be transmitted by that Government to the Government of the United States.

In witness whereof the undersigned plenipotentiaries have signed this Treaty.

Done in duplicate at Washington this thirtieth day of August 1951.

No. 3. Security Treaty between the United States and Japan[3]

Japan has this day signed a Treaty of Peace with the Allied Powers. On the coming into force of that Treaty, Japan will not have the effective means to exercise its inherent right of self-defense because it has been disarmed. There is danger to Japan in this situation because irresponsible militarism has not yet been driven from the world. Therefore, Japan desires a Security Treaty with the United States of America to come into force simultaneously with the Treaty of Peace between the United States of America and Japan. The Treaty of Peace recognizes that Japan as a sovereign nation has the right to enter into collective security arrangements, and further, the Charter of the United Nations recognizes that all nations possess an inherent right of individual and collective self-defense.

In exercise of these rights, Japan desires, as a provisional arrangement for its defense, that the United States of America should maintain armed forces of its own in and about Japan so as to deter armed attack upon Japan.

The United States of America, in the interest of peace and security, is presently willing to maintain certain of its armed forces in and about Japan, in the expectation, however, that Japan will itself increasingly assume responsibility for its own defense against direct and indirect aggression, always avoiding any armament which could be an offensive threat or serve other than to promote peace and security in accordance with the purposes and principles of the United Nations Charter.

Accordingly, the two countries have agreed as follows:

Article I. Japan grants, and the United States of America accepts the right, upon the coming into force of the Treaty of Peace and of this Treaty, to dispose United States land, air and sea forces in and about Japan. Such forces may be utilized to contribute to the maintenance of the international peace and security in the Far East and to the security of Japan against armed attack from without, including assistance given at the express request of the Japanese Government to put down large-scale internal riots and disturbances in Japan, caused through instigation or intervention by an outside Power or Powers.

Article II. During the exercise of the right referred to in Article I, Japan will not grant, without the prior consent of the United States of America, any bases or any rights, power or authority whatsoever, in or relating to bases or the right of garrison or of maneuver, or transit of ground, air or naval forces to any third power.

Article III. The conditions which shall govern the disposition of armed forces of the United States of America in and about Japan shall be determined by administrative agreements between the two Governments.

Article IV. This Treaty shall expire whenever in the opinion of the Governments of the United States of America and of Japan there shall have come into force such United Nations arrangements or such alternative individual or collective security dispositions as will satisfactorily provide for the maintenance by the United Nations or otherwise of international peace and security in the Japan Area.

Article V. This Treaty shall be ratified by the United States of America and Japan and will come into force when instruments of ratification thereof have been exchanged by them at Washington.

IN WITNESS WHEREOF the undersigned plenipotentiaries have signed this Treaty.

DONE in duplicate at the city of San Francisco, in the English and Japanese languages, this eighth day of September, 1951.

No. 4. Treaty of Mutual Cooperation and Security between the United States and Japan (Signed at Washington, D.C., January 19, 1960)[4]

The United States of America and Japan,

Desiring to strengthen the bonds of peace and friendship traditionally existing between them, and to uphold the principles of democracy, individual liberty, and the rule of law,

Desiring further to encourage closer economic cooperation between them and to promote conditions of economic stability and well-being in their countries,

Reaffirming their faith in the purposes and principles of the Charter of the United Nations, and their desire to live in peace with all peoples and all governments,

Recognizing that they have the inherent right of individual or collective self-defense as affirmed in the Charter of the United Nations,

Considering that they have a common concern in the maintenance of international peace and security in the Far East,

Having resolved to conclude a treaty of mutual cooperation and security,

Therefore agree as follows:

Article I. The Parties undertake, as set forth in the Charter of the United Nations, to settle any international disputes in which they may be involved by peaceful means in such a manner that international peace and security and justice are not endangered and to refrain in their international relations from the threat or use of force against the territorial integrity or political independence of any state, or in any other manner inconsistent with the purposes of the United Nations.

The Parties will endeavor in concert with other peace-loving countries to strengthen the United Nations so that its mission of maintaining international peace and security may be discharged more effectively.

Article II. The Parties will contribute toward the further development of peaceful and friendly international relations by strengthening their free institutions, by bringing about a better understanding of the principles upon which these institutions are founded, and by promoting conditions of stability and well-being. They will seek to eliminate conflict in their international economic policies and will encourage economic collaboration between them.

Article III. The Parties, individually and in cooperation with each other, by means of continuous and effective self-help and mutual aid will maintain and develop, subject to their constitutional provisions, their capacities to resist armed attack.

Article IV. The Parties will consult together from time to time regarding the implementation of this Treaty, and, at the request of either Party, whenever the security of Japan or international peace and security in the Far East is threatened.

Article V. Each Party recognizes that an armed attack against either Party in the territories under the administration of Japan would be dangerous to its own peace and safety and declares that it would act to meet the common danger in accordance with its constitutional provisions and processes.

Any such armed attack and all measures taken as a result thereof shall be immediately reported to the Security Council of the United Nations in accordance with the provisions of Article 51 of the Charter. Such measures shall be terminated when the Security Council has taken the measures necessary to restore and maintain international peace and security.

Article VI. For the purpose of contributing to the security of Japan and the maintenance of international peace and security in the Far East, the United States of America is granted the use by its land, air and naval forces of facilities and areas in Japan.

The use of these facilities and areas as well as the status of the United States armed forces in Japan shall be governed by a separate agreement, replacing the administrative Agreement under

Article III of the Security Treaty between the United States of America and Japan, signed at Tokyo on February 28, 1952, as amended, and by such other arrangements as may be agreed upon.

Article VII. This Treaty does not affect and shall not be interpreted as affecting in any way the rights and obligations of the Parties under the Charter of the United Nations or the responsibility of the United Nations for the maintenance of international peace and security.

Article VIII. This Treaty shall be ratified by the United States of America and Japan in accordance with their respective constitutional processes and will enter into force on the date on which the instruments of ratification thereof have been exchanged by them in Tokyo.

Article IX. The Security Treaty between the United States of America and Japan signed at the city of San Francisco on September 8, 1951 shall expire upon the entering into force of this Treaty,

Article X. This Treaty shall remain in force until in the opinion of the Governments of the United States of America and Japan there shall have come into force such United Nations arrangements as will satisfactorily provide for the maintenance of international peace and security in the Japan area.

However, after the Treaty has been in force for ten years, either Party may give notice to the other Party of its intention to terminate the Treaty, in which case the Treaty shall terminate one year after such notice has been given.

IN WITNESS WHEREOF the undersigned Plenipotentiaries have signed this Treaty.

DONE in duplicate at Washington in the English and Japanese languages, both equally authentic, this 19th day of January, 1960.

No. 5. Agreed Minute to the Treaty of Mutual Cooperation and Security⁵

Japanese Plenipotentiary:

While the question of the status of the islands administered by the United States under Article 3 of the Treaty of Peace with Japan has not been made a subject of discussion in the course of treaty negotiations, I would like to emphasize the strong concern of the Government and people of Japan for the safety of the people of these islands since Japan possesses residual sovereignty over these islands. If an armed attack occurs or is threatened against these islands, the two countries will of course consult together closely under Article IV of the Treaty of Mutual Cooperation and Security. In the event of an armed attack, it is the intention of the Government of Japan to explore with the United States measures which it might be able to take for the welfare of the islanders.

United States Plenipotentiary:

In the event of an armed attack against these islands, the United States Government will consult at once with the Government of Japan and intends to take the necessary measures for the defense of these islands, and to do its utmost to secure the welfare of the islanders.

Washington, January 19, 1960   C. A. H[erter]
                                                N. K[ishi]

*No. 6. Exchange of Notes Incorporating Agreed Consultation Formula*⁶

(Japanese Note)

Washington, January 19, 1960

Excellency: I have the honour to refer to the Treaty of Mutual Cooperation and Security between Japan and the United States of America signed today, and to inform Your Excellency that the following is the understanding of the Government of Japan concerning the implementation of Article VI thereof:

Major changes in the deployment into Japan of United States armed forces, major changes in their equipment, and the use of of facilities and areas in Japan as bases for military combat operations to be undertaken from Japan other than those conducted under Article V of the said Treaty, shall be the subjects of prior consultation with the Government of Japan.

I should be appreciative if Your Excellency would confirm on behalf of your Government that this is also the understanding of the Government of the United States of America.

I avail myself of this opportunity to renew to Your Excellency the assurance of my highest consideration.

Nobusuke Kishi

(Note: The key sentence of Secretary of State Christian Herter's

reply under the same date is: "I have the honor to confirm on behalf of my Government that the foregoing is also the understanding
of the Government of the United States of America.")

No. 7. Exchange of Notes Re Establishment of the
Security Consultative Committee[7]
Washington, January 19, 1960

Dear Secretary Herter: . . . Under Article IV of the Treaty,
the two Governments will consult together from time to time regarding the implementation of the Treaty, and, at the request of
either Government, whenever the security of Japan or international peace and security in the Far East is threatened. The exchange of notes under Article VI of the Treaty specifies certain
matters as the subjects of prior consultation with the Government
of Japan.

Such consultations will be carried on between the two Governments through appropriate channels. At the same time, however,
I feel that the establishment of a special committee which could as
appropriate be used for these consultations between the Governments would prove very useful. This committee, which would meet
whenever requested by either side, could also consider any matters underlying and related to security affairs which would serve
to promote understanding between the two Governments and contribute to the strengthening of cooperative relations between the two
countries in the field of security.

Under this proposal the present "Japanese-American Committee
on Security" established by the Governments of the United States
and Japan on August 6, 1957, would be replaced by this new committee which might be called "The Security Consultative Committee." I would also recommend that the membership of this new committee be the same as the membership of the "Japanese-American
Committee on Security," namely on the Japanese side, the Minister for Foreign Affairs, who will preside on the Japanese side,
and the Director General of the Defense Agency, and on the United
States side, the United States Ambassador to Japan, who will serve
as chairman on the United States side, and the Commander-in-
Chief, Pacific, who will be the Ambassador's principal advisor on
military and defense matters. The Commander, United States
Forces, Japan, will serve as alternate for the Commander-in-
Chief, Pacific.

I would appreciate very much your views on this matter.

Most Sincerely,
Nobusuke Kishi

(Note: Secretary Herter's reply under the same date expresses full agreement with the proposals concerning both the committee and its membership.)

No. 8. Mutual Defense Treaty between the United States and the Republic of Korea[8]

The Parties to this Treaty,

Reaffirming their desire to live in peace with all peoples and all governments, and desiring to strengthen the fabric of peace in the Pacific area,

Desiring to declare publicly and formally their common determination to defend themselves against external armed attack so that no potential aggressor could be under the illusion that either of them stands alone in the Pacific area,

Desiring further to strengthen their efforts for collective defense for the preservation of peace and security pending the development of a more comprehensive and effective system of regional security in the Pacific area,

Have agreed as follows:

Article I. The Parties undertake to settle any international disputes in which they may be involved by peaceful means in such a manner that international peace and security and justice are not endangered and to refrain in their international relations from the threat or use of force in any manner inconsistent with the Purposes of the United Nations, or obligations assumed by any Party toward the United Nations.

Article II. The Parties will consult together whenever, in the opinion of either of them, the political independence or security of either of the Parties is threatened by external armed attack. Separately and jointly, by self-help and mutual aid, the Parties will maintain and develop appropriate means to deter armed attack and will take suitable measures in consultation and agreement to implement this Treaty and to further its purposes.

Article III. Each Party recognizes that an armed attack in the Pacific area on either of the Parties in territories now under their respective administrative control, or hereafter recognized by one of the Parties as lawfully brought under the administrative control of the other, would be dangerous to its own peace and safety and declares that it would act to meet the common danger in accordance with its constitutional processes.

Article IV. The Republic of Korea grants, and the United States of America accepts, the right to dispose United States land, air and sea forces in and about the territory of the Republic of Korea as determined by mutual agreement.

Article V. This Treaty shall be ratified by the United States of America and the Republic of Korea in accordance with their respective constitutional processes and will come into force when instruments of ratification thereof have been exchanged by them at Washington.

Article VI. This Treaty shall remain in force indefinitely. Either party may terminate it one year after notice has been given to the other party.

In witness whereof, the undersigned plenipotentiaries have signed this Treaty.

Done in duplicate at Washington, in the English and Korean languages, this first day of October 1953.

No. 9. Mutual Defense Treaty between the United States and the Republic of China[9]

The Parties to this Treaty,

Reaffirming their faith in the purposes and principles of the Charter of the United Nations and their desire to live in peace with all peoples and all Governments, and desiring to strengthen the fabric of peace in the West Pacific Area,

Recalling with mutual pride the relationship which brought their two peoples together in a common bond of sympathy and mutual ideals to fight side by side against imperialist aggression during the last war,

Desiring to declare publicly and formally their sense of unity and their common determination to defend themselves against external armed attack, so that no potential aggressor could be under the illusion that either of them stands alone in the West Pacific Area, and

Desiring further to strengthen their present efforts for collective defense for the preservation of peace and security pending the development of a more comprehensive system of regional security in the West Pacific Area,

Have agreed as follows:

Article I. The Parties undertake, as set forth in the Charter of the United Nations, to settle any international dispute in which they may be involved by peaceful means in such a manner that international peace, security and justice are not endangered and to refrain in their international relations from the threat or use of force in any manner inconsistent with the purposes of the United Nations.

Article II. In order more effectively to achieve the objective of this Treaty, the Parties separately and jointly by self-help and mutual aid will maintain and develop their individual and collective capacity to resist armed attack and communist subversive activities directed from without against their territorial integrity and political stability.

Article III. The Parties undertake to strengthen their free institutions and to cooperate with each other in the development of economic progress and social well-being and to further their individual and collective efforts toward these ends.

Article IV. The Parties, through their Foreign Ministers or their deputies, will consult together from time to time regarding the implementation of this Treaty.

Article V. Each Party recognizes that an armed attack in the West Pacific Area directed against the territories of either of the Parties would be dangerous to its own peace and safety and declares that it would act to meet the common danger in accordance with its constitutional processes.

Any such armed attack and all measures taken as a result thereof shall be immediately reported to the Security Council of the United Nations. Such measures shall be terminated when the Security Council has taken the measures necessary to restore and maintain international peace and security.

Article VI. For the Purposes of Articles II and V, the terms "territorial" and "territories" shall mean in respect of the Republic of China, Taiwan and the Pescadores; and in respect of the United States of America, the island territories in the West Pacific under its jurisdiction. The provisions of Articles II and V will be applicable to such other territories as may be determined by mutual agreement.

Article VII. The Government of the Republic of China grants, and the Government of the United States of America accepts, the right to dispose such United States land, air and sea forces in and about Taiwan and the Pescadores as may be required for their defense, as determined by mutual agreement.

Article VIII. This Treaty does not affect and shall not be interpreted as affecting in any way the rights and obligations of the

Parties under the Charter of the United Nations or the responsibility of the United Nations for the maintenance of international peace and security.

Article IX. This Treaty shall be ratified by the United States of America and the Republic of China in accordance with their respective constitutional processes and will come into force when instruments of ratification thereof have been exchanged by them at Taipei.

Article X. This treaty shall remain in force indefinitely. Either Party may terminate it one year after notice has been given to the other Party.

In witness whereof the undersigned plenipotentiaries have signed this Treaty.

Done in duplicate, in the English and Chinese languages, at Washington on this second day of December of the year One Thousand Nine Hundred and Fifty-four, corresponding to the second day of the twelfth month of the Forty-third year of the Republic of China.

No. 10. *Southeast Asia Collective Defense Treaty (Manila Pact)*[10]

The Parties to this Treaty [Australia, France, New Zealand, Pakistan, Republic of the Philippines, Thailand, United Kingdom, the United States],

Recognizing the sovereign equality of all the Parties,

Reiterating their faith in the purposes and principles set forth in the Charter of the United Nations and their desire to live in peace with all peoples and all governments,

Reaffirming that, in accordance with the Charter of the United Nations, they uphold the principle of equal rights and self-determination of peoples, and declaring that they will earnestly strive by every peaceful means to promote self-government and to secure the independence of all countries whose peoples desire it and are able to undertake its responsibilities,

Desiring to strengthen the fabric of peace and freedom and to uphold the principles of democracy, individual liberty and the rule of law, and to promote the economic well-being and development of all peoples in the treaty area,

Intending to declare publicly and formally their sense of unity, so that any potential aggressor will appreciate that the Parties stand together in the area, and

Desiring further to coordinate their efforts for collective defense for the preservation of peace and security,

Therefore agree as follows:

Article I. The Parties undertake, as set forth in the Charter of the United Nations, to settle any international disputes in which they may be involved by peaceful means in such a manner that international peace and security and justice are not endangered, and to refrain in their international relations from the threat or use of force in any manner inconsistent with the purposes of the United Nations.

Article II. In order more effectively to achieve the objectives of this Treaty, the Parties, separately and jointly, by means of continuous and effective self-help and mutual aid will maintain and develop their individual and collective capacity to resist armed attack and to prevent and counter subversive activities directed from without against their territorial integrity and political stability.

Article III. The Parties undertake to strengthen their free institutions and to cooperate with one another in the further development of economic measures, including technical assistance, designed both to promote economic progress and social well-being and to further the individual and collective efforts of governments towards these ends.

Article IV. 1. Each Party recognizes that aggression by means of armed attack in the treaty area against any of the Parties or against any State or territory which the Parties by unanimous agreement may hereafter designate, would endanger its own peace and safety, and agrees that it will in that event act to meet the common danger in accordance with its constitutional processes. Measures taken under this paragraph shall be immediately reported to the Security Council of the United Nations.

2. If, in the opinion of any of the Parties, the inviolability or the integrity of the territory or the sovereignty or political independence of any Party in the treaty area or of any other State or territory to which the provisions of paragraph 1 of this Article from time to time apply is threatened in any way other than by armed attack or is affected or threatened by any fact or situation which might endanger the peace of the area, the Parties shall consult immediately in order to agree on the measures which should be taken for the common defense.

3. It is understood that no action on the territory of any State designated by unanimous agreement under paragraph 1 of this Article or on any territory so designated shall be taken except at the invitation or with the consent of the government concerned.

Article V. The Parties hereby establish a Council, on which each of them shall be represented, to consider matters concerning the implementation of this Treaty. The Council shall provide for consultation with regard to military and any other planning as the situation obtaining in the treaty area may from time to time require. The Council shall be so organized as to be able to meet at any time.

Article VI. This Treaty does not affect and shall not be interpreted as affecting in any way the rights and obligations of any of the Parties under the Charter of the United Nations or the responsibility of the United Nations for the maintenance of international peace and security. Each Party declares that none of the international engagements now in force between it and any other of the Parties or any third party is in conflict with the provisions of this Treaty, and undertakes not to enter into any international engagement in conflict with this Treaty.

Article VII. Any other State in a position to further the objectives of this Treaty and to contribute to the security of the area may, by unanimous agreement of the Parties, be invited to accede to this Treaty. Any State so invited may become a Party to the Treaty by depositing its instrument of accession with the Government of the Republic of the Philippines. The Government of the Republic of the Philippines shall inform each of the Parties of the deposit of each such instrument of accession.

Article VIII. As used in this Treaty, the "treaty area" is the general area of Southeast Asia, including also the entire territories of the Asian Parties, and the general area of the Southwest Pacific not including the Pacific area north of 21 degrees 30 minutes north latitude. The Parties may, by unanimous agreement, amend this Article to include within the treaty area the territory of any State acceding to this Treaty in accordance with Article VII or otherwise to change the treaty area.

Article IX. 1. This Treaty shall be deposited in the archives of the Government of the Republic of the Philippines. Duly certified copies thereof shall be transmitted by that government to the other signatories.

2. The Treaty shall be ratified and its provisions carried out by the Parties in accordance with their respective constitutional processes. The instruments of ratification shall be deposited as soon as possible with the Government of the Republic of the Philippines, which shall notify all of the other signatories of such deposit.

3. The Treaty shall enter into force between the States which have ratified it as soon as the instruments of ratification of a ma-

jority of the signatories shall have been deposited, and shall come into effect with respect to each other State on the date of the deposit of its instrument of ratification.

Article X. This Treaty shall remain in force indefinitely, but any Party may cease to be a Party one year after its notice of denunciation has been given to the Government of the Republic of the Philippines, which shall inform the governments of the other Parties of the deposit of each notice of denunciation.

Article XI. The English text of this Treaty is binding on the Parties, but when the Parties have agreed to the French text thereof and have so notified the Government of the Republic of the Philippines, the French text shall be equally authentic and binding on the Parties.

Understanding of the United States of America

The United States of America in executing the present Treaty does so with the understanding that its recognition of the effect of aggression and armed attack and its agreement with reference thereto in Article IV, paragraph 1, apply only to communist aggression but affirms that in the event of other aggression or armed attack it will consult under the provisions of Article IV, paragraph 2.

In witness whereof, the undersigned Plenipotentiaries have signed this Treaty.

Done at Manila, this eighth day of September, 1954.

No. 11. Protocol to the Southeast Asia Collective Defense Treaty[11]

Designation of states and territories as to which provisions of Article IV and Article III are to be applicable:

The Parties to the Southeast Asia Collection Defense Treaty unanimously designate for the purpose of Article IV of the Treaty the States of Cambodia and Laos and the free territory under the jurisdiction of the State of Vietnam.

The Parties further agree that the above-mentioned states and territory shall be eligible in respect of the economic measures contemplated by Article III.

This Protocol shall enter into force simultaneously with the coming into force of the Treaty.

In witness whereof, the undersigned Plenipotentiaries have signed this Protocol to the Southeast Asia Collective Defense Treaty.

Done at Manila, this eighth day of September, 1954.

No.12. Pacific Charter[12]

The Delegates of Australia, France, New Zealand, Pakistan, the

Republic of the Philippines, the Kingdom of Thailand, the United Kingdom of Great Britain and Northern Ireland, the United States of America,

Desiring to establish a firm basis for common action to maintain peace and security in Southeast Asia and the Southwest Pacific,

Convinced that common action to this end, in order to be worthy and effective, must be inspired by the highest principles of justice and liberty,

Do hereby proclaim:

First, in accordance with the provisions of the United Nations Charter, they uphold the principle of equal rights and self-determination of peoples and they will earnestly strive by every peaceful means to promote self-government and to secure the independence of all countries whose peoples desire it and are able to undertake its responsibilities;

Second, they are each prepared to continue taking effective practical measures to ensure conditions favorable to the orderly achievement of the foregoing purposes in accordance with their constitutional processes;

Third, they will continue to cooperate in the economic, social and cultural fields in order to promote higher living standards, economic progress and social well-being in this region;

Fourth, as declared in the Southeast Asia Collective Defense Treaty, they are determined to prevent or counter by appropriate means any attempt in the treaty area to subvert their freedom or to destroy their sovereignty or territorial integrity.

Proclaimed at Manila, this eighth day of September, 1954.

NOTES

Complete citations for abbreviations used in these notes are contained in the bibliography following this section.

Chapter 1
1. MacMurray, I, 18-22.
2. *Nihon Gaikō Monjo (Japanese Diplomatic Documents)*, XXVIII, No. 2, 17. This is the Japanese Government's English translation of the Russian Government's note in French presented to the Japanese government on April 23, 1895. It was concurred in by the German and French governments.
3. *Ibid.*, pp. 63-64. This is the message from Foreign Minister Mutsu to Vice-Foreign Minister Hayashi to be transmitted to the Russian government. Mr. Hayashi was instructed to deliver similar replies to the French and German governments. It was dated April 30, 1895.
4. MacMurray, I, 50-51. Excerpts only.
5. *Ibid.*, pp. 119-21. Excerpts only.
6. *Ibid.*, pp. 223-35. Secretary of State Hay's correspondence on the Open Door was addressed to the governments of France, Germany, Great Britain, Italy, Japan, and Russia. Given here are only items and excerpts which bear most directly on the nature of the policy and of the response of the powers to it. The Choate-Salisbury letter for the most part was identical with the Hay-White letter; the excerpt given here sheds additional light on the nature of the Open Door policy.
7. MacMurray, I, 324-25.
8. *Ibid.*, pp. 516-18. Only items significantly different from the 1902 agreement are given here.
9. *Ibid.*, pp. 900-1. Only this article differs significantly from anything in the 1905 agreement.

10. *Ibid.*, pp. 522-26.

11. *Ibid.*, p. 24, n. 1.

12. *Annual Report for 1907 on Reforms and Progress in Korea,* compiled by His Imperial Japanese Majesty's Residency General, Seoul, December, 1908. Appendix A, pp. 101-2.

13. *Annual Report on Reforms and Progress in Chosen (Korea): (1910-11),* compiled by Government-General of Chosen, Keijo (Seoul). December, 1911. Appendix A, pp. 235-36.

Chapter 2

1. MacMurray, II, 1167.

2. *Ibid.*

3. *Ibid.*, p. 1153.

4. *Ibid.*, p. 1488. Only that section of the treaty dealing with the former German holdings in Shantung is given here.

5. *Papers Relating to the Foreign Relations of the United States, 1915.* Department of State, Washington, D. C., pp. 159-60.

6. *Ibid.*, pp. 160-61.

7. *Ibid.*, pp. 105-11. Excerpts only.

8. *Ibid.*, p. 146.

9. *Ibid.*, pp. 171-72.

10. *Ibid.*, p. 172.

11. *Ibid.*, pp. 172-73. Only the first four articles, dealing directly with the Demands, are given here.

12. *Papers Relating to the Foreign Relations of the United States, 1918, Russia.* (In three volumes.) Department of State, Washington, D. C., II, 67-68.

13. *Ibid.*, pp. 262-63.

14. *Ibid.*, pp. 324-25.

15. *Ibid.*, pp. 328-29.

16. *LN Treaty Series*, XXV, 184-89.

17. *Ibid.*, pp. 202-25.

18. *LN Treaty Series*, XXXVIII, 278-84.

19. *LN Treaty Series*, X, 310-22.

20. *LN Treaty Series*, XXXVII, 176-82.

21. *LN Treaty Series*, XXXIV, 32-36.

22. *Ibid.*, pp. 36-38.

23. *Ibid.*, pp. 40-42. Excerpts only.

Chapter 3

1. *Foreign Relations: Japan,* I, 11-12.

2. *Ibid.*, p. 76.

3. *Japan-Manchoukuo Year Book: 1934,* pp. 593-94.

4. *League of Nations. Appeal by the Chinese Government: Report of the Commission of Enquiry.* Series of League of Nations Publications, Vol. VII; Political (1932) Vol. VII, No. 12. Dated October 1, 1932. Excerpts only.

5. *League of Nations. Official Journal,* 14th Year, No. 5, May, 1933, pp. 657-58.

6. *Nouveau Recueil Général de Traités et Autres Actes Relatifs aux Rapports de Droit International,* continuation du *Grand Recueil* de G. Fr. de Martens, 3rd Series, XXX, 3rd Ed., (1935) 649-61. Excerpts only.

7. *Ibid.,* pp. 666-67. Excerpts only.

Chapter 4

1. *Foreign Relations: Japan,* I, 477-78.

2. *Ibid.,* pp. 482-83.

3. *China Year Book: 1939,* pp. 422-26. Given here are only excerpts which present the essence of the argument against Japan's policy toward China.

4. *The Far East Year Book: 1941,* pp. 90-91.

5. *Foreign Relations: Japan,* II, 117-19.

6. *Ibid.,* p. 122.

7. *LN Treaty Series,* CLXXXI, 102, 104.

8. *Foreign Relations: Japan,* II, 153-55.

9. *Documents on German Foreign Policy, 1918-1945, from the Archives of the German Foreign Ministry.* Series D (1937-1945). Vol. I. From "Neurath to Ribbentrop." (September 1937-September 1938). U. S. Department of State (jointly with the British Foreign Ministry). 1949. This document appears as Note 2a on p. 734.

10. *Foreign Relations: Japan,* II, 159-60.

11. *LN Treaty Series,* CCIV, 386.

12. *Soviet Documents on Foreign Policy,* selected and edited by Jane Degras (Oxford University Press, 1953), III (1933-41) 486-87.

13. *Foreign Relations: Japan,* II, 768-70.

14. *Ibid.,* pp. 787-92.

15. From a book entitled *The Imperial Rescript Declaring War on United States and British Empire,* by Iichiro "Soho" Tokutomi, translated by Hanama Tasaki, Tokyo, 1942.

Chapter 5

1. *Daitōa Jōyaku Shū,* I, 798-800. Text in French, translated by the present editor.

2. *Ibid.,* pp. 801-3. Text in French, translated by the present editor.

3. Dispatch of Dōmei, the official Japanese news agency, appearing in the *Syōnan Shimbun* (Singapore newspaper), March 12, 1945, No. 711, p. 4. This newspaper was published in English, although its title was in Japanese.

4. *Daitōa Jōyaku Shū*, I, 447-49. Text in French, translated by the present editor.

5. *Ibid.*, p. 705. Text in Japanese, translation by the present editor.

6. *Ibid.*, pp. 701-3. Text in French, translation by the present editor.

7. *Ibid.*, p. 704. Text in French, translation by the present editor.

8. *Ibid.*, p. 809.

9. *Ibid.*, pp. 7-8.

10. *Daily Report: Foreign Radio Broadcasts*, Foreign Broadcast Intelligence Service, Federal Communications Commission (Washington, D. C.), April 23, 1945, p. A3.

11. *New York Times*, April 1, 1944, reporting a wireless transmission by Dōmei (see Note 3 above).

12. *New York Times*, April 6, 1945.

13. *Ibid.*, August 9, 1945.

Chapter 6

1. *China White Paper*, p. 519.

2. Department of State *Bulletin*, XII, No. 307 (May 13, 1945) 886.

3. *China White Paper*, pp. 113-14.

4. Department of State *Bulletin*, XIII, No. 318 (July 29, 1945) 137-38.

5. *Nippon Times*, August 15, 1945.

6. Department of State *Bulletin*, VIII, No. 326 (September 23, 1945) 423-27.

7. *U. S. Treaties*, III, 3169-91.

8. *UN Treaty Series*, CXXXVIII, 38-44.

9. *Ibid.*, pp. 44-48. Given here are the only two items which were of more than routine significance. The terms of the protocol constituted an integral part of the treaty.

10. *Ibid.*, CCLXIII, 112-16.

11. *Ibid.*, CCLXXXV, 24-36.

Chapter 7

1. *China White Paper*, pp. 607-9.

2. *Ibid.*, pp. 689-94. Only the concluding paragraphs given here.

3. *Ibid.*, pp. 686-89.
4. *UN Treaty Series*, X, 334-38.
5. *Ibid.*, p. 340.
6. *Ibid.*, pp. 342-44.
7. *Ibid.*, pp. 346-54. Excerpts only.
8. *Ibid.*, pp. 354-56. Excerpts only.
9. *Ibid.*, pp. 358-60. Excerpts only.
10. *Ibid.*, pp. 364-66. Excerpts only.
11. *Soviet Monitor*, issued by Tass Agency, London, No. 11, 311, February 15, 1950.
12. *Ibid.*,
13. *Ibid.*,

Chapter 8
1. See p. 119, Cairo Declaration.
2. Department of State *Bulletin*, XIII, No. 340 (December 30, 1945) 1027-30. Only portion dealing with Korea is given here.
3. *United Nations. Official Records of the Second Session of the General Assembly. Plenary Meetings of the General Assembly. Verbatim Record. 16 September-29 November 1947.* I, *80th-109th Meetings*, 21-22. Only the section dealing with Korea is given here.
4. *Yearbook of the United Nations: 1947-48*, p. 88.
5. Department of State *Bulletin*, XIX, No. 477 (August 22, 1948) 242.
6. *United Nations: General Assembly. Official Records: Third Session, Resolutions, 21 September-12 December 1948*, pp. 25-27.
7. *United Nations. Security Council. Official Records. Fifth Year. 473rd Meeting: 25 June 1950.* No. 15. Note 2, p. 2.
8. *Yearbook of the United Nations: 1950*, p. 222.
9. *Ibid.*, pp. 223-24.
10. Department of State Bulletin, XXIII, No. 574 (July 3, 1950) 5.
11. *Yearbook of the United Nations: 1950*, p. 230.
12. *United Nations. Security Council. Official Records. Fifth Year. Supplement for June, July, August, 1950*, pp. 77-78.
13. *United Nations. General Assembly. Official Records. Fifth Session, Supplement No. 20 (A/1775), Resolutions Adopted*, pp. 9-10.
14. *United Nations. Security Council. Official Records. Fifth Year. 527th Meeting: 28 November, 1950*, No. 69, pp. 2-26. Excerpts only.
15. *Yearbook of the United Nations: 1951*, pp. 224-25.
16. *Armistice in Korea: Selected Statements and Documents.* U.S. Department of State. Publication 5150. Far Eastern Series 61. Re-

leased August, 1953. Only the major provisions are given here.
17. *Ibid.*, Only the major provisions are given here.

Chapter 9
1. *Further Documents relating to the discussion of Indo-China at the Geneva Conference June 16-July 21, 1954.* Presented by the Secretary of State for Foreign Affairs to Parliament by Command of Her Majesty, August, 1954. Command Paper 9239. Miscellaneous No. 20 (1954), pp. 9-10.
2. *Ibid.*, pp. 27-38. The agreement is long and extremely detailed; only the major points are given here.
3. Department of State *Bulletin*, XXI, No. 788 (August 2, 1954) 162-63.
4. *Daily Bulletin*, New China News Agency, London, No. 1342, (July 8, 1945) pp. 2-5.
5. Given here is only the concluding section of the communique as it appears on p. 244 in *Conflict in Indo-China & International Repercussions* as quoted from *Translations from the Soviet Press*, No. 553 (July 27, 1955), issued by the Embassy of the U.S.S.R., Washington, D.C. The long section preceding this is virtually identical with the similar section in the "Joint Sino-Vietnamese Communique."

Chapter 10
1. *U.S. Treaties*, III, Part III, 3420-24.
2. *Ibid.*, pp. 3948-51.
3. *Ibid.*, pp. 3329-32.
4. Department of State *Bulletin*, XLII, No. 1072 (February 8, 1960) 184-85.
5. *Ibid.*, p. 185.
6. *Ibid.*, p. 198.
7. *Ibid.*, pp. 200-1.
8. *U.S. Treaties*, V, Part III, 2368-74.
9. *U.S. Treaties*, VI, Part I, 433-38.
10. *Ibid.*, pp. 81-92.
11. *Ibid.*
12. *Ibid.*

BIBLIOGRAPHY

Listed below in alphabetical order are the principal sources uti-' lized in the compilation of this collection. Other sources are cited in the notes.

Japan. Ministry of Foreign Affairs. Treaties Bureau. *Daitōa Jō- yaku Shū (Collection of Greater East Asia Treaties)*. July, August, and November, 1943. Seven volumes: Vol. I. Treaties between Japan and the Countries of Greater East Asia; Vol. II. Treaties between Manchoukuo and Countries other than Japan; Vol. III and Vol. IV. Treaties between the Republic of China and Countries other than Japan; Vol. V. Treaties concerning Indochina between France and Countries other than Japan; Vol. VI. Treaties between Thailand and Countries other than Japan; Vol. VII. Treaties between Burma and Countries other than Japan.
This collection is mainly in Japanese. However, in almost all cases the text of treaties also appears in another appropriate language. Although most of the treaties are available elsewhere, this collection is particularly valuable for treaties concluded by Japan with other Asian countries during the Second World War and for the treaties between the puppet state of "Manchoukuo" and the governments recognizing it.

League of Nations. Secretariat. *League of Nations. Treaty Series. Publication of Treaties and International Engagements registered with the Secretariat of the League.* Referred to in the notes as *LN Treaty Series.*

MacMurray, John V. A., *Treaties and Agreements with and Concerning China, 1894-1919.* New York: Oxford University Press, 1921. 2 vols. Referred to in the notes as MacMurray. Although unofficial, this collection is generally regarded as authoritative.

United Nations. Secretariat. *United Nations. Treaty Series. Treaties and international agreements registered or filed and re-*

corded with the Secretariat of the United Nations. Referred to in the notes as *UN Treaty Series*.

United States of America. Department of State. *Bulletin*. I have used this mainly for official statements and policy papers other than treaties. Most of the items cited as coming from the *Bulletin* are available elsewhere, but I have preferred to use it as a source because it is official.

United States of America. Department of State. *Papers Relating to the Foreign Relations of the United States. Japan: 1931-1941*. Publication 2008. U.S. Government Printing Office. 1943. 2 vols. Referred to in the notes as *Foreign Relations: Japan*. This work is useful for United States and Japanese official statements as well as American-Japanese diplomatic correspondence in the 1931-41 period.

United States of America. Department of State. *United States Relations with China: With Special Reference to the Period 1944-49*. U.S. Government Printing Office. 1949. This is popularly known as the "China White Paper" and is so referred to in the notes.

United States of America. Department of State. *United States Treaties and Other International Agreements*. Referred to in the notes as *U.S. Treaties*.

INDEX

Entries are limited to (1) titles of documents; (2) major signatories of treaties, agreements, and so forth; (3) subject matter as indicated in titles; and (4) personal names which have become identified with documents. This index will only assist the reader to locate documents; it cannot be used to find specific items in the texts of documents.

Anglo-Japanese Alliance of 1902, 16; renewal of 1905, 17; renewal of 1911, 18

ANZUS Pact, 215

Australia. *See* ANZUS Pact

Axis Alliance: Japan-Germany agreement (1936), 91; supplementary protocol to, 92; secret additional agreement to, 92; Italy-Germany-Japan Protocol (1937), 93; Japan-Germany-Italy Mutual Assistance Pact (1940), 94

Burma: alliance with Japan, 110

Bryan, Secretary of State, letter on Twenty-one Demands, 35

Cairo Declaration, 119; excerpt on Korea, 180

Cambodia. *See* Geneva Conference

Chiang Kai-shek: reply to Japanese statements of policy, 81

China (Imperial): Treaty of Peace with Japan (Shimonoseki), 5. *See also* Liaotung Peninsula

China, People's Republic of (communist):

–on Korea: General Assembly resolution attacking aggression in, 197; truce agreement, 198

–and U. S. S. R. : Treaty of Friendship, Alliance and Mutual Assistance, 172; Agreement on Chinese Changchun Railway, Port Arthur and Dalny, 174; agreement on credits, 176

–and United States: attack in Security Council on U. S. policy in Korea and Formosa, 195

–Viet Nam, Joint Communique with, 208. *See also* Geneva Conference

China, Republic of:

–and Japan: Japanese government statement on, 78; Konoye statement on, 79; Treaty of Peace (1952), 146; Protocol to, 147. *See also* Chiang Kai-shek

–and U. S. S. R. : agreement of 1924, 54; Treaty of Nonaggression (1937), 90; Treaty of Friendship and Alliance (1945), 165; note accompanying, 167; Agreement on Chinese Changchun Railway, 168; note on Outer Mongolia, 168; Agreement on Dairen, 170; Agreement on Port Arthur, 170; Agreement on Three Eastern Provinces (Manchuria), 171

–and United States: Mutual Defense Treaty (1954), 226. *See also* Marshall, General George C. ;

"Open Door" Notes; Truman, President Harry S. ; Twenty-one Demands; Washington Conference; Yalta Agreement

Chinese Changchun Railway: U. S. S. R. –Republic of China agreement on, 168; U. S. S. R. –Communist China agreement on, 174

Chinese Eastern Railway: U. S. S. R. cession of rights to Manchoukuo, 74; Japanese note on U. S. S. R. cession of rights, 76

Choate to Salisbury letter on "Open Door," 14

Dairen (Dalny): U. S. S. R. –Republic of China agreement on, 170; U. S. S. R. –Communist China agreement on, 174

Eastern Inner Mongolia, treaty respecting, 40

Five-Power Pact, 47

Four-Power Pact, 46

France: protocol with Japan on security and political understanding, 107; protocol with Japan on Indochina, 108; Japanese Removal of French Authorities in Indochina, 109. See also Five-Power Pact; Four-Power Pact; Geneva Conference; Southeast Asia Collective Defense Treaty

Free India; Japanese statement on, 112

Geneva Conference: Final Declaration on Indochina, 203. See also Indochina; U. S. declaration; Viet Nam; agreement on cessation of hostilities

Germany: Japanese Ultimatum to, 28; Japanese declaration of war on, 29. See also Axis Alliance; Three-Power Intervention; Treaty of Peace between Allied and Associate Powers and Germany

Great Britain: statement regarding Japan's participation in World War I, 28. See also Anglo-Japanese Alliance; Geneva Conference; Washington Conference; Yalta Agreement

Greater East Asia: Joint Declaration on, 112; Declaration of 1945, 113

Hay to White letter on "Open Door," 12

Imperial Rescript on the End of the War, 123

Indochina: U. S. Declaration on, 206. See also France; Geneva Conference; Viet Nam

Italy. See Axis Alliance; Five-Power Pact

Japan: Liaotung Peninsula, retrocession of, 11; British statement regarding participation in World War I, 28; League of Nations, withdrawal from, 72; Burma, alliance with, 110; Treaty of Peace (general of 1951), 132

–and China, Imperial: treaty of peace (Shimonoseki), 5

–and China, Republic of: government statement on, 78; Konoye statement on, 79; Statement on Establishment of New Central Government of China, 85; treaty with, 87; treaty of peace (1952), 146; protocol to, 147

–and Germany: ultimatum to, 28; declaration of war on, 29

–and Korea: alliance with, 23; protocol with, 23; annexation of, 24

–and the Philippines: alliance with, 111; Terms of Understanding Annexed thereto, 112; Reparations Agreement with, 150

–Russia, treaty of peace with (Portsmouth), 18

–Thailand, alliance with, 110

–and U. S. S. R. : Convention of 1925, 57; Protocol on concessions in Saghalien, 60; Protocol on troops in Saghalien, 60; Neutrality Pact, 95; Soviet denunciation thereof, 115; transfer of concessions in Sakhalin, 114; declaration of war, 116; Joint Declaration (1956), 148

–and United States: U. S. outline of proposed agreement with (1941), 95; Nomura memorandum to Hull, 98; declaration of war on, 104; Truman

Statement on Meaning of Unconditional Surrender, 120; World War II,
Imperial Rescript on End of, 123;
U. S. Initial Postsurrender Policy
for, 124; Security Treaty (1951),
219; Treaty of Mutual Cooperation
and Security (1960), 220; Exchange
of notes on Consultation Formula
thereunder, 223; Agreed Minute
concerning islands under U. S. administration, 222; exchange of
notes on Security Consultative
Committee, 224
See also Anglo-Japanese Alliance; Axis Alliance; France;
Free India; Germany; Greater
East Asia; Manchoukuo; Manchurian crisis; Potsdam Declaration; Siberian Intervention;
Three-Power Intervention;
Twenty-one Demands; Wang
Ching-wei regime; Washington
Conference; Yalta Agreement;
Yonai, Premier Admiral

Kato, Baron, instructions on Twenty-
one Demands, 30
Konoye, Premier Prince, Statement
on China, 79
Korea: Cairo Declaration excerpt
on, 180; Moscow Agreement concerning, 180; Chinese communist
attack on U. S. in, 195; truce agreement, 198; prisoners of war,
agreement on, 201
–and Japan: alliance with, 23; protocol with, 23; annexation of, 24
–and United Nations: General Assembly, presentation of problem by
U. S. , 181; General Assembly Resolution of 1947, 183; of 1948, 186; of
1950, 192; UN Commission report
of attack on, 188; Security Council
Resolution of June 25, 1950, 188;
of June 27, 1950, 189; of July 7,
1950, 191; U. S. S. R. statement on
July 7 Resolution, 192; resolution
concerning Chinese communist aggression, 197
–and United States: U. S. statement
of Policy (1948), 184; Truman
statement of policy regarding attack

on, 190; Mutual Defense Treaty,
225

Laos. *See* Geneva Conference
League of Nations. *See* Manchurian
crisis
Liaotung Peninsula: Japanese retrocession of, 11; Convention for Lease
to Russia, 11
Lytton Commission Report, 67

Manchoukuo: Protocol with Japan, 66;
Joint Declaration with Japan and
Wang Ching-wei regime, 89. *See
also* Chinese Eastern Railway;
Manchurian crisis
Manchurian crisis: Japanese government statement, 63; Stimson Doctrine, 65; Japan-Manchoukuo Protocol, 66; Lytton Commission Report, 67; Japanese withdrawal from
the League of Nations, 72. *See also*
Chinese Eastern Railway
Manila Pact. *See* Southeast Asia Collective Defense Treaty
Marshall, General George C. , statement on mission to China, 161
Moscow Agreement on Korea, 180

Naval Limitation Treaty. *See* Five-
Power Pact
New Central Government of China.
See Wang Ching-wei regime
New Zealand. *See* ANZUS Pact
Nine-Power Pact, 51
Nomura, Admiral, memorandum to
Secretary of State Hull, 98

"Open Door" Notes: Hay to White
letter stating policy, 12; Choate to
Lord Salisbury stating additional
points, 14; von Bulow to White
(German reply), 14; Department of
State instructions regarding, 15
Outer Mongolia, Chinese note to
U. S. S. R. on, 168

Pacific Charter, 231
Philippines: alliance with Japan, 111;
terms of understanding annexed
thereto, 112
Philippines, Republic of: Reparations

Agreement with Japan, 150; Mutual
Defense Treaty with U. S., 217
Port Arthur: U. S. S. R. – Republic of
China agreement on, 170; U. S. S. R.
– Communist China agreement on,
174
Portsmouth, Treaty of, 18
Potsdam Declaration, 121

Russia (Imperial): treaty of peace
with Japan (Portsmouth), 18. *See
also* Liaotung Peninsula; Three-
Power Intervention

Saghalien. *See* Sakhalin
Sakhalin: Concessions, U. S. S. R. –
Japan Protocol on, 60; Japanese
Troops, Protocol on, 60; transfer
of concessions, U. S. S. R. – Japan
Protocol on, 114
SEATO. *See* Southeast Asia Collec-
tive Defense Treaty
Shantung: Japan-China treaty and note
respecting, 54. *See also* Treaty of
Peace between Allied and Associate
Powers and Germany; Twenty-one
Demands
Shimonoseki, Treaty of, 5
Siberian Intervention: U. S. Acting
Secretary of State to U. S. Ambas-
sador in Japan, 40; White House
conference on, 41; Japanese Am-
bassador to U. S. Acting Secretary
of State, 42; U. S. declaration
against, 44
South Manchuria and Twenty-one De-
mands, 40
Southeast Asia Collective Defense
Treaty, 228; Protocol to, 231
Stimson Doctrine of nonrecognition,
65

Thailand: alliance with Japan, 110.
See also Southeast Asia Collective
Defense Treaty
Three Eastern Provinces (Man-
churia): U. S. S. R. – Republic of
China agreement on, 171. *See also*
U. S. S. R. – Communist China agree-
ment on Chinese Changchun Rail-
way, Port Arthur, and Dalny
Three-Power Intervention: Japanese

reply to Russian note, 10; Russian
note to Japan, 10; retrocession of
Liaotung Peninsula, 11
Treaty of Peace between Allied and
Associate Powers and Germany
(Treaty of Versailles), 30
Treaty of Peace with Japan (1951),
132
Truman, President Harry S.: Statement on Meaning of Unconditional
Surrender of Japan, 120; Statement
of Policy on China (1945), 157;
Statement of Policy on China (1946),
160; statement on Korea and Formosa, 190
Twenty-one Demands, 32; Japanese
instructions regarding, 30; U. S.
reaction to (Bryan letter), 35; U. S.
statement of policy concerning (Secretary of State to Ambassador
Guthrie), 38; Treaty and Note respecting Shantung, 39; Treaty respecting South Manchuria and Eastern Inner Mongolia, 40

Unconditional Surrender, Meaning of
for Japan, 120
Union of Soviet Socialist Republics:
statement on UN Security Council
Resolution of July 7, 1950, 192;
Viet Nam (communist), Joint Communique with, 211. *See also* Geneva
Conference; Manchoukuo; Manchurian crisis; Siberian Intervention;
Yalta Agreement
– and China, People's Republic of
(communist): Treaty of Friendship,
Alliance, and Mutual Assistance,
172; Agreement on Chinese Changchun Railway, Port Arthur and
Dalny, 174; agreement on credits,
176
– and China, Republic of: Agreement
of 1924, 54; Treaty of Nonaggression
(1937), 90; Treaty of Friendship and
Alliance, 165; note accompanying
treaty, 167; Agreement on Chinese
Changchun Railway, 168; Outer
Mongolia, note on, 168; Agreement
on Dairen, 170; Agreement on Port
Arthur, 170; Agreement on Three
Eastern Provinces (Manchuria), 171

–and Japan: Convention of 1925, 57; Protocol on Japanese Troops in Saghalien, 60; Protocol on Japanese concessions in Saghalien, 60, 114; Neutrality Pact, 95; denunciation of, 115; declaration of war on, 116; Joint Declaration (1956), 148

United Nations and Korea: Commission on Korea, report of attack, 188; truce agreement, 198

–General Assembly: presentation by U. S. of Korean problem to, 181; Resolution of 1947, 183; Resolution of 1948, 186; Resolution of 1950, 192; Resolution condemning communist Chinese aggression, 197; prisoners of war agreement, 201

–Security Council: Resolution of June 25, 1950, 188; of June 27, 1950, 189; of July 7, 1950, 191; U. S. S. R. statement on July 7 resolution, 192; communist Chinese attack on U. S. in, 195

United States: Declaration on Indochina, 206; Mutual Defense Treaty with Republic of the Philippines, 217. *See also* ANZUS Pact; Geneva Conference; "Open Door" Notes; Siberian Intervention; Truman, President Harry S. ; Twenty-one Demands; Washington Conference; Yalta Agreement

–and China: communist Chinese attack on, in Security Council, 195; Mutual Defense Treaty with Republic of, 226. *See also* Marshall, General George C. ; "Open Door" Notes; Truman, President Harry S. ; Twenty-one Demands; Washington Conference; Yalta Agreement

–and Japan: Outline of Proposed Basis of Agreement with, 95; Nomura memorandum to Hull, 98; Japanese declaration of war, 104;

Initial Postsurrender Policy for, 124; Security Treaty (1951), 219; Treaty of Mutual Cooperation and Security (1960), 220; Agreed Minute to, 222; Exchange of Notes on Consultation Formula, 223; Exchange of Notes on Security Consultative Committee, 224. *See also* Stimson Doctrine of nonrecognition

–and Korea: Présentation of Korean Problem to UN General Assembly, 181; Policy toward New Korean Government, 184; Truman statement on defense of, 190; Mutual Defense Treaty with, 225

United States Initial Postsurrender Policy for Japan, 124

Viet Nam, Agreement on Cessation of Hostilities in, 206. *See also* Geneva Conference; Southeast Asia Collective Defense Treaty

Viet Nam, Democratic Republic of: Joint Communique with communist China, 208; Joint Communique with U. S. S. R. , 211

von Bulow letter to White on "Open Door," 14

Wang Ching-wei regime: Yonai statement on, 85; Treaty with Japan, 87; Joint Declaration with Japan and Manchoukuo, 89

Washington Conference: Four-Power Pact, 46; Five-Power Pact, 47; Nine-Power Pact, 51; Japan-China Treaty respecting Shantung, 54

White House Conference on Siberian Intervention, 41

Yalta Agreement, 120

Yonai, Premier Admiral, Statement on Establishment of New Central Government of China, 85